Teaching Performance Practices in Remote and Hybrid Spaces

This collection of insightful essays gives teachers' perspectives on the role of space and presence in teaching performance. It explores how the demand for remote teaching can be met while at the same time successfully educating and working compassionately in this most 'live' of disciplines.

Teaching Performance Practices in Remote and Hybrid Spaces reframes prevailing ideas about pedagogy in dance, theatre, and somatics and applies them to teaching in face-to-face, hybrid, and remote situations. Case studies from instructors and professors provide essential, practical suggestions for remotely teaching a vast range of studio courses, including tap dance, theatre design, movement, script analysis, and acting, rendering this book an invaluable resource. The challenges that teachers are facing in the early twenty-first century are addressed throughout, helping readers to navigate these unprecedented circumstances whilst delivering lessons, guiding workshops, rehearsing, or even staging performances.

This book is invaluable for dance and theatre teachers or leaders who work in the performing arts and related disciplines. It is also ideal for any professionals who need research-based solutions for teaching performance online.

Jeanmarie Higgins is a new works dramaturg and an Associate Professor in the School of Theatre at the Pennsylvania State University, University Park.

Elisha Clark Halpin is an Associate Professor of Theatre and Dance at the Pennsylvania State University. After retiring from the concert stage her research focus has been on using somatic practices as interventions to stress and trauma.

Teaching Performance Practices in Remote and Hybrid Spaces

Edited by
Jeanmarie Higgins and
Elisha Clark Halpin

LONDON AND NEW YORK

Cover image: © Getty Image/Orbon Alija

First published 2022
by Routledge
4 Park Square, Milton Park, Abingdon, Oxon OX14 4RN

and by Routledge
605 Third Avenue, New York, NY 10158

Routledge is an imprint of the Taylor & Francis Group, an informa business

© 2022 selection and editorial matter, Jeanmarie Higgins and Elisha Clark Halpin; individual chapters, the contributors

The rights of Jeanmarie Higgins and Elisha Clark Halpin to be identified as the authors of the editorial material, and of the authors for their individual chapters, has been asserted in accordance with sections 77 and 78 of the Copyright, Designs and Patents Act 1988.

All rights reserved. No part of this book may be reprinted or reproduced or utilised in any form or by any electronic, mechanical, or other means, now known or hereafter invented, including photocopying and recording, or in any information storage or retrieval system, without permission in writing from the publishers.

Trademark notice: Product or corporate names may be trademarks or registered trademarks, and are used only for identification and explanation without intent to infringe.

British Library Cataloguing-in-Publication Data
A catalogue record for this book is available from the British Library

Library of Congress Cataloging-in-Publication Data
Names: Higgins, Jeanmarie, editor. | Halpin, Elisha Clark editor.
Title: Teaching performance practices in remote and hybrid spaces / edited by Jeanmarie Higgins and Elisha Clark Halpin.
Description: First edition. | Abingdon, Oxon ; New York : Routledge, 2022. | Includes bibliographical references and index.
Identifiers: LCCN 2021059466 (print) | LCCN 2021059467 (ebook) | ISBN 9781032134079 (hardback) | ISBN 9781032134055 (paperback) | ISBN 9781003229056 (eBook)
Subjects: LCSH: Performing arts—Study and teaching (Higher) | Acting—Study and teaching (Higher) | Teaching—Technological innovations.
Classification: LCC PN1576 .T435 2022 (print) | LCC PN1576 (ebook) | DDC 790.2—dcundefined
LC record available at https://lccn.loc.gov/2021059466
LC ebook record available at https://lccn.loc.gov/2021059467

ISBN: 978-1-032-13407-9 (hbk)
ISBN: 978-1-032-13405-5 (pbk)
ISBN: 978-1-003-22905-6 (ebk)

DOI: 10.4324/9781003229056

Typeset in Galliard
by codeMantra

For all who taught during the 2020 pandemic

Contents

List of figures	xi
List of contributors	xiii
Acknowledgments	xvii
Foreword: In Defense of "Stuff": Teaching the Ephemeral Theatre of Things	xix
SARAH BAY-CHENG	

Introduction: Teaching Performance Practices in Remote and Hybrid Spaces   1
JEANMARIE HIGGINS AND ELISHA CLARK HALPIN

PART I
Pedagogies of Care for Digital Spaces   9

1 Reevaluating Rigor with 2020 Hindsight—A Manifesto for the Ungraded Classroom   11
JANE BARNETTE

2 Solving the Real Crisis in Virtual Education: Strategies for Training Arts Practitioners in Social and Emotional Learning   21
ELIZABETH COEN

3 Practicing Academic Grace: Pedagogical Experiments with *Mr. Burns* in Digital Play Analysis Classrooms   32
SAMUEL YATES

4 I Hope This Email Finds You (Well): Teaching in Traumatic Spaces during the COVID-19 Pandemic   44
LES GRAY

PART II
Dance and Movement 55

5 Imaginative Deixis and Distributed Fictions in the
Suzuki Method of Actor Training 57
CHRISTOPHER J. STALEY

6 New Geographies of Space in Virtual and Hybrid
Performance Classrooms 69
KELLEY HOLLEY

7 Dramaturgy and Social Media: New Tools for Composition 78
ELISHA CLARK HALPIN

8 Teaching Alexander Technique (without Hands) Online:
A Study of Kindness 85
GWENDOLYN WALKER

9 Turn on Original Sound: Releasing Expectations in the
Digital Dance Studio 99
MICHELE DUNLEAVY

PART III
Doing Theatre Online: Research, Rehearsal, Production 107

10 An Archive by Any Other Name: The Historiographic,
the Digital, the Hybrid 109
DANIEL CIBA

11 Building Trust Across Miles: New Play Dramaturgy in
Virtual Rehearsal Rooms 122
KRISTIN LEAHEY AND SHELLEY ORR

12 Re-Making Rehearsal and Performance: Intersections of
Collaboration and Accessibility in a Hybrid *Romeo & Juliet* 134
DENNIS SCHEBETTA

13 Walking Backward on a Global Tightrope: Interview
with Nassim Soleimanpour about the Virtual
Performance of *White Rabbit, Red Rabbit* 145
MARJAN MOOSAVI

PART IV
Materiality/Ephemerality: Teaching Design and Production Now   155

14 Reclaiming Materiality in Remote Theatrical Design Instruction   157
MICHAEL SCHWEIKARDT

15 Reframing Beauty and Gender in Stage Makeup   169
CHARLENE GROSS

16 Lighting Design Dramaturgy and Practice in the Post Pandemic World of Online Streaming: *The Juditha Triumphans* Case Study   183
CHRISTINA THANASCULA

17 Standby Life as We Know It...Life as We (Now) Know It, Go: A Case Study in the Hybrid Stage Management Classroom   190
MEG HANNA-TOMINAGA

Index   197

Figures

0.1	Screen capture of prefab house design. Second Life, 9 December 2021	xxii
0.2	Adolphe Appia, "The Staircase" from Rhythmic Spaces, c. 1913	xxiii
5.1	A schematic of deictic axes originating from the Deictic Ground through the actor's Origo, or Deictic Center	63
8.1	Person in downward pull	89
8.2	Side view of head and neck skeleton illustrating where the top of the spine meets the bottom of the head (superior facets of the atlas meet the occipital condyles of the skull)	91
8.3	Person illustrating where the bottom of their head is by placing their hand underneath their cheekbones	92
11.1	Trauma informed teaching and learning during a global health crisis	130
14.1	A student drawing of two figures in an embrace	164
14.2	A student writes in the margin of their drawing, "I miss hugs"	165
14.3	A student drawing of a figure trying to calm themself	166
14.4	A student expresses their anxiety and terror in a drawing	167

Contributors

Jane Barnette is an Associate Professor in the Department of Theatre and Dance at the University of Kansas, where she teaches courses in dramaturgy, theatre history and analysis, and theatrical adaptation. She is the author of *Adapturgy* and has a forthcoming book about the performance and representation of Witch characters.

Daniel Ciba received a Ph.D. in Theatre and Performance Studies from Tufts University. Daniel is currently the Educational Programs Manager for Quintessence Theatre Group, the Associate Editor for the University of Iowa Press's Studies in Theatre History and Culture Series, and the Book Review Editor for *Theatre Annual*.

Elizabeth Coen serves as the School Programs and Partnerships Manager at Seattle Children's Theatre and plays an integral role in developing arts programming that focuses on teenagers' social-emotional growth. She is also a scholar of theatre history and a professional dramaturg. Her work can be found in *Theatre History Studies* and the *Journal of Dramatic Theory and Criticism*, among other publications.

Michele Dunleavy has choreographed and performed extensively throughout the Mid-Atlantic region. She works in a variety of dance forms including tap, jazz, and modern, and her choreography has been presented in Chicago, Pittsburgh, Philadelphia, Minneapolis, New York City, Maryland, and West Virginia. Michele is Professor at Penn State University and Artistic Director of Dunleavy Dance Projects. She has danced with Kompitus Rhythm Collective, Take it Away Productions, Pittsburgh Opera, Junction Dance Theatre, Physical Theatre Project, DANA Movement Ensemble, ETCH Dance Co., and B3W.

Les Gray is a postdoctoral scholar at the University of Missouri. Their work has appeared in *Prompt: A Journal of Theatre Theory* and *Performing Ethos*. Their research focuses on cultural production and its relationship to trauma and terror ranging from blues dancing to police brutality videos. Les is interested in performances of spectacular Black pain as well as the potential for joy, healing, and solidarity.

Charlene Gross is an Assistant Professor of Costume Design at the Pennsylvania State University School of Theatre. Her opera, theatre, and dance designs have been seen on and off Broadway, across the country, and on the West End London stage. Charlene was an Innovator-in-Residence at PSU's Center for Pedagogy in Arts and Design for the work cited. She holds an MFA from NYU and is a member of USA 829.

Elisha Clark Halpin is an Associate Professor of Dance and Theatre at the Pennsylvania State University School of Theatre and a Ph.D. candidate in Somatics and Transpersonal Psychology. Her research centers on embodiment, trauma, and sites of memory. Halpin uses somatics principles and practices as a pathway of conscious disruption to deepen curiosity and develop leadership skills. Her performance and teaching work has taken her around the world, most notably the Dublin Dance Festival, Bates Dance Festival, Amsterdam's de Theaterschool, and DanceLab Prague.

Meg Hanna-Tominaga is the current chair and resident scenic designer for the Department of Theatre & Dance at Converse University, where in addition to a variety of design-related courses, she also teaches Stage Management, Puppetry, Playwriting, and Intro to Asian Theatre. She received her MFA from the University of Hawaii – Mānoa. Meg has worked for Sony and Nickelodeon Animation Studios on a number of shows including *Spongebob Squarepants*, *Hey Arnold!*, and *Invader Zim*; she has worked for theatres, opera companies, and on independent films in various capacities all across the mainland, from Florida to California, and in Hawaii as well.

Jeanmarie Higgins is an Associate Professor in the Pennsylvania State University School of Theatre. A new works dramaturg in dance and theatre, Jeanmarie publishes widely on the intersection of theory and practice. Co-editor for *Prompt: A Journal of Theatre Theory, Practice, and Teaching,* Jeanmarie is the 2021 recipient of the Oscar Brockett Outstanding Teacher Award from the Association of Theatre in Higher Education.

Kelley Holley is a Ph.D. candidate at the University of Maryland, College Park. Her research interests include site-specific performance and audience studies. As a dramaturg, she has worked with companies such as New Rep Theatre and Company One Theatre. She is the co-curator of "Rebels and Revels," a virtual photo exhibit of the theatre of the Middle East from 1950 to 1970.

Kristin Leahey (she/her) is an Assistant Professor at Boston University. She served as the Director of New Works at Seattle Repertory Theatre and the Literary Manager at Woolly Mammoth Theatre. Leahey has dramaturged with the Oregon Shakespeare Festival, Dallas Theater Center, Denver Center, Guthrie Theater, Steppenwolf Theatre, The Goodman Theatre, The Kennedy

Center, The Old Globe, and Ireland's Galway Arts Festival, among others. Her publications include articles in *Theatre Topics*, *Theatre Journal*, and *Theatre History Studies*.

Marjan Moosavi is, by turns, a lecturer, researcher, digital curator, and dramaturg. She is the Roshan Lecturer in Persian Studies and Performing Arts and a member of the Roshan Initiative in Persian Digital Humanities. She holds a Ph.D. in Theatre and Performance Studies from the University of Toronto. Her work, whether academic or artistic, examines the dynamics of theatre-making and performance in the Persianate world, and their intersection with gender, religion, and politics. Her scholarly articles are published in The *Drama Review (TDR)*, *New Theatre Quarterly*, *Modern Drama*, *Theatre Journal*, and *Asian Theatre Journal*. She is the principal investigator of "Rebels and Revels," a virtual photo exhibit on the theatre of the Middle East, and a longstanding Regional Managing Editor for TheTheatreTimes.com.

Shelley Orr is an Associate Professor at San Diego State University. She heads SDSU's MA in Theatre Arts. Her publications have appeared in *Review: the Journal of Dramaturgy*, *Theatre Journal*, *TheatreForum*, and *Theatre Topics*. She co-edited the collection *Performance and the City*. She served as a dramaturg for the San Diego REP, New York's Classic Stage Company, and La Jolla Playhouse. She is a past president of Literary Managers and Dramaturgs of the Americas (LMDA).

Dennis Schebetta is an actor, writer, and director for film and theatre. He is currently an Assistant Professor at Skidmore College where he teaches acting and directing. He has worked off-Broadway and regionally in works ranging from Shakespeare to devising to new play development at organizations such as Ensemble Studio Theater, 13th Street Rep, Vital Theater, Pittsburgh Playhouse, Saratoga Shakespeare Festival, and the NY Fringe. A graduate of the William Esper Studio, where he studied with William Esper, he also holds an MFA from Virginia Commonwealth University.

Michael Schweikardt enjoys a successful career as a set designer. He currently teaches scenic design and theatre studies at The Pennsylvania State University. Essays in *Teaching Critical Performance Theory in Today's Theatre Classroom, Studio, and Communities* (Routledge 2020) and *Text and Presentation, 2019* (McFarland 2020) demonstrate his research focus on the tension between materiality and ephemeral performances. He serves as managing editor for design at *thetheatretimes.com* and is co-editor of *Prompt: A Journal of Theatre Theory, Practice, and Teaching*.

Christopher J Staley is an actor, director, and teaching artist. He currently is a Ph.D. candidate in Theatre and Performance Studies at the University of Pittsburgh. Additional compendium contributions include *Theatre and the Macabre* (University of Wales, 2022). Onstage appearances include the

American Repertory Theatre, OBERON, Indiana Repertory Theatre, Opera Carolina, the Moscow Art Theatre Studio, and performance venues such as the Watermill Center and Locust Projects. Christopher has had multiple training experiences each with SITI Company, the Moscow Art Theatre, Theatre Nohgaku, Pacific Performance Project, Robert Wilson, and the Suzuki Company of Toga.

Christina Thanasoula is a Europe-based freelance lighting designer. Since 2002, she has designed lighting for over 250 operas, theatre and dance performances, in most of Greece's largest venues, including the National Theatre and the ancient theatre of Epidaurus. She holds a Master of Arts in Advanced Theatre Practice, strand of Lighting Design from the Royal Central School of Speech and Drama, and a degree in Theatre Studies from the University of Athens where she currently teaches lighting design. She is the author of the Greek national occupational standard and educational curriculum of the lighting technician profession and author of the book *Lighting design: painting on stage in four dimensions* published in 2021.

Gwendolyn Walker (she/her) is an Assistant Professor of Voice in Penn State's BFA Musical Theatre program and a graduate of the Contemporary Alexander School. Her unique approach to training young artists from a somatic perspective as well as from a contemporary commercial vocal perspective has made her a sought-after guest artist around the world (Juilliard, Oslo, London, Paris). She maintains an active Voice and Alexander Technique Studio in New York City.

Samuel Yates, Ph.D., is a deaf artist and researcher who is currently an Assistant Professor in the School of Theatre and Dance at Millikin University. They are the recipient of a George J. Mitchell Scholarship, the Helen Krich Chinoy Fellowship, and ASTR's Grant for Researchers with Heavy Teaching Loads for their work on disability and performance. Samuel's work is published or forthcoming in the *Journal of Dramatic Theory and Criticism, Music Theatre Today, Studies in Musical Theatre, Medicine and Literature, The Matter of Disability* (U Michigan), and *A Cultural History of Disability in the Modern Age* (Bloomsbury).

Acknowledgments

Teaching Performance Practices in Remote and Hybrid Spaces was collectively written by theatre and performance practitioners who were too busy to commit to writing anything in 2020 and 2021. And yet they did, and for this we are grateful. We are also grateful to Sarah Bay-Cheng, whose front essay embodies the best of kind of optimism, one informed by her distinct way of calling on theatre histories in order to embrace what's next for our fields.

The place we work, the Pennsylvania State University, University Park, is filled with artists and scholars who contribute to—and often define—their respective fields. We are fortunate to teach alongside all of these folks, but we would specifically like to thank the theatre studies and dance faculty—Elizabeth Bonjean, Michele Dunleavy, Megan Moore, Michael Schweikardt, Sebastian Trainor, and Malcolm Womack—for their friendship and collaborative spirit throughout one of the most challenging periods of our teaching lives. Penn State authors represent a significant part of this book's authorship primarily because they agreed to write chapter proposals at one of the most stressful times of the pandemic, when we convinced them that their time would be well spent helping others to strengthen their classes held in remote and hybrid spaces.

We are also grateful to the Penn State School of Theatre and College of Arts and Architecture, whose research support continued during the pandemic. We are fortunate to have institutional support for our pedagogy research, especially through the Center for Pedagogy in Arts and Design under the leadership of Susan Russell.

Thank you to the Penn State graduate students in directing, design, and technology who were taking a pedagogy seminar in Spring 2020, and who contributed to the creation of a new online theatre pedagogy and practice journal, taking part in so many online teaching experiments in our course as students and instructors—Ryan Douglass, Alison Morooney, Grisele Gonzalez-Ledezma, Beatriz Chung, Keagan Styes, Tyler Phillips, Jessica Hill, Jen Delac, Rosalind Isquith, and Alyssa Ridder. A special shout-out goes to our editorial assistant, Rozy, without whom we never could have gotten our manuscript submitted. As always, thank you to Routledge and especially to our fearless editor, Ben Piggott.

Jeanmarie Higgins and Elisha Clark Halpin

In Defense of "Stuff"
Teaching the Ephemeral Theatre of Things

Sarah Bay-Cheng

Although it doesn't accord with the desire to live an elegantly minimalist lifestyle, I am a gear-head at heart. I might pretend to enjoy the simplicity of running, but I truly love the sports that require a good kit. Cycling, triathlons, kayaking, and rock climbing are as enjoyable for their accessories as for the sports themselves, perhaps even more so. As any aficionado knows, the pleasures of gear are many. There's the actual use, of course, as well as the maintenance, the packing and unpacking, organizing and upgrading, preparation, care, and display of all the *stuff*. No matter the endeavor, gear provides a tactile connection to activity that extends before and after the action itself.

This preference extends to theatre as well. I appreciate simple staging and great acting in the so-called "empty space," but I'd rather someone or something fill it up. Pina Bausch's work does this exceptionally well. *Palermo Palermo* (1989), for example, opens by crashing an enormous cinderblock wall on the stage. The subsequent performance progressively layers innumerable objects and bodies across the resulting rubble. Even Bausch's minimalism can become maximal, as in the sea of empty chairs that dancers noisily move about the setting of *Café Müller* (1978). The sound of the objects fills the space as much as the chairs themselves.

Or, take Big Art Group's *Broke House* (2012), a loose adaptation of Anton Chekhov's *Three Sisters* that built—and destroyed—a physical and virtual community on stage. At the 2012 production for the American Realness Festival in New York, the set was constructed as a series of boxes made out of brightly colored plastic tarps and filled with piles of debris that continued to multiply throughout the show, eventually becoming costumes that the characters built up on their bodies. In characteristic style, Big Art Group linked the layered physical stage spaces together through real-time video that projected the world of the characters on to surfaces and screens within the built space. Using techniques they've coined "real-time film" to produce what Jennifer Parker-Starbuck calls "cyborg theatre," Big Art Group creates works that maximize the materiality of physical theatre alongside the pleasurable excesses of digital video. Stitched across theatrical time and space, Big Art Group creates witty, irreverent, and moving performances that fill the senses through both tactile and remote technologies.

Company founders Caden Manson and Jemma Nelson have been ready for their Zoom close-up for a long time. As Parker-Starbuck herself wrote as early as 2006, "There is no future by the cyborg theatre." Surveying the state of performance over the course of the global pandemic in 2020 and 2021—or what I'm calling ACV (*Anno Coronavirus*)—I'm inclined to agree with her.

As theatres and other live performance venues closed in the wake of COVID-19 and many turned to theatre, dance, and other performances on screen, the artistry and scholarship of those creating and investigating digital performance feels more timely, more prescient than ever. The coronavirus took so much from those who work in the theatre: audiences, spaces, revenue, physical co-presence, intimacy. Whatever limited security and opportunities the theatre ever offered was further eroded during the pandemic. According to a report from the US Recovery Support Function Leadership Group (RSFLG), the theatre and the performing arts were among the most severely affected industries. According to their weekly report of January 4, 2021, among the broader arts and cultural sector, "nowhere has the effect been more direct, deep, and immediate than on the performing arts." According to data from the National Endowment of the Arts (NEA), revenue from tax-exempt performing arts companies declined nearly 54% in quarter 3 of 2020 from almost $1.9 billion in 2019.[1] Unemployment in the performing arts more than quadrupled in some areas. Musicians, singers, and related workers saw unemployment rise from 1.1% in 2019 to more than 27.1% in 2020.

Amid these painful realities, new opportunities and resources emerged. Online performance collections, archives, and documents became available as never before, with numerous and varied recordings previously locked behind paywalls circulating freely (for a while at least). For example, after decades of reading Bertolt Brecht's accounts of Helene Weigel's performance in *Mother Courage and Her Children* and trying to imagine what might have been happening on stage, I could watch the Berliner Ensemble's film of her performance from 1957. Amazing! (And humbling, as I realize that my imaginings fell far short of the actual show.) In mid-2015, Lin-Manuel Miranda's theatrical juggernaut, *Hamilton* (2015) became available on the Disney+ streaming video service. After years in which the price of a ticket for the show soared to the hundreds of dollars or more and the original cast disbanded, audiences could watch the original Broadway cast (on repeat!) for roughly $7 USD per month, a price that includes the Marvel Universe among other offerings from the Disney vault.

Whatever one thinks about the show, *Hamilton* is probably the most (re)mediated theatrical production of all time. The show itself remediates both musical theatre history and 1980s and 1990s hip-hop music and aesthetics to compelling effect. Part of what makes the video version of the live performance work so well is that its original staging owes a great deal to music video aesthetics of the 1980s and 1990s, influencing not only the show's dramatic structure (e.g., "Rewind") and audio but also choreography and staging. Much of the original staging echoes filmic techniques. For example, the stage revolve creates the effects of a tracking shot in film, while the use of lighting in numbers such as "Dear Theodosia" echoes the cinematic split screen. The camera placements and (re)choreography for the screen performance offer perspectives and views not visible to a live audience in the theatre.

Beyond the remediation of stage production itself, the show built an extensive fan culture through the intersection of live and social media encounters in pre-show performances shared as #Ham4Ham posts, and original cast album and Hamilton mix-tape recordings (and re-recordings), amid proliferating bootlegs and imitations since the musical's Broadway premiere in 2016. According to Google, there are 36.9 million videos online related to "Hamilton the musical." Even if every video were only ten seconds (and, of course, most of these are much longer), it would take one person watching 24 hours per day, over 11 and half years to watch every available video.

But what about the stuff?

One of the many challenges of 2020–2021 was that so many of our habitual activities were flattened into a single mode: the two-dimensional televisual screen. Work-related meetings, social gatherings, family conversations suddenly and overwhelmingly transpired through screens. Whether this screen is a flat-panel television, computer, tablet, or phone, the aesthetics are comparable. I enjoy watching television as much as the next person, but even as someone who has been watching and writing about mediated performance over the past 20 years, I never imagined that these might become the *only* theatre available. Although I've been accused of not appreciating the "magic" of live performance on more than one occasion, I'd never stopped attending live performances until March 2020. Indeed, over the past two decades, I've come to enjoy some forms of performance more in person (most dance, music) and other forms equally but in different ways (sports).[2] With unprecedented access to screen performances from around the world, I both loved what I could watch on screen during the pandemic, and deeply missed the experience of sitting in a shared physical space waiting for a performance to begin.

Even with so many performances available as never before, there was still so much missing, most especially the stuff.

I stand by my earlier writing that the experience of live performance on screen can be as rich and even as visceral as the in-person experience, albeit in different and distinguishing ways. (If you're inclined to disagree that media can be visceral, remember that audiences literally vomited during screenings of *The Blair Witch Project* [1999] with similar reports of nausea reported from too many video-conference meetings.) However, I readily acknowledge that all of the tertiary elements of attending live theatre cannot be so easily simulated or replaced: the anticipatory dinner before the show, or the drinks and discussion after; the physical sensations of sitting among a group of strangers, either thrillingly aligned with my own reactions or revealing distinct perspectives; the tactile familiarity of velvet-covered seats or the bite of well-used (and slightly splintered) rehearsal cubes. Most of all, I miss the risk that comes with seeing a show in a new space for the first time, of encountering not only new stories and unfamiliar people, but entering a space and forming a new community for however long the show will last. This doesn't happen at home where the images flicker in the same space as social media feeds, meetings, amid scores of television shows. The living room is where it sort of happens.

Long before the pandemic crisis, we find evidence of a similar longing for physicality, presence, and spontaneous unfamiliar community in other simulated environments. The virtual reality space, Second Life, for instance, allows its avatars to fly, teleport, and otherwise move in ways completely outside the realm of bodily human experience. So what did its earliest users build? Perhaps the most unnecessary and potentially uninteresting of objects: stairs and chairs (Figure 0.1).

Sometimes these stairs and chairs were historical or simply decorative (modernist furniture was especially popular in the first decade of Second Life), but often they were used as well by the world's avatars. It is almost as if the image of physical spaces and items particular to bodily use, such as walking or sitting, encouraged a kind of conceptual affinity between a user's primary experience in real life (IRL) and their virtual projection in Second Life, even when the latter was required to neither sit nor walk.[3]

Especially in the early years of Second Life, these stairs reminded me of Adolphe Appia's drawing series, *Rhythmic Spaces*, and I think they serve the same function (Figure 0.2). Appia's conceptual theatrical spaces and the Second Life stairs are notable for their orientation to human experience (i.e., presumably embodied audiences) and yet are notably absent any people, including avatars.

Figure 0.1 Screen capture of prefab house design. Second Life, 9 December 2021.

This is surprising for Appia, who argued vigorously for the centrality of the three-dimensional actor as integral to the creation of design. Why does he omit the human figure from his images? It is possible that the very emptiness of these spaces is what invites opportunity to the embodied viewer, who is implicitly addressed in both these conceptual spaces. That is, these are physical spaces for the viewer to imaginatively locate one's own body across the barrier of the two-dimensional frame.

Stairs are particularly evocative and effective in such settings because their reliance on perspective works against the two-dimensionality of the image. Both Second Life and Appia's drawings seek to convey a virtual reality in which viewers can project themselves into the image. The stairs suggest a bridge between the three dimensionality of the viewer's body and the two-dimensional image. This effect is even more pronounced when the stairs face the viewer directly as a kind of visual imperative. Looking at the image one might imagine walking up the stairs presented. After all, what else does one do with stairs? These images remind us not only of the sensations of being in shared physical space, but of the bodily actions required to navigate it. The three-dimensionality of the stairs restores a sensation of performance materiality even when expressed in two dimensions.

And, so we come to the present moment in which we find ourselves experiencing simultaneously a scarcity and an abundance of theatrical experience.

Figure 0.2 Adolphe Appia. "The Staircase" from Rhythmic Spaces, c. 1913.

In response to the limitations and opportunities of the present moment, those teaching theatre, dance, and performance practice and theory face unprecedented challenges. One of the most significant, of course, is how to teach certain parts of theatre without access to these physical spaces or the things that fill them. In other words, how do we teach theatre without "stuff"? Can we convey theatre and all its possible experiential dimensions across digital divides?

The essays included in *Teaching Performance Practices in Remote and Hybrid Spaces* offer compelling examples of the potential for new forms of performance pedagogy in a post-COVID landscape. The examples here provide ways to work through the present (and future?) limitations by reimagining theatre's materiality across screens, bodies, environments, social relations, and experiences. Like the virtual stairs of Appia's drawings and Second Life, the authors here provide bridges from the familiarity of the theatre pedagogy pre-pandemic and its physical experience in three dimensions to new forms of engagement in digital and hybrid spaces.

In our present context, new performances of all kinds require attention to both theatre and film and media studies, with a rethinking of how principles of composition function in the context of the screen. Teaching theatre remotely is not about simply conveying pre-existing techniques of theatre through new media, but rather teaching effectively today requires us to invent new techniques from the synthesis of theatricality and media specificity. We're still making theatre with things, but the "things" have changed. As we navigate this transition, we can't let the medial become immaterial.

Although it's hard to feel celebratory in the midst of a continuing global pandemic, new developments, techniques, and ideas are nevertheless exciting. As we look to the current moment for new opportunities to rewrite and revise our approach to teaching theatre and performance studies, there are many new opportunities. As many others have noted, these are not only formal, but more importantly social, cultural, and economic. In my most optimistic moments, I am persuaded by those who are working to write new and improved rules for theatrical creation, reception, and education. I believe in this mission and will continue to work in whatever ways I can to create opportunities for new generations of students. I'm excited to see what comes next.

I'll get my gear ready.

Notes

1 https://www.arts.gov/sites/default/files/COVID-Outlook-Week-of-1.4.2021.pdf.
2 The exception to this is baseball, which benefits from a hybrid approach, including live presence at the game with radio commentary. I am still waiting for the Wooster Group to create a performance based on baseball (and, yes, I am available to dramaturg this). Note: I stand by my completely biases belief that Toronto Raptors basketball is superior to all other performances regardless of format and OG Anunby is a gifted performance artist on par with Andy Kaufman. (If you don't know what I'm talking about, look him up now).

3 I'm tempted to draw a similar equivalence with the popularity of cooking shows that coincided with a decline in people actually cooking at home. That reality television about how things *taste* continues to be so popular suggests again that the connection between physical embodiment and media is not as well defined as we might think.

Introduction
Teaching Performance Practices in Remote and Hybrid Spaces

Jeanmarie Higgins and Elisha Clark Halpin

This essay collection, *Teaching Performance Practices in Remote and Hybrid Spaces*, is our most recent collaboration; we have been partners in performance pedagogy at the Pennsylvania State University for five years. In addition to leading a praxis-based BA Theatre Studies program, beginning in 2017 we developed and wrote Performance & Society, a large-format general education course for non-arts majors specifically designed to fulfill a new "intercomain" course requirement for all Penn State undergraduate students. We first taught Theatre 101N, a course that combines arts and social sciences knowledge domains, in Spring 2020 as co-instructors to 220 students in one of Penn State's largest and most hospitable classrooms. The sound system worked beautifully; our PowerPoint presentations were displayed on two separate screens. Best of all, a space between the podium and the first row of student seating functioned as a theatre stage. Students recited poetry in this "mystic gulf;" we demonstrated the principles of Laban, Forum theatre, and Viewpoints; PSU's Center for the Performing Arts guest artists Step Afrika! and jazz singer Lizz Wright performed in our class. Theatre 101N's premise is that performance happens everywhere and in many ways. As such, the course topics range from dance and theatre, to sports, everyday life, and politics. With the US Democratic presidential debates in full swing, during one memorable class, students "voted" for president in a physical mapping exercise that asked them to align themselves with a candidate based on where they chose to stand in the classroom (interestingly, Kamala Harris won that election).

Scalable from 25 to 750 students, Theatre 101N is assessed without quizzes or exams regardless of enrollment. Instead, students are asked to complete a set of creative projects and discussions, all of which are submitted online through the learning management system. Some of the assignments are art projects. Other assignments are performance-based—a dance, a monologue—and still others ask students to find performance in unexpected places—family photographs, a random throw of a handful of coins. Students also write performance reviews and short plays. If the student completes all the assignments, they receive an A for the course. So, although the stress of moving to online delivery in March 2020 was significant, Theatre 101N did not suffer as much as other courses in

DOI: 10.4324/9781003229056-1

general education, specifically because we developed it to be taught in a range of modes depending on curricular and student needs.[1]

By developing this course to be taught online, we discovered much more than how to teach online. We diversified our assessment methods to align with research on how students learn best. We created assignments to which we respond, not grade. Although it might strain the imagination, thanks to our LMS (Canvas), the work required to maintain the course was no more than other large general education courses we had taught that used attendance and exams as primary methods of assessment. Although we did not know it at the time, we had created a class that privileged joy over rigor, and in such a way that we were not overly taxed as instructors. In March 2020, this feature of our course design made the transition to remote learning less onerous for us than for others in our university. We were also team teaching, a luxury that is more efficient than many administrators who must count FTE's might think.

Author Jane Barnette's chapter resonates clearly to us in this moment—after what we hope is the worst of the COVID-19 crisis. In Chapter 1, "**Reevaluating Rigor with 2020 Hindsight—A manifesto for the ungraded classroom**," Barnette says: "Particularly for remote performance classrooms, where risk-taking and failure are crucial steps in the artistic process, flexible pedagogy has never been more necessary." She continues, "Without the necessity of change, brought on by a lethal airborne virus, I likely would have continued teaching as I had for decades: in a graded classroom, with expectations of 'rigor' at the root of my curriculum." (12) Part I of *Teaching Performance Practices in Remote and Hybrid Spaces*, Pedagogies of Care for Digital Spaces, is a collective response to what many of us learned when needing to switch from teaching in-person to teaching online, that is, to release expectations of "rigor" in favor of employing a pedagogy of care for students. With the onslaught of stress from online learning and the pandemic itself, many educators found themselves knee deep in waters they had not before been forced to traverse. While educators were by no means oblivious to the mental health issues and other struggles their students experienced, as we entered virtual and hybrid space, our previously held professional boundaries seemed to be melting away. Our students needed us in ways we had not experienced before, and most of us tried to rise to the challenge of putting students' mental health needs first.

But as a field, we did not know what we did not know. As Elizabeth Coen reminds us:

> It is frequently argued that theatre education naturally accords certain social-emotional competencies, like empathy and emotional awareness. Yet the fact remains that undergraduates enrolled in theatre and performance classes still struggle with applying emotional knowledge gained through coursework to support their academic growth. College students need skills to manage stress and self-motivate, especially when taking classes in remote settings. (21)

In Chapter 2, "**Solving the real crisis in virtual education: strategies for training arts practitioners in social and emotional learning**," Coen sounds the call to implement strategies of Social and Emotional learning to address mental wellness and equitable learning outcomes in the virtual classroom, citing SEL as a bridge to help students apply that emotional knowledge. Samuel Yates likewise scrutinizes idealized notions of theatre education. In Chapter 3, "**Practicing Academic grace: Pedagogical Experiments with *Mr. Burns* in Digital Play Analysis Classrooms**," Yates asks us to center student learning by first breaking through academic ableism, a practice that begins with acknowledging the harm done by failing to notice what we have internalized as foundational texts and ideas, which Yates terms "forms of academic violence" such as "the uncritical assignment of 'canonical' syllabus content …; citational practices that reinforce cultural biases towards senior white male scholars; racial and gendered microaggressions in the classroom; … or the disability-exclusionary practices that Jay T. Dolmage calls 'academic ableism'" (33).

Chapter 4, "**I hope this email finds you (well): teaching in traumatic spaces during the COVID-19 pandemic**," is Les Gray's first-person account of teaching trauma as a subject during the pandemic, realizing from March onward that "after proposing and designing a course about trauma and terror, my students and I were met with lives saturated with trauma and terror." (44) Using what their students were learning to inform *how* they were learning it, it is fitting that Gray completes this book's first section with a poetic conflation of the pandemic's medical and spiritual effects:

> I breathed into a time where breath was pathologically being stolen from us, trusting that if I continued to show up for my students, they would absorb the knowledge that was of the utmost importance; I held them and their survival in far higher regard than any grade or deadline. (46–7)

What all of us might have learned teaching during 2020 and 2021 was just this—that caring about students is the first step in preparing them to learn. As dedicated educators, our foundational study of Paulo Freire's notion of love, Augusto Boal's provocation to recognize coercion in our methods, and bell hooks's directive to transgress in order to liberate, inspire the authors in this book as they argue for undoing ableism, questioning the value of rigor, collaborating with students on syllabuses, and "ungrading" (Blum).

Though dance and movement arguably present the most legible challenges to online teaching—their primary subject being the body—the authors in Part II: Dance and Movement write of the unforeseen benefits that the move to online and hybrid forms of teaching and performing has revealed. Part II looks at the new life emerging in teaching embodied practices and the innovative approaches to thinking about dance space. Authors Elisha Clark Halpin and Kelley Holley invite curiosity about the dramaturgical process in composition classes and the use of virtual performance spaces, while Christopher Staley, Michele Dunleavy, and Gwendolyn Walker investigate and re-envision pedagogies steeped in tradition. This section begins with Chapter 5, "**Imaginative deixis and distributed fictions in the Suzuki method of actor training.**" Here Staley finds correspondences between Suzuki's own pedagogy and the pedagogy required from all teachers during the pandemic. "A larger benefit [of Suzuki training] comes from … extending their imaginative conception of the other person—to remember that while the embodied realities of another person are not actually accessible, they are imaginatively available" (66). Relating his experiences in Suzuki training over the years, he focuses on the workshop he took online in Summer 2021, drawing correspondences between the actor's need to imagine another on stage while also acting completely alone, a state that resonated with most of us in that prolonged 2020–2021 moment of isolation from our theatre-making partners.

In Chapter 6, "**New geographies of space in virtual and hybrid performance classrooms,**" Holley shares her experience leading performance in virtual spaces when the performers are rehearsing and performing at home. Holley extends her notion of a space that is where students actually live, to performance spaces always already being "where a student lives:" "Pedagogy that is attentive to the student's space, in many ways, resembles a pedagogy of care: it is attuned and responsive to the individual conditions each student learns in, investigating their environments and building the performance from these contexts." (75) Chapter 7, "**Dramaturgy and social media: new tools for composition,**" continues this book's exploration of virtual performance spaces as co-editor Halpin explores social media as a ripe landscape for young artists to pay attention to their work, providing opportunities to develop their voices and apply dramaturgical tools in their compositions.

> What began as a reaction to studios closing and stages going dark now looks like an opportunity to cultivate a new relationship with the compositional study. Armed with personal digital studios like Instagram and TikTok, dancers capitalized on what they already knew, and created work from the spaces (inner and outer) they were inhabiting. (80)

During the pandemic Walker taught Alexander Technique in the virtual classroom. In Chapter 8, "**Teaching Alexander Technique (without hands) Online: A Study of Kindness,**" she shares how she taught without touch, but nonetheless discovered that the pandemic made Alexander Technique all the more necessary, whether in a studio space or a virtual space: "Our nervous systems are in a state of high alert due to the pandemic, and AT offers unique solutions to coping with stress so that the trauma we experience does not turn into misuse, pain, or disease" (85). Like many educators thrown into online teaching, Dunleavy found meaning in the subtexts that became context, requiring new tools and modes of navigation. In Chapter 9, "**Releasing expectations in the digital dance studio,**" Dunleavy explores how teaching tap online in a rigorous musical theatre training program led her to rethink pedagogy in the arts more broadly, noting: "Conversations that previously lived at the margins of the arts community are suddenly center stage. Conversations that propose a new paradigm based on models of abundance, not scarcity, security instead of precarity, and collaboration rather than competition" (105). The space that can exist between the values we hold and the pedagogies we employ has never been clearer. Dunleavy's chapter is a case study in bridging the gaps we may find in teaching online, but also provokes questions about the ethics of rigorous training in BFA performance programs.

The authors in Part III: Doing Theatre Online: collectively ask "What is theatre in the absence of its historical home?" For Daniel Ciba, this home is the theatre archive, historical records kept in physical places, all of which were closed to in-person visitors during 2020 and much of 2021 In **"An archive by any other name: the historiographic, the digital, the hybrid,"** dramaturg and queer theorist Ciba details the frustration he experienced in 2020 while working on a book about Tennessee Williams. He ultimately expresses gratitude for the discoveries he made—both historical and pedagogical—because of (rather than despite) his circumstances. He concludes: "Archival research would benefit from the exploration of hybrid teaching because this forces teachers and students alike to think about how they access and explicate evidence." (119) As in so many chapters in *Teaching Performance Practices*, access is at the front of the researcher's mind as he invites "in-person archives [to] change their policies based on how closures highlighted the issues of access existent long before the pandemic" (119). In Chapter 11, **"Building trust across miles: new play dramaturgy in virtual rehearsal rooms,"** new play dramaturgs Kristin Leahey and Shelley Orr detail their experiences developing student plays during the pandemic in their respective university departments. New play development processes are so often gatherings, processes that unfold in such idyllic places as the O'Neill Center or Hedgebrook Women's Writers retreat, or else in the incubator spaces of noted regional theatres. What Leahey and Orr discovered in their respective university new works projects is that the values and skills that drove pandemic teaching are the same that will drive their future in-person new play development projects: "a focus on student-centered learning, applying a process-over-product lens, and implementing a cadre of antiracist rehearsal practices" (133).

Chapter 12, **"Re-making rehearsal and performance: intersections of collaboration and accessibility in a hybrid *Romeo & Juliet*,"** will be familiar to anyone who was directing a university production in March 2020. When the pandemic halted rehearsal and production on a production of *Romeo and Juliet* at Siena College, director Dennis Schebetta scrambled to find ways to rehearse online. When it became clear that in-person activities would be canceled, he shifted to finding ways to perform online. Like so many stories in this book, Schebetta discovered much more than how to perform Shakespeare remotely. He made key discoveries about acting pedagogy, concluding that acting for both platforms—theatre and film—could benefit from each other's methods. Schebetta, too, finds the message of access at the end of his story, reminding all of us that a digital future provides an opportunity to meet the access needs of students and audiences alike: "How you adapt your productions to meet the needs of your students is how you will move forward in reaching your goals for inclusion and accessibility." Schebetta concludes that "this model of hybrid rehearsal and performance is a multi-dimensional methodology of theatre-making that integrates accessibility with collaboration." (144)

In the last chapter of Part III, Chapter 13, **"Walking backward on a global tightrope: interview with Nassim Soleimanpour about the virtual performance of** *White Rabbit, Red Rabbit*,**"** Iranian playwright Soleimanpour talks with Marjan Moosavi about the virtual performance of *White Rabbit Red Rabbit* on the global stage during the pandemic. Soleimanpour brings out the political in the absence of material theatre spaces as he articulates our common, current predicament: "The virtual platforms market themselves as reunion opportunities while at their core they are testaments to our isolation." (149) His outlook on the future of theatre organizations that depend on material spaces is not optimistic:

> [T]hese beautiful empty spaces, the heartbroken theatres which had to sit idly and watch us move on without them, have … gone through tragic changes in the course of the pandemic. Not only systematically or financially but more deeply philosophically or even deeper existentially. (150)

Scenic design professor Michael Schweikardt convenes the conversation of Part IV: Materiality / Ephemerality: Teaching Design and Production Now with Chapter 14 **"Reclaiming materiality in remote theatrical design instruction."** Switching to remote instruction for an introduction to design course, Schweikardt's pedagogy changed less than he would have imagined. Notably, Schweikardt's students continued drawing on paper, creating journals that documented not only their progress as emerging designers but their individual and often troubling experiences of Spring 2020. He concludes:

> [B]ranching out into digital spaces in 2020 … opened new spaces for collaboration; it made class delivery equitable for students with varied and ever-changing situations; it made the submission of material assignments more efficient and allowed for consistent instructor feedback; and it left behind an archive of embodied practice that captures the moment. (166)

In Chapter 15, **"Reframing beauty and gender in stage makeup,"** costume design professor Charlene Gross discovered that being asked to teach online led to discovering a wealth of resources, in this case makeup tutorials from drag performers commissioned through a grant Gross received. These discoveries, in turn, underlined the need to change course language:

> As I reimagined individual projects, the need to step back and reframe the language for the class became apparent. How can the course terminology,

along with the project titles, be more inclusive to diverse student populations, and be as clear as possible to convey the meaning? (170)

Without the need to teach online, Gross might not have discovered these makeup demonstration videos with their attendant array of ways to describe beauty.

Finally, Christina Thanasoula and Meg Hanna-Tominaga call for us to cross-train in various technical and design areas to meet the moment (and the future) of theatre production. In Chapter 16, "**Lighting design dramaturgy and practice in the post pandemic world of on-line streaming,**" lighting designer Thanasoula concludes that "hybrid theatre is in need of hybrid theatre practitioners who will embrace digital transformation" and will eventually form "a workforce with the necessary skills" (183). In "**Standby life as we know it … Life as we (now) know it, Go: a case study in the hybrid stage management classroom,**" professor Hanna-Tominaga concludes that "much like running a show that must put in an understudy who knows none of her lines or blocking, teaching during the pre-vaccine pandemic pushed my preparedness and adaptability to extreme edges." (190) Hanna-Tominaga highlights the use of the stage manager's golden rules of flexibility and clarity not only when running a production, but also in managing the stage management classroom to keep students thriving in difficult scenarios.

To close this introductory essay, we offer another thought from Staley's chapter on Suzuki training online, something we hope that our readers will take away from all the essays collected here. Like Staley, we "aim to remind [our] colleagues and [ourselves] of all the rich insights provided by this extended interval of remote practice," as we "hope to recuperate this period of experimentation, frustration, and successful failings" (67). As we move on (or back) to in-person training, teaching, learning, and production, may the lessons we learned about access, inclusion, and care take a primary place in our pedagogies.

Note

1 We are grateful for the course development grant funding we received from the Penn State Office of Digital Learning.

References

Blum, Susan Debra, editor. 2020. *Ungrading: why rating students undermines learning (and what to do instead)*. Morgantown: West Virginia University Press.

Boal, Augusto. 1985. *Theatre of the oppressed*. New York: TCG.

Dolmage, Jay T. 2017. *Academic Ableism: disability and higher education*. Ann Arbor: University of Michigan Press.

Freire, Paulo. 2020. *Pedagogy of the oppressed: 50th anniversary edition*. New York: Bloomsbury.

hooks, bell. 1994. *Teaching to transgress: education as the practice of freedom*. London: Routledge.

Part I

Pedagogies of Care for Digital Spaces

Chapter 1

Reevaluating Rigor with 2020 Hindsight—A Manifesto for the Ungraded Classroom

Jane Barnette

In recent years, public institutions of higher education have become more reliant on tuition revenue for survival and the process of learning, in turn, has become more transactional. "Transactional models of education identify students as consumers and teachers as retail workers who must please their customers (an inhumane model for retail sales as well as the world of learning)" (Denial 2016). In response to this pressure, many professors have doubled-down on their commitment to what they define as academic excellence, as evidenced by (what they consider) rigorous assignments. However, it is not coincidental that the word "rigor" is short-hand for rigor-mortis and derives from the Latin word for stiffness. As digital pedagogy trailblazer Jesse Stommel suggests, "most meanings of the word 'rigor' have no productive place in education, unless you believe school (and disciplinary culture) should be about policing, punishing, and gatekeeping—again with the effect of excluding already marginalized voices" (@Jessifer, *Twitter* June 27, 2021). Indeed, demanding rigor in the classroom accomplishes exactly what its Latin root suggests: it hardens and freezes students, encouraging them to create and labor from a place of fear. Conversely, to teach in/through *compassion* enlivens students, allowing them to stretch and grow, not only in the subject matter of the course being taught but in their very humanity and capacity for empathy.

Approaching the labor of teaching with kindness or compassion at the forefront also aligns with neuroscience discoveries—contrary to previous beliefs that students' emotions impede learning, we now recognize that "emotion and cognition are supported by interdependent neural processes" (Immordino-Yang 2016). Learning depends not only on intellectual capacity, then, but also on emotional receptivity. Students are more receptive when they feel brave and can trust their classmates and teacher, but this connection between emotion and knowing goes further when we recognize "that we only think deeply about things we care about" (Immordino-Yang 2016). Teaching critical thinking relies on having the capacity and emotional range to attach meanings to feelings and the courage to allow those emotional connections to form.

Arguably, students who select theatre courses (and especially those who major or minor in theatre or performance studies) are already familiar with the

DOI: 10.4324/9781003229056-3

vulnerability required of actors, whose emotional flexibility and accessibility has long been part of actor-training. Yet to assume that all students in any class, including an advanced acting class, are neurotypical would be foolhardy and discriminatory, so these insights about emotions and cognition only help teachers recognize part of the problem; they do not offer pedagogical solutions.

While teachers cannot control the emotional range or wellbeing of our students, we can improve our affective approach to teaching, by embracing kindness as well as offering an ungraded experience. As historian and pedagogy scholar Catherine Denial offers, "a pedagogy of kindness asks us to apply compassion in every situation we can, and not to default to suspicion or anger." Doing so "means recognizing that our students possess innate humanity, which directly undermines the transactional educational model to which too many of our institutions lean, if not cleave" (Denial 2019). When this approach is coupled with techniques of ungrading, the entire experience of teaching and learning transforms.

Particularly for remote performance classrooms, where risk-taking and failure are crucial steps in the artistic process, flexible pedagogy has never been more necessary. To learn performance analysis, design, or technique without the benefit of face-to-face interaction encourages increasingly deeper rifts between teacher and student, as well as between students perceived as "talented" and their peers whose skills are not yet obvious. In contrast, ungraded pedagogy empowers students to take control over how (much) they learn and establishes a foundation of trust for the professor that enables everyone's creativity to flourish.

With appreciation for the irony that the phrase "20/20 hindsight" now evokes, I recognize that the following provocations for teaching performance practices were made possible (or at least, rendered visible) because of the shared trauma that those of us who taught (and learned) during 2020 in the wake of stay-at-home orders and widespread digital (and hybrid) education mandates endured. Without the necessity of change, brought on by a lethal airborne virus, I likely would have continued teaching as I had for decades: in a graded classroom, with expectations of "rigor" at the root of my curriculum. And the students, in turn, would have evaluated me based on how well their learning and life obstacles could be balanced against my (perceived) rigor. Instead, thanks to the precarity brought on by the events of 2020 in the United States, we became hyper-aware of our needs and limitations—our innate humanity, as Denial would have it, rose to the surface, and made it all the more evident how inhumane the practice of rating students has always been.

What follows, then, is my proposal for radical change in university teaching methods. Because this proposal is so very situated in the "hindsight of 2020"—because it emerged out of the collective trauma wrought by the near-global mismanagement of COVID-19, alongside the strategic cruelty of the 45th US president—it takes the form of a manifesto, rather than a traditional essay. "To write a manifesto," after all, "is to announce one's participation, however discursive, in a struggle against oppressive forces" (Janet Lyon, qtd. in Gane, 2006, 219). I choose this format to mark a break with the past and to provoke others to do the same. In doing so, I call upon Donna Haraway's observation that "there is a kind of fantastic hope that runs through a manifesto" (qtd. in Gane, 2006, 222). I write this manifesto to conjure and nurture the *joy* of teaching and learning that so many of us mourn losing, or believe is possible, even if we have yet to experience it ourselves.

The Invocation

I call upon curiosity, which is related to care.
My muses are Natalie Loveless and Julia Frodahl.
—This is citational practice.
"Etymologically, *curious* has the same root as *careful* or *curate*: to care. It brings warning (caution), desire (to know), and considered choice (the *care* at stake in curation) together as the name of the (pedagogical) game."
(Loveless, 47, emphasis original)

"Compassion is the willingness and ability to feel someone else's suffering, and to wish to help alleviate that suffering. The word passion originally means suffering ... from a Buddhist perspective, where there's passion there tends to be attachment, and attachment is a cause of suffering."
(Frodahl, Interview)

I assert that **curiosity** is crucial for genuine learning to take place. The student must be driven by an abiding *desire to discover*.[1]

I claim that the **economy of grading students interferes with cultivating their curiosity**. By the economy of grading, I refer to the transactional qualities of contemporary higher education—the *banking model of education* defined by Paolo Freire (1970) that "understands knowledge as information bits that are depositable [*sic*], retrievable, and usable at some moment completely separate from the original scene of learning—like a toolkit that ... protects us—all of us!— from the anxiety associated with ignorance" (Loveless 49). From this perspective, teachers hold knowledge that they can transfer to students who earn grades worthy of receiving that knowledge. The language reveals the intent: to *earn* suggests the transaction assumed in grading. It presumes worthiness connected in the transaction and situates learning in a capitalist, consumer-driven setting. **Students are not consumers. They cannot earn knowledge**. The empty thing they receive—a grade—only matters because it benefits the transactional model by providing the capital—the grade—upon which neoliberal education depends.

Adding the "l" to earning to make learning entirely transforms the gerund. We learn because we want to know, because we study, **because we *care***.

When students care more about earning (a grade, a wage, a role) than learning, teachers become gatekeepers and supervisors who judge worthiness rather than mentors who inspire discovery.

I want to inspire students; I want students to inspire me. I want to cultivate compassion and curiosity in my classroom.

Therefore, I commit to a pedagogy of kindness, without traditional grading.

Three Parts of the Ritual

Having invoked curiosity and care, I turn now to the ritual at hand: teaching. Because all aspects of the ritual cannot be covered here, I highlight three distinctive parts, all of which are crucial to an ungraded pedagogy of kindness: (1) the flexible syllabus, (2) compassionate conversations, and (3) offering constructive feedback based on kindness.

The ritual begins with the syllabus, which is traditionally crafted before the course begins, before the teacher interacts with the students enrolled. While it is prudent to have boundaries in mind before the class begins, **I assert that syllabi must be written *in collaboration with students*, incorporating their collective decisions**. Curating the syllabus in cooperation with students aligns the ethics of the course with my intention to cultivate curiosity and compassion. Here, we are reminded of the shared root that curating, care, and curiosity share—the three Cs of this ritual.

Curating honors the expertise of the instructor, who has (presumably) chosen the scope of the course, and (or) chosen key readings and experiences that will facilitate exploring the subject at hand. **Once these decisions have been made, however, they must be ordered, both in *time* and *space*.** Within the restrictions set by the university (the dates of the term, the meeting days and times of the course, and any breaks or exam dates designated by the academic calendar, for example), students-as-curators *can and should* have the flexibility to rearrange *the timing* at will, until they reach consensus. The question of *space* applies to all classrooms, but especially those grounded in performance in digital and hybrid formats: in what digital and/or in-person spaces the scholarship will be presented, and to whom, are decisions **to be made by the students**, from among options offered (or agreed upon) by teachers.

Once these basics are established—*when* and *where* we will study and present—the real work begins. Variations abound for approaching student labor in ungraded paradigms, but one constant cannot be overlooked: the importance of **metacognition**. Knowing *what* and *how* you comprehend is crucial to teaching and learning, as scholars have established, but ungraded approaches move the needle beyond simply thinking about thinking. "Grading and assessment are two distinct things, and spending less time on grading does not mean spending less time on assessment. Assessment is inevitable," as Stommel (2020) claims (36). In addition to the instructor's inevitable contributions to evaluating the learning, however, in an ungraded classroom it is vital for students to evaluate themselves.

This can take several forms, occurring in small ways throughout the term, but I find it useful to require self-evaluations at least at midterm and before the university final exam period begins. True followers of the ungraded path (who are nevertheless obligated to enter university-sanctioned grades, rather than pass/fail or the like) will enter the exact grade a student assigns themselves for the course, but I reserve the right to adjust these proposed grades, typically so that I can raise them for students (usually female-identifying or members of the global majority) whose assessment is too modest or too harsh, in light of their peers.[2]

In addition to whatever self-evaluation checkpoints the class agrees upon, the expected *labor* of the students must be considered. There are numerous options for approaching this, including establishing a contract with a baseline grade for all students, contingent on an agreed-upon number of assignments completed, as well as (in many cases) an agreed-upon number and degree of absences or tardies allotted.[3] While my department—like many theatre departments—has a tacit expectation that students must attend virtually every class period, and adheres to the industry standard of timeliness ("to be early is to be on time"), with the hindsight of 2020 I no longer take attendance. Central to the premise of compassionate pedagogy is the tenet of believing students, and believing *in* them (Denial 2019)—therefore, if a student misses class, I must assume they had good reason. Ultimately, those students who have excessive absences but cannot (or will not) drop the course have opportunities to consider the weight of these absences in their self-evaluations, based on their unique challenges.

Once the syllabus has been determined as a class collective (a process that will take at least the first week, if not the first two-three weeks to establish), the next consideration for the ritual of teaching is **how we might foster compassionate conversations**. This concept is tangential to "difficult" conversations, a term that usually signals the discussion of "hot button" issues, such as "varying interpretations of religion; race, gender, and sexuality; genetic testing; evolution; immigration; and many more" ("Difficult Dialogues" 2021). Scholarship about discussions in educational settings also frequently evoke the concept of brave and safe spaces.[4] While similar, my use of *compassionate conversations* is meant to designate an approach based on both the pedagogy of kindness and an ungraded classroom. At the root of the difficulty experienced in discussing "hot button" topics, leading to the need to designate spaces as either brave or safe, is *judgment*. As Frodahl notes,

> compassion (and the changes it makes possible) comes from the ability to see beneath the surface. Specifically, to see the suffering that lies beneath every single act of harm and every dangerous belief... Because here's the thing: shaming, judging, and severing almost never has a transformative result.

That said, as she recognizes, "anyone subjected to racism, homophobia, and misogyny shouldn't also have to bear the burden of enlightening everyone" (2021). Unlike brave spaces, which can easily fall into the trap of falsely equating experiences and suggesting that *"historical inequities and power dynamics are irrelevant,"* **compassionate conversations are grounded in contemplation and meditation** (Zheng 2016).

Depending on the nature of the course at hand, introducing meditation into teaching can take different formats, but I insist that some form of meditation occur before we introduce conversations about controversial subjects. From the simplest option of inserting a moment of silence into the lesson—a reflective pause, during which perhaps the students write their questions on an index card or into a shared electronic document with anonymity—to more structured meditation practice, as long as students are asked to *expand their awareness* before the conversation begins, the discussion will be more likely to be grounded in kindness. The goal of meditation-based pauses like these is to **expand the capacity to listen and speak with heightened attention**. Additional guidelines to structure the conversation abound (for example, the acronym THINK: is it True? is it Helpful? will it Improve the dialogue? is it Necessary? and is it Kind?), but at their root they share the goal of contemplation or reflection as a crucial part of joining the conversation ("THINK Acronym" 2016).

Students will have a greater stake in these conversations once they get to know their peers, a process that I facilitate through including **peer review opportunities** throughout the course. Of the many digital platforms that offer systems for peer review, I have found Kritik to be the most rewarding. Based out of Canada, Kritik bills itself as "the only peer-to-peer solution designed to enhance students' higher order and critical thinking skills in online or in-person classes" ("About Us" 2021), and features three steps to each assignment: anonymous peer review, an evaluation of the review by the recipient, and feedback on the evaluation of the review (by the peer who did the initial review).[5] Thus, if Student X reviewed Students Y and Z, for example, after they received these reviews, Students Y and Z would, in turn, assess the helpfulness of the review they received (without knowing who in class wrote it), and then Student X would have an opportunity to rate the assessments received from Students Y and Z (who remain anonymous to Student X). This *triple tier of feedback* makes several things possible: first, it ensures that students are receiving feedback immediately upon turning material in; second, by virtue of reviewing their peers, students learn how others have approached the assignment, which, in turn, makes them more likely to fully digest the lesson itself. Finally, students learn how challenging it is to provide helpful critique, a lesson that is emphasized by the algorithms at the heart of Kritik that offer ongoing and adaptive input about how well their own peer reviews (and their ratings of others' reviews) were received by their classmates. The dynamic response of this algorithm makes the student Kritik interface akin to game-play, offering an incentive for students that is unrelated to grades yet still ignites the drive and potential satisfaction of tracking one's improvement. Crucially, none of these steps occur without the potential of intervention, allowing students to "flag" reviews they consider unfair or unreasonable, and instructors the option to override scores or feedback offered among students.

Of course, in an ungraded classroom, the stakes for adopting a peer-based grading system like Kritik are substantially lower (as are the incentives for completing all the steps of review). Even without full participation, however, I find peer review to be essential in ungraded courses. The impulse to share evaluation among the classroom community aligns with the ethos I hope to cultivate: I am not the "sage on the stage," nor am I simply the "guide on the side"; instead, **all of us**—students, teaching assistant/s, and instructor—**participate in the feedback process.**[6]

And this brings us to the final part of the ritual to consider: **how to provide constructive yet caring feedback.** While a crucial part of their feedback should come from their peers, without grades as a summary, students rightfully expect attentive critiques of their labor. Indeed, the primary draw to the ungraded approach for many teachers stems from their recognition that students rarely integrate written evaluations when grades are attached—instead, they skim through the words to see the score or letter grade, because that's the currency of the transaction.

When offering feedback (and on the student's end, completing assignments), *format matters*. Although I shift forms depending on what I'm reviewing, my preference for most assignments is to craft my response *as a letter*. The epistolary style feels familiar without being informal, while also modeling a style of writing that may be less familiar to students yet remains a pivotal part of many job (and graduate or professional school) application processes. Traditionally, I structure feedback letters with three sections: (1) what I received from their assignment—depending on the work, this could be the thesis of a paper, the theme of a play, or the overall vibe generated by a talkback, for example; (2) what worked best and where they can improve—the meat of the assessment itself; (3) questions generated by their work, and specific examples of opportunities forthcoming in the class (or beyond) where they might (begin to) answer these lingering questions. I close these letters with an invitation for conversation or follow-up questions they might have, and thank them for their labor.

As I have discussed elsewhere, **I maintain that one-on-one consultations are essential for student learning.**[7] Therefore, especially in an ungraded scenario, I will usually require a short meeting (via video conference, phone call, or face-to-face) at least once during the term, preferably early on, so that I can learn more about how the student receives the feedback I offer. Depending on the setting and the assignment in question, I frequently ask students to *read parts of their work (or my feedback letter) aloud to me* during this session. Hearing their own words (or mine) in their voice inevitably leads to discovery (for them and for me)—perhaps in hearing them speak a sentence they've written, for example, either or both of us might realize how to make the sentence clearer, or understand a difference of emphasis between the student's reception of the letter and my intention. Regardless of what they learn during the read-aloud portion, this request encourages us both to *slow down*, to listen more closely (or accurately), and to connect the words on the page with the human being behind it.[8]

The intimacy fostered by these consultations is crucial as well. While our first instinct for defining "intimacy" is physical or even sexual, my usage for it in teaching cites popular culture self-help mentor Iyanla Vanzant's quip that intimacy means "into me see." Outside of the group dynamic that is a classroom setting, when I meet with students individually, we have an opportunity to allow them to see me (and for me to see them) differently—if trust is established, we may allow each other to glimpse our full selves, under the public masks of "student" and "teacher" we otherwise wear.

The Offering

At the close of the ritual is the offering. What have we learned here? In what ways (if any) has this manifesto mattered?

While I cannot know your experience, dear reader, I suspect that at least a few of you will consider my offerings too "woo woo," emotional, or risky for your practice. I respect that, but hope you'll consider this last piece before discarding my call to action altogether: how might teaching and learning change if they were both based on cultivating curiosity and compassion? As Loveless asks in her own (book-length) manifesto, "What does it mean to enact *an ethics of care* in a time so marked by cultural and intra-species violence?" (2019, 102, emphasis added). What impact might this approach have *beyond the classroom*?

Ungrading is a wakeup call—to teaching and learning, of course, but it has the potential to revolutionize far further. While it (decidedly!) does *not* reduce the labor required to educate, it profoundly changes the *nature* of that labor, for both teacher and student. For many instructors (including myself) who have embraced the pedagogy of kindness in ungraded settings, these changes have led to the (re)discovery of *pleasure* and *hope* in our teaching. Similar insights occur with students encountering this approach: as one anonymous student phrased it, in response to a Spring 2020 class, the "groundwork of the pedagogy of kindness, [Jane's] vulnerability and her transparency allowed us all to do the same and grow into our best selves." From the same semester (but another course), another student writes, "Because of your teaching style, I feel more engaged in the material because I'm truly interested in it, not because I feel threatened with low grades or punishment."[9]

Ultimately, my commitment to this approach pays homage to the lessons learned in Julia Frodahl's "Training A Million Compassionate Americans," one she undertook to address "a longing to move from a culture of Me to a culture of We" in 2020. With the hindsight of all we have survived and lost in 2020 (and the years surrounding it), and in the face of increasing pressures to quantify and homogenize our research, creative work, and teaching "through put," I resist these pressures however I can.[10] Because, like Loveless, "*pedagogy* is how I care," I integrate compassion-based methods into my teaching (2019, 105). Of all the methods I have piloted thus far, however, ungrading my curriculum has had the most immediate and far-reaching—dare I say it? *joyful*—impact. It has reignited my love for teaching, and my curiosity for learning even as the world falls apart around us. May it be an equally transformative tool for you and your students!

Notes

1 Regarding students' motivation and desire to learn, see astrophysicist Mario Livio's book *Why?: What Makes Us Curious* (New York: Simon & Schuster, 2017).
2 My experience (that self-evaluations exhibit a gender bias and that female/femme students tend to undervalue their labor by assigning lower grades) appears to be typical among colleagues who also feature the ungraded model. See Blum (2020), especially Aaron Blackwelder's chapter, "What Going Gradeless Taught Me about Doing the 'Actual Work'," pp. 42–52.
3 When I have used contracts for ungraded teaching, I have followed the model used by Inoue (2019).
4 See "Moving from Safe Classrooms to Brave Classrooms" (2021); Zheng (2016).
5 Significantly, access to Kritik (when I used it last) was not free, necessitating institutional (or departmental) buy-in and/or ethical consideration regarding student cost. I am grateful to KU's Department of Theatre & Dance for sponsoring my students' use of Kritik in 2020.
6 See Morrison (2014) for more details about the "sage on the stage" and "guide on the side" guidance.
7 See Barnette (2015). My commitment to one-on-one consultations is made possible, of course, by manageable class sizes—I do not suggest (or know) that (whether) such a practice is feasible in classes with more than 25 students enrolled.
8 For more about the impulse to slow down within academia, see Conti (2019) as well as Gearhart and Chambers (2019).
9 These anonymous comments came from students enrolled in the Spring 2020 semester at University of Kansas. Specifically, they are for THR 380: Witches in Popular Culture (featuring Renee Cyr as GTA) and THR 308: Script Analysis (featuring Timmia Hearn Feldman as GTA). Both teaching assistants were pivotal in the success of these courses, and I am grateful for their contributions to the classroom community we built.
10 The metric of "through put" has been proposed at KU by our provost, as a way of addressing budget shortfalls. Not surprisingly, this vague tool, meant to correspond to the number of student credit hours each professor/department produces, has been met with resistance from faculty, without satisfactory response (yet)

References

"About Us." 2021. Accessed June 15, 2021. *Kritik.* https://www.kritik.io/about
Barnette, Jane. 2015. "Embracing the 'Foggy Place' of Theatre History: The Chautauqua/Colloquium Model of Public Scholarship as Performance." *Theatre Topics* 25, no. 3: 231–242.
Blum, Susan D, editor. 2020. *Ungrading: Why Rating Students Undermines Learning (And What to Do Instead).* Morgantown: University of West Virginia Press.
Conti, Meredith. 2021. "Slow Academic Travel: An Antidote to 'Fly Over' Scholarship in the Age of Climate Crisis." *Theatre Topics* 31, no. 1 (March): 17–29.
Denial, Catherine. 2019. "A Pedagogy of Kindness." Accessed June 15, 2021. *Hybrid Pedagogy.* Last modified August 15, 2019.
"Difficult Dialogues." 2021. Accessed July 1, 2021. *Center for Teaching at Vanderbilt University.* https://cft.vanderbilt.edu/guides-sub-pages/difficult-dialogues/
Freire, Paolo. 1970. *Pedagogy of the Oppressed.* New York: Herder and Herder.
Frodahl, Julia. 2020. "Training A Million Compassionate Americans." Accessed July 1, 2021. https://www.amillioncompassionateamericans.com

Frodahl, Julia. April 16, 2021. Interview with Jane Barnette. https://www.juliafrodahl.com

Gane, Nicholas. 2006. "When We Have Never Been Human, What Is to Be Done? An Interview with Donna Haraway." *Theory, Culture, Society* 23, nos. 7–8: 135–158, at 152.

Gearhart, Stephannie S., and Jonathan Chambers, editors. 2019. *Reversing the Cult of Speed in Higher Education: The Slow Movement in the Arts and Humanities.* New York: Routledge.

Immordino-Yang, Mary Helen. 2016. "Why Emotions are Integral to Learning." Accessed June 30, 2021. *MindShift, KQED.* Last modified May 31, 2016. https://www.kqed.org/mindshift/45201/why-emotions-are-integral-to-learning

Inoue, Asao B. 2019. *Labor-Based Grading Contracts: Building Equity and Inclusion in the Compassionate Writing Classroom.* Fort Collins: WAC Clearinghouse and University Press of Colorado.

Loveless, Natalie. 2019. *How to Make Art at the End of the World: A Manifesto for Research-Creation.* Durham: Duke University Press.

Lyon, Janet. 1991. *Manifestoes: Provocations of the Modern.* Ithaca: Cornell University Press.

Morrison, Charles D. 2014. "From 'Sage on the Stage' to 'Guide on the Side': A Good Start." *International Journal for the Scholarship of Teaching and Learning* 8, no. 1 (January): Article 4.

"Moving from Safe Classrooms to Brave Classrooms." 2021. Accessed July 1, 2021. *Anti-Defamation League.* https://www.adl.org/education/resources/tools-and-strategies/moving-from-safe-classrooms-to-brave-classrooms

Stommel, Jesse. 2020. "How to Ungrade." *Ungrading: Why Rating Students Undermines Learning (And What to Do Instead).* Morgantown: University of West Virginia Press: 25–41.

"THINK Acronym for Kinder and More Effective Communications." 2016. Accessed July 1, 2021. The *Coaching Tools Company* (February 16). https://www.thecoachingtoolscompany.com/think-acronym-for-kinder-and-more-effective-communications/

Weeks, Kathi. 2013. "The Critical Manifesto: Marx and Engels, Haraway, and Utopian Politics." *Utopian Studies* 24, no. 2: 216–231.

Zheng, Lily. 2016. "Why Your Brave Space Sucks." Accessed July 1, 2021. *The Stanford Daily.* Last modified May 15, 2016. https://www.stanforddaily.com/2016/05/15/why-your-brave-space-sucks/

Chapter 2

Solving the Real Crisis in Virtual Education

Strategies for Training Arts Practitioners in Social and Emotional Learning

Elizabeth Coen

With the onset of the COVID-19 pandemic, educators teaching kindergarten through college turned to remote and hybrid instructional models. As a result, many students disengaged from their computer screens. In the spring of 2021, undergraduates taking remote and hybrid classes voiced increased feelings of loneliness and worry (Ezarik 2021). High school students similarly described problems concentrating on schoolwork, feeling isolated from peers, and struggling to stay motivated in their online courses (Prothero 2021). For learners already vulnerable to the inequities of US educational systems, studies from this time paint an even bleaker picture. In a nationally representative survey of 2,000 respondents, 77% of Black and Latinx high school students reported more challenges with mental health in 2021 than they did prior to the pandemic, nine percentage points higher than their white peers. Students who identified as low-income and LGBTQ+ likewise felt a greater sense of anxiety and distress (EdWeek Research Center 2021, 5, Sparks 2021).

In response to this mental health crisis, leaders of primary and secondary schools across the United States prioritized the integration of social and emotional learning (SEL) into core curricula and programs. Defined as "the process through which children enhance their ability to integrate thinking, feeling, and behaving to achieve important life tasks," SEL is a pedagogy known to increase learning outcomes and high school graduation rates (Zins et al. 2004, 6). Experts in education suggest that children who gain competencies in SEL are more equipped to negotiate the challenges of life because they can recognize and manage their emotions, maintain healthy relationships, and make responsible decisions (Zins et al. 2004, 6). While not typically discussed within the context of higher education, SEL can also benefit undergraduate students transitioning into adulthood. As more and more post-secondary instruction is conducted online—mediated by educational software and a camera lens—the imperative to support students' social and emotional development is essential.

It is frequently argued that theatre education naturally accords certain social-emotional competencies, like empathy and emotional awareness. Yet the fact remains that undergraduates enrolled in theatre and performance classes still struggle with applying emotional knowledge gained through coursework

DOI: 10.4324/9781003229056-4

to support their academic growth. College students need skills to manage stress and self-motivate, especially when taking classes in remote settings. Instructors who integrate SEL into their course design can help them gain abilities to realize academic success. So too, when instructors use SEL to examine inequities within their own teaching practice, a methodology called transformative SEL, they can champion students furthest from educational justice (Schlund, Jagers, Schlinger 2020, 3). Practitioners in the field of theatre for young audiences (TYA) already generate equity-focused curricula in support of the social and emotional development of children and teens. Prioritizing transformative SEL at the post-secondary level, will not only promote mental wellness in virtual classrooms but also effectuate more equitable learning outcomes for the next generation of artists who are eager to make a positive impact in the communities that they serve.

Situating SEL within Theatre and Performance Pedagogies

This chapter's pedagogical framework and practical suggestions for implementing SEL into college curricula is inspired by several years of intensive research, training, and teaching for community-based organizations. In 2018, two years after completing a Ph.D. in theatre history, and ten years after I began my career working in post-secondary classrooms, I joined AmeriCorps to *learn from* and *collaborate with* educators who specialize in serving under-resourced students. As an AmeriCorps tutor for the non-profit Northwest Education Access, I participated in concentrated trainings on youth reengagement and equitable teaching while mentoring more than 50 students as they earned a G.E.D. diploma and successfully transitioned into college. Since that time, I have maintained my commitment to under-resourced youth by overseeing the development of SEL curricula for grades 6–12 at Seattle Children's Theatre.

Like so many instructors in higher education, I began my career feeling like I lacked the pedagogical knowledge to serve the diverse students in my classrooms, especially those historically marginalized by educational systems in the United States. Moreover, as a white woman from a middle-class background, I wanted to augment the teachings that I did receive in social justice with methods to improve the educational experience of every student in my classrooms. SEL with a "transformative" focus "is a process where young people and adults build strong, respectful, and lasting relationships that facilitate co-learning to critically examine root causes of inequity, and to develop collaborative solutions that lead to personal, community, and societal well-being" (Schlund, Jagers, Schlinger 2020, 3). In sum, SEL intersects with social justice and anti-racism pedagogies but concentrates first on the personal facets of education; specifically, instructional practices recognized to enhance students' sense of belonging, identity, and agency within learning environments.

The methods outlined in this chapter improve learning outcomes within remote and hybrid courses in theatre and performance by bridging the values of artistic study with clear and actionable strategies that foster success in distance education. I first examine SEL through a theoretical lens, focusing largely on learner-centered psychological principles in service to SEL competencies, and then consider its practical applications. To illustrate these ideas, I draw from my own experiences teaching undergraduates, and provide sample assignments that can be adapted to any performance course. I want to emphasize that I do not offer SEL as a replacement for social justice curricula and anti-racist efforts, nor do I discount the fact that students with mental health disorders such as clinical anxiety, depression, and post-traumatic stress require serious medical attention. SEL is designed to help students thrive in education. It is not a band-aid solution for mental illness or social injustice.

What Is Social Emotional Learning?

In 1989, Daniel Goleman, a psychologist and reporter for the *New York Times*, described a revolutionary discovery about the brain. This finding, and other research conducted in the fields of neuroscience and psychology during the 1980s and 1990s, dramatically changed how leaders in education think about the learning process. He wrote:

> The power of emotions to override even the most rational decisions may be explained by a new discovery about the brain, researchers say. The data suggests that the brain is arranged so key aspects of emotional life, like primitive fears, can operate largely independent of thought. This arrangement may explain why certain emotional reactions, like phobias, are so tenacious despite their obvious irrationality. It may also explain other baffling facts of emotional life, such as why troubling experiences from life's earliest years can have such powerful effects decades later.
> (Goleman 1989)

While it was once believed that the thinking part of the brain (the neocortex) could operate independently from the brain's emotional center (the amygdala), neuroscience revealed that emotions could effectively impede cognitive functioning. In addition, psychologists who pioneered research on emotional intelligence proved a clear correlation between the emotional, behavioral, and cognitive facets of learning (Mayor, Salovey, Caruso 2008). Goleman, who reported on these studies for the *Times* and published his bestselling book *Emotional Intelligence* in 1995, played a considerable part in making this work accessible to the public. He also captivated the interest of educators. As *Emotional Intelligence* received critical attention, he co-founded the Collaborative for Academic, Social and Emotional Learning (CASEL), a research institution and resource for educational leadership seeking effective evidence-based guidance in SEL for primary and secondary schools.

Today, it is widely believed that both children and adults can manage, or regulate, emotional response. In short, when the amygdala is triggered, one can effectually reengage the brain's intellective capacity. Thus, leaders in education emphasize that students must *learn* to self-motivate and persist in the face of challenging or frustrating situations and regulate their moods so that feelings of stress and anxiety do not hinder their ability to think and perform in school. CASEL categorizes the development of these abilities and other forms of inter-/intra-personal knowledge within five conceptual domains, quoted here in condensed form:

1. Self-awareness: involves understanding one's emotions, personal and social identities, goals, and values.
2. Self-management: skills and attitudes that facilitate the ability to regulate emotions and behaviors.
3. Social awareness: having the critical historical grounding to take the perspective of those with the same and different backgrounds and cultures and to appropriately empathize and feel compassion.
4. Relationship skills: the interpersonal sensibilities and facility needed to establish and maintain healthy and rewarding relationships.
5. Responsible decision-making: requires the cultivation of knowledge, skills, and attitudes to make caring, constructive choices about personal and group behavior in social interactions within and across diverse institutional settings (Jagers, Rivas-Drake, Williams 2019, 167).

By assisting students in gaining competency within these five areas, SEL provides a kind of roadmap to effectively train the brain (i.e., build emotional intelligence) in pursuit of academic success and personal growth.

The performing arts can serve as an ideal vehicle for promoting social and emotional skill building. Studies conducted by the University of Chicago Consortium on School Research suggest that arts education, which combines opportunities for both reflection and action (e.g., choosing, tinkering, practicing), may strengthen neural pathways to support understanding and metacognition (Farrington and Shewfelt 2020, 32). To take a case in point, Seattle Children's Theatre's high school residency *Creative Drama for Mental Wellness* uses these principles in theatre games to boost students' skills in self-awareness and self-management. As part of the curriculum, participants perform personal moments of happiness and joy in contrast to moments when they are feeling isolated or down. They then rehearse mediation strategies using somatic first aid and grounding techniques to prepare for future events that may trigger feelings of stress or sadness. The program's emphasis on reflection and practice is intended to elucidate how students can negotiate challenges and setbacks. As instructors of SEL, teaching artists emphasize that intellectual and emotional capacities are not irreparable or fixed, to promote what is variously described as a growth mindset, grit, and resilience. Understanding that the brain can evolve to develop new mindsets and abilities substantiates the argument that learning is an ongoing process.

Still, I would like to underscore that an SEL-informed curriculum is most effective when applied through a transformative lens, namely, when it is paired with culturally responsive teaching and a strong mandate for educational equity. As one of the foremost leaders in culturally responsive instructional design, Zaretta Hammond asserts that educators who rely solely on their students' grit or mindset to propel the learning process are not helping them develop new cognitive skills. To boost students' academic achievement, especially those marginalized by educational systems, she writes, educators must "recognize students' cultural displays of learning and meaning making and respond positively and constructively with teaching moves that use cultural knowledge as a scaffold to connect what the student knows to new concepts and content" (2015, 15). This directive does not imply that teachers must become acquainted with the cultural background of every student enrolled in their class. Although it does prompt teachers to reflect upon their own culture and upbringing, as well as the culture and experience of their students (2015, 24–28).

Hammond also contends that culturally responsive education is different from social justice education. Social justice education, as Hammond outlines in her teachings on distinctions of equity, "centers around raising students' consciousness about inequity in everyday social, environmental, economic, and political situations; [and] concerns itself with creating a lens to recognize and interrupt inequitable patterns and practices in society." Culturally responsive education, on the other hand, "centers around the affective and cognitive aspects of teaching and learning… pushing back on dominant narratives about people of color" (2020). Within the field of performing arts education, I see the difference between these two pedagogic concerns manifest as follows. A professor creates a syllabus on performance theory, which includes critical race and postcolonial theory. A significant amount of the curricula considers oppressive structures that impede the professional ambitions of playwrights of color. Yet in class, the students of color sit at the margins of the room and rarely speak. At the end of the semester, these same students are in the bottom quartile of the grading scale. Thus, an instructor may be proficient in social justice education but struggle with culturally responsive teaching. The course content clearly demonstrated an imperative to disrupt social injustice. However, the course instruction failed to sustain students' engagement with the material, perpetuating a cycle of educational inequity.

I offer this anecdote to highlight a trend that I have seen happen over and over in college classrooms by some of the most well-intentioned instructors. In giving students a lens to analyze oppression within artistic contexts, instructors fail to consider how their own actions align with attitudes that have historically excluded students from higher education. Culturally responsive instructors are aware that both their teaching practice (e.g., how they support students in acquiring knowledge) and their policies (e.g., how they articulate and uphold expectations) can inform whether students absorb the course content or disengage. They reimagine their relationships with students as partnerships, dedicated to the transmission of knowledge and the learning process. In essence, transformative SEL helps students gain a sense of identity, agency, and belonging in school settings (Jagers, Rivas-Drake, Williams 2019, 166). Developmental psychologist Robert Jagers and other members of the CASEL Assessment Workgroup suggest that this framework is essential to achieving equity in educational institutions (163–166).

Planning for a Learner-Centered Online Course: Setting a Foundation for Policy and Practice

There are innumerable how-to guides for implementing SEL into K-12 education; three are listed in this chapter's references section (Elias et al. 1997, Zins et al. 2004, Goleman and Senge 2014). However, the literature for implementing SEL into post-secondary courses is sparse. Perhaps this is due to a widespread belief that students who graduate high school already possess the social and emotional skills needed to complete a college education. Data collected during the COVID-19 pandemic suggest otherwise (EdWeek Research Center 2021, Ezarik 2021, Prothero 2021, Sparks 2021). If the turn toward remote instruction during a tumultuous two years caused high school students to struggle with concentration, isolation, and general anxiety, it is likely that these same feelings will manifest in post-secondary environments. Moreover, psychologists argue that the pandemic's long-term effects on students' mental health will take years to fully understand (Prothero 2021, Sparks 2021). My framework for integrating SEL into remote and hybrid courses derives from my experience in post-secondary classrooms as well as publications on SEL written principally for primary and secondary school leadership.

My method is also informed by the American Psychological Association's (APA) *Learner-Centered Psychological Principles.* "What defines learner-centeredness in both K-12 and college classrooms," writes APA author Barbara McCombs, "is not solely a function of particular instructional practices or programs. Rather it is a complex interaction of teacher qualities in combination with characteristics of instructional practices – as perceived by individual learners" (2004, 30). Indeed, much like Hammond, McCombs points to the importance of serving students as individuals with unique attitudes, experiences, and goals.

When teaching remotely, this task requires careful planning. Because there are fewer occasions to become acquainted with students informally, instructors must *create* opportunities to gain information about their students. I see this process as akin to data collection in community-based program design, a collaborative and reflective approach to working discussed in scholarship by Jen Plants (2020), as well as Monica Prendergast and Juliana Saxton (2016). When addressing a social or political challenge, community leaders survey their constituents, examine the problems at hand, and analyze prior attempts at finding a solution. Why don't instructors apply a similar approach to teaching? The more educators learn about their students, the better they'll be able to serve them.

Using an introductory survey to gather student data is a quick way to gain a baseline understanding of who they are as learners. Survey responses can also be used to cultivate a rapport with students in meetings and correspondence. When I taught a remote dramatic literature course to Boston University undergraduates in the spring of 2021, I knew little about the culture of the school and those enrolled, a scenario that is quite common for contingent faculty increasingly called upon to teach online courses. I therefore asked students to complete the following questions before our first synchronous class meeting. Note that I too completed the survey and posted my answers to the course's asynchronous learning platform:

1. What is your first and last name?
2. If you have a preferred name or nickname, please write it here.
3. Do you have a tip for pronouncing your name? Please include it here.
4. What are your pronouns?
5. What year are you?
6. What is your major?
7. Are you residing outside of the Eastern Time Zone?
8. Rate your knowledge of the following plays and topics. *I included a comprehensive list from my syllabus with the following rating system: I know nothing about this topic; I've studied this topic a little in high school/college; I know a lot about this topic.*
9. Name one of your strengths as a student/emerging professional? Are there skills or an area of knowledge that you wish to improve upon?
10. Are you worried that something will prevent you from doing well in this course? If you are comfortable, please share.
11. What career do you wish to pursue after you graduate?

After reviewing the students' responses, I adjusted my readings and lectures so that they aligned with their knowledge of the material. And, in taking this action, I showed that previous experience is relevant to continued development and professional ambition. Survey information also served as a point of reference in email communications throughout the semester. Since the class met synchronously once a week and had an enrollment of 65, I was glad to have some foundation from which to build a relationship with each and every student.

I often hear instructors articulate a desire to be likeable as they prepare for the start of a new semester. This approach puts a great deal of onus on subjective matters that are challenging to measure. Student success should not pivot on likability. Instead, instructors might concentrate on strategies that foster positive and personal connections to the course curriculum and learning process. Research has shown that when school environments satisfy students' basic psychological requirements, they are more likely to bond with school staff and accept school values (McCombs 2004, 34). Collecting data to evaluate students' interests and knowledge is a first step toward meeting their needs and championing their mental wellness.

Collaborative policymaking is another way to nurture learning and trust in the virtual classroom. As McCombs argues, when teachers overly control the learning process, students may comply, but they won't gain a sense of responsibility for their actions as learners. Conversely, if given the opportunity to engage in the decision-making process, students are likely to abide by decisions that they made (2004, 34). In keeping with this idea, I designed a community agreement assignment for the synchronous portion of my online dramatic literature class and put students into breakout groups to complete it. I offer an abbreviated example of the assignment here:

In this breakout room, I'd like you to discuss the following topics with your groupmates. Please have one person fill out this form and submit it. I will read the responses to assemble our class community agreement.

1 Please list the first names of everyone in your group and one fun fact about each person.
2 In this course, we actively embrace anti-racism. Please review the classroom meeting agreements. Is there anything you would like to add?
3 Please respond as a group to the following. Check either Agree, Disagree, or Ambivalent.
   a   Cameras can be on or off while the instructor is talking.
   b   Cameras should be on in large group discussions.
   c   Cameras should be on in breakout groups. *Strongly encouraged by the professor.*
4 Video record all class sessions? Check either Agree or Disagree.
5 What can the instructor do to support your learning?
6 What can your fellow classmates do to support your learning?

When I introduced this assignment, I emphasized that the responsibility for creating a positive learning environment was not mine alone; everyone in the virtual classroom needed to care for one another. Asking students to consider how each member of the learning community could accomplish this goal prompted reflection upon personal needs as well as the needs of others, advancing SEL competencies in self and social awareness.

The practice of offering choice within various instructional contexts is both culturally responsive and learner centered. In fact, the allowance of choice can significantly improve students' motivation to prepare for classes, participate in discussions, and complete assignments. Many instructors already provide options in assigning paper topics and large projects. However, in an SEL-centered course, instructors offer choice in all facets of their teaching practice. For instance, I allow students to choose questions for discussion within synchronous breakout sessions. Prompts for my class on Roman comedy might include the following: "(1) Do you think Terence is questioning Roman values in his play *Phormio*? (2) How does comedy reveal the truths of a given society? (3) What happens when playwrights cannot overtly question their government or political leaders?" The questions invite students to discuss what they feel is personally relevant and urges them to negotiate with their peers. As a result, they develop two SEL proficiencies: self-awareness and relationship skill building.

Granting undergraduates' freedom in low-stakes situations is groundwork for navigating challenging conversations about mental health. As I noted earlier, studies suggest that online coursework can foster feelings of depression and anxiety. When students express that they are struggling with their mental health, I have found that relaxing hard deadlines for completing assignments improves engagement in the course and reduces failure and dropout rates. Yet in keeping with SEL principles, I tether accommodations to self-management skills. I encourage students seeking an extension to propose an alternative due date. This practice compels a greater sense of accountability in meeting self-imposed deadlines. Furthermore, when working with students contending with significant hardship, this technique—coupled with regular check-ins over email and virtual meetings—can prove the difference between academic success and failure. For example, once, when teaching an online course, I worked with a student who had recently lost a friend to violence. The pressure to write a paper while grappling with loss and other responsibilities proved paralyzing, and he missed the deadline for submission. In noticing this disengagement, I called for a virtual meeting. Together, we agreed upon a schedule for completing the paper. The student chose dates for submitting drafts and a final version that he felt he could meet, and the process proved successful. At midterm, he was in danger of failing the course. At the end of the semester, he received an A-.

Scheduling time to meet one-on-one with students can be an immediate and important form of emotional support. Yet when teaching online courses with large enrollment numbers, scheduling individual meetings may not be a practical option. The integration of SEL into curricula is not a substitute for mentorship, but it serves as a scaffold for students to reflect on their emotional needs and find critical resources. The best way to ensure that SEL is happening in remote settings is to pronounce at every opportunity that learning is a process and emotions inform that learning process.

There are numerous ways to convey this idea in action. One easy strategy is to routinely check-in with students at the start of a synchronous class. The performance of an emotional state can be readily incorporated into acting warm-ups. Because I routinely teach courses in writing and research, I like to use the chat function on Zoom to have students type how they are doing. Sometimes, I ask what their academic workload looks like for the week or what they will do to take care of themselves over the weekend. This intrapersonal practice provides an ongoing opportunity to collect data on their feelings and attitudes, so that I can calibrate my instruction and show investment in their wellbeing.

Another way to lend transparency to the teaching of SEL is to devote instructional time to helping students understand that caring for their mental and physical health can bolster their academic success. I like to teach this concept by assigning a writing reflection or small video performance. A few prompts to get started might include: What time of the day do you do your best concentrated thinking? What is a song that inspires you and gets you excited to work? When can you make time in your schedule for completing schoolwork, and just as importantly, take time to rest and recharge? By simply asking students to engage with questions related to how they learn, instructors can highlight how "thinking about thinking" and considering one's emotional and physical needs is just as critical to the learning process as studying for a test.

Encouraging theatre and performance students to reflect on these connections in coursework will better prepare them to serve as justice-oriented artists after they graduate. Because teaching is undervalued as a career choice, leaders in the arts overlook the obvious benefits of promoting a strong correlation between SEL and artistic practices. Most post-secondary theatre and dance programs do not train students in pedagogies of performance, nor do they prepare them to be teaching artists. This is a great disservice, as leaders in primary and secondary education are looking to community partners for guidance and support to help both students and teachers process the emotional challenges of working in virtual and hybrid classrooms. Moreover, research suggests that students in K-12, across income brackets and racial/ethnic divides, achieve higher learning outcomes in SEL when under the tutelage of culturally responsive arts instructors and teaching artists (Farrington, et al. 2019, Arts Corps 2019). For all of these reasons, post-secondary performance instruction must prepare artists to address the mental health crisis in education.

References

American Psychological Association. 1997. *Learner-Centered Psychological Principles: A Framework for School Reform & Redesign*. Washington, DC: Center for Psychology in Schools and Education.

Arts Corps. 2019. *Liberating Academic Mindsets through Culturally Responsive Arts Integration*. Seattle: Highline Creative Schools Initiative (HCSI). "CASEL. 2021. https://casel.org/." is a separate reference entry.

EdWeek Research Center. 2021. *Student Mental Health during the Pandemic: Educator and Teen Perspectives*. Bethesda, MD: Editorial Projects in Education.

Elias, Maurice J., Joseph E. Zins, Roger P. Weissberg, Karin S. Frey, Mark T. Greenberg, Norris M. Haynes, Rachael Kessler, Mary E. Schwab-Stone, and Timothy P. Shriver. 1997. *Promoting Social and Emotional Learning: Guidelines for Educators*. Alexandria, VA: Association for Supervision and Curriculum Development.

Ezarik, Melissa. 2021. "Students Struggle but Don't Seek Colleges' Help." *Inside Higher Ed*, April 14, 2021. https://www.insidehighered.com/news/2021/04/14/students-struggling-not-seeking-campus-mental-health-support.

Farrington, Camille A., Joseph Maurer, Meredith R. Aska McBride, Jenny Nagaoka, J.S. Puller, Steve Shewfelt, Elizabeth M. Weiss, and Lindsay Wright. 2019. *Arts Education and Social-Emotional Learning Outcomes Among K-12 Students: Developing a Theory of Action*. Chicago, IL: Ingenuity and the University of Chicago Consortium on School Research.

Farrington, Camille A., and Steve Shewfelt. 2020. *How Arts Education Supports Social-Emotional Development: A Theory of Action*. Alexandria, VA: National Association of State Boards of Education.

Goleman, Daniel. 1989. "Brain's Design Emerges as a Key to Emotions." *New York Times*, August 15, 1989. https://www.nytimes.com/1989/08/15/science/brain-s-design-emerges-as-a-key-to-emotions.html.

Goleman, Daniel. 2020. *Emotional Intelligence: The 25th Anniversary Edition*. New York: Bantam Books.

Goleman, Daniel, and Peter Senge. 2014. *The Triple Focus: A New Approach to Education*. Florence, MA: Key Step Media.

Hammond, Zaretta. 2015. *Culturally Responsive Teaching & the Brain: Promoting Authentic Engagement and Rigor Among Culturally and Linguistically Diverse Students*. Thousand Oaks, CA: Corwin.

Hammond, Zaretta. 2020. "Distinctions of Equity." https://www.crtandthebrain.com/wp-content/uploads/Hammond_Full-Distinctions-of-Equity-Chart.pdf.

Jagers, Robert J., Deborah Rivas-Drake, and Brittney Williams. 2019. "Transformative Social and Emotional Learning (SEL): Toward SEL in Service of Educational Equity and Excellence." *Educational Psychologist* 54, no. 3: 162–184.

Mayer, John D., Peter Salovey, and David R. Caruso. 2008. "Emotional Intelligence: New Ability or Eclectic Traits?" *American Psychologist* 63, no. 6 (September): 503–517.

McCombs, Barbara. 2004. "The Learner-Centered Psychological Principles: A Framework for Balancing Academic Achievement and Social-Emotional Learning Outcomes." In *Building Academic Success on Social and Emotional Learning: What Does the Research Say?*, edited by Joseph E Zins, Roger P. Weissberg, Margaret C. Wang, and Herbert J. Walberg, 23–39. New York: Teachers College Press.

Plants, Jen. 2020. "Life First: Interdisciplinary Placemaking for the Theatre." In *Teaching Critical Performance Theory: In Today's Theatre Classroom, Studio, and Communities*, edited by Jeanmarie Higgins, 183–194. New York: Routledge.

Prendergast and Juliana Saxton. 2016. *Applied Theatre: International Case Studies and Challenges for Practice*. Bristol: Intellect.

Prothero, Arianna. 2021. "The Pandemic Will Affect Students' Mental Health for Years to Come. How Schools Can Help." *Education Week*, March 31, 2021. https://www.edweek.org/leadership/the-pandemic-will-affect-students-mental-health-for-years-to-come-how-schools-can-help/2021/03.

Schlund, Justina, Robert J. Jagers, and Melissa Schlinger. 2020. *Emerging Insights on Advancing Social and Emotional Learning (SEL) as a Lever for Equity and Excellence*. Chicago, IL: CASEL.

Seattle Children's Theatre. 2021. "High School Programs." https://www.sct.org/education-programs/sct-at-your-school/high-school-programs/.

Sparks, Sarah D. 2021. "Data: What We Know About Student Mental Health and the Pandemic." *Education Week*, March 31, 2021. https://www.edweek.org/leadership/data-what-we-know-about-student-mental-health-and-the-pandemic/2021/03.

Zins, Joseph E., Michelle R. Bloodworth, Roger P. Weissberg, and Herbert J. Walberg. 2004. "The Scientific Base Linking Social and Emotional Learning to School Success." In *Building Academic Success on Social and Emotional Learning: What Does the Research Say?*, edited by Joseph E. Zins, Roger P. Weissberg, Margaret C. Wang, and Herbert J. Walberg, 3–22. New York: Teachers College Press.

Chapter 3

Practicing Academic Grace

Pedagogical Experiments with *Mr. Burns* in Digital Play Analysis Classrooms

Samuel Yates

"Academic grace" is a concept familiar to the many higher education administrators and faculty who have carefully combed through their institution's policies and to those students who may have eagerly accepted scholarships and positions in graduate study programs. As a noun, "grace" indicates favor or benevolence; as a verb, the primary definitions of grace coalesce around giving thanks or conferring permission (OED Online 2021). Academic grace has a variety of uses that govern expectations of scholarly performance. In many university handbooks and departmental policy guides, such as those in the Yale Religious Studies Graduate Student Handbook, "grace" is nearly synonymous with probation (Yale University, n.d.). In this model, a student who fails to meet functional benchmarks towards degree progression is placed on academic probation for one semester, after which they may be barred from registering for future terms of study. Many undergraduates who receive merit-based scholarships have similar "academic grace" probationary periods in their first semester of study, during which they can work without fear of immediately losing their funding if they do not achieve a high GPA at the semester's end. For professional scholars, academic grace is a laurel of community acceptance conferred through institutional gatekeeping. Swiss aesthetics scholar Michael J. Böhler characterizes the gatekeeping of prestige in his 1998 *PMLA* Forum letter: "My reputation was dramatically enhanced; I had truly come in from the cold – all because I had been endorsed by that benign bestower of academic grace *PMLA*" (1129). Böhler explicitly describes his position as a geographic outsider who gains success through a highly respected interdisciplinary journal that speaks to many fields simultaneously. Böhler's use of passive voice explicitly signals how academic grace functions as a systemic conferral of accepting one's place within the academy in student policies and career accolades.

In this essay, I argue that theatre and performance scholars should extend frameworks of academic grace beyond the good standing earned by completion of coursework or as a transactional conferral of permission and prestige. Instead, I propose that abdicating "permission" models of scholarship is a more productive mode of academic grace in the university classroom, studios, and performance spaces. Suppose one goal of the theatre and performance studies classroom is to communicate how the field is "theoretically ... wide open," and acts "on or act[s] against settled hierarchies of ideas, organizations, and people," as Richard Schechner (2014) frames his oft-assigned *Performance Studies: An Introduction*. In that case, we must attend to how our classrooms reiterate academic violence through the very "settled hierarchies" our fields presume to unbraid (1–4). These forms of academic violence appear in the uncritical assignment of "canonical" syllabus content (including primers like Schechner's); citational practices that reinforce cultural biases towards senior white male scholars; racial and gendered microaggressions in the classroom, as Bert María Cueva details in her study (2014) of testimonios drawn from 21 female-identifying Chicana and Native American doctoral students; or the disability-exclusionary practices that Jay T. Dolmage calls "academic ableism" (2017). If our field is indeed "sympathetic to the avant-garde, the marginal, the offbeat, the minoritarian, the subversive, the twisted, the queer, people of color, and the formerly colonized," in the ways Schechner posits, then it is incumbent upon us to change our teaching methods. Otherwise, there is an inherent conflict between the capacious vantage that performance studies scholars imagine for themselves and the mechanics of pedagogy that ensure the maintenance of academic grace on behalf of our institutions even as they disproportionately impact disabled, queer, low-income, and non-white students.

Moreover, acknowledging these contradictions without taking actionable countermeasures, Dolmage concludes, excuses these acts of violence by cloaking them in the guise of administrative fatigue and elitism – "an excusable problem or a [necessary] byproduct of the culture of universities" (2017, 39). Abdicating permission models of academic grace invites a transfer of some course control from the instructor to the student. It requires that students take more ownership in generating course connections and identifying personal use-value.

On a practical basis, there are two dominant models for what this shift from "permission" modes of scholarship looks like. Ungrading and contract grading offer two holistic approaches. Ungrading, Alfie Kohn (2020) describes, is a practice of "eliminating the control-based function of grades, with all its attendant harms" (xv). This often means submitting final grades in consultation with students who reflect on what grade they feel they have earned based on their performance throughout the course. Contract grading similarly emphasizes process over product. Contract grading takes the view of the syllabus as a "contract" and makes it explicit: students earn specific grades through completion (open to instructor definition) of a set number of assignments rather than functional "correctness." Contract assessment allows the instructor and student to both focus on feedback and processual development rather than grades. Functionally, contract grading achieves a similar effect to ungrading – increased transparency, less subjectivity, a greater emphasis on the development process, reducing student anxiety, and more significant classroom equity (Melzer et al., n.d.) Susan D. Blum further details this practice in her introduction to *Ungrading: Teaching and Learning in Higher Education* and amplifies the concerns of Cueva,

Dolmage, and others: the basis and consequences of a grade-based system are unnecessarily mechanistic, dehumanizing in that its standardized approaches flatten nuance, and it further begets a transactional system with a focus on the exchange value of labor for marks (2020, 2–3). Following Blum, it is difficult to imagine traditional grading as a pedagogical fit within Theatre and Performance Studies if we are indeed "sympathetic" to minoritarian ways of being, committed to openness and change, seeking to indigenize and decolonize our classrooms, and laboring to create accessible and equitable classrooms.

Transitioning to these systems requires careful recalibration of one's teaching style, clear communication with students, and, frequently, departmental support. While I am an advocate for both ungrading and contract grading in performance studies and studio-based classes, many departments and university administrations bristle at the lack of traditional metrics and fear it will damage their sense of "rigor." As an instructor at a regional teaching-centered university who has also spent considerable time adjuncting, I am also sensitive to the labor these forms of grading require – especially if you teach high enrollment courses. For this reason, this essay offers one model that utilizes the ideas of contract grading and ungrading without the need for committing to a wholesale reorientation.

Since there was no manual for transitioning into teaching during a pandemic, I used online teaching as an opportunity to examine my pedagogical impulses – my classroom goals and outcomes, behaviors, assignments, values – and test changes that continue to inform my teaching now that vaccines are available and universities across the globe negotiate our returns to face-to-face work. In short, I sought to experiment with academic grace as an open-ended pedagogical tool to center student-learning outcomes over rigid syllabus adherence in Play Analysis, a fundamental theatre and performance course. I conducted the class in synchronous online sessions, although I engineered asynchronous iterations of the work so that international students working in separate time zones might access the course during more hospitable working hours. No assignment was mandatory aside from the final project (a collaborative group project establishing a dramaturgical arc for *Woyzeck*). Students were free to choose which assignments they wanted to complete, but with the understanding that there would be no makeup work at the end of the semester. Some assignments, such as the short close reading paper I discuss later in this essay, had a specific due date. Students could choose when to submit others, such as the "reader reports" about play texts in the class. To ensure no one fell too far behind or that I would not receive an onslaught of material to mark at the end of the term, I had three check-in dates by which students had to submit any work related to certain plays. With each play, students had two thematic areas explicitly linked to elements of the play's artistic production: storytelling and text analysis. Students were graded primarily on participation and completion in each area, although each used rubrics that set out the terms of successful completion to allow students to work towards the desired grade.

The unit that follows uses a play text that exists in the shadow of pandemics and catastrophe. Anne Washburn's *Mr. Burns: A Post-Electric Play* (2014) is a post-apocalyptic play that challenges students to imagine the future of theatre after the world is remade – finding new remediations for their art. *Mr. Burns* occurs in time jumps over 75 years after a global nuclear disaster wipes out all electricity, decimating governments and normative social structures in the process. Spectators follow a band of storytellers sharing the story of an episode from the popular animated television series *The Simpsons*: first, to distract themselves from their dire situation; next, to barter items and skills for survival; finally, to celebrate the mythology central to the "post-electric" culture that emerged in catastrophe's wake. Asking students to engage in this catastrophic plot amidst a global pandemic may seem counterintuitive or even cruel – but opening the formats of engagement with the play enabled students to come to the playtext in modalities that felt manageable, specific to their interests, and invested in the connections they could offer.

As an instructor, this also provided flexibility and helped establish more solid work-life boundaries during class preparation. In *Care Work: Dreaming Disability Justice*, disability activist and artist Leah Lakshmi Piepzna-Samarasinha reminds us that, "It's OK if you build in boundaries … You are a renewable and also limited resource" (2018, 224). Practicing academic grace requires that we acknowledge that care work is *work* – embodied, felt, labor. In doing so, we must ask: How, as instructors, are you building accessibility and inclusivity into your work for yourself and your students? Are you creating more work for yourself? Is your pedagogical system unnecessarily complicated? What is the relationship between the accessible, inclusive, and justice-oriented materials you make for your students and your teaching load or workload? How can you practice grace in your classroom? What would it mean for you to abandon "permission" models of scholarship?

Between *The Simpsons* and Screen Time: Finding *Mr. Burns* on Zoom

How do we make theatre during a pandemic? Does our relative distance from each other impact how we read, discuss, and imagine theatrical worldmaking? Do digital technologies that alternatively facilitate ways of holding space together change our dramaturgical engagement with plays scripted for face-to-face, in-person engagement? Rather than shy away from the questions that drove the theatre community amidst the Covid-19 crisis, I used these questions to reassess my approach to a foundational course in Theatre and Performance Studies: Play Analysis. Play Analysis (PA) is where many first encounter different forms of dramatic structure and genre, the vocabularies of "beats" and motivation, and the movements of theatre history. Many of us teach a mixture of classic texts and contemporary voices, ranging from Sophocles to Lynn Nottage, *Hamlet* to *The Thanksgiving Play*. Given the multiple forms and formats that online pedagogy presents, and that many students in these sections are first-years still learning how to navigate the demands of university-level study successfully, PA is a good testing ground for experimenting with traditional expectations of an introductory-level course.

In this section, I mobilize the "benchmark" aspect of academic grace to reinvent ways of dramaturgical exploration in PA. When teaching online, it is tempting to create more course rules so that your expectations of the students are clear. This shift is a natural response to the comparative lack of in-person face-to-face time; without the unscripted comments, questions, clarifications, and contextualization that occur before, after, and during in-person classes, you may feel as though the connective threads that hold your course together are less apparent. For those of us working in hybrid or asynchronous models, the need for transparency feels more critical because students will rely almost solely upon instructor-generated recordings or text as they complete their coursework. Using *Mr. Burns: A Post-Electric Play* as the basis for exploration, in my PA classes, students were able to demonstrate their competency in one of three areas: storytelling, design, and text analysis. Each comes with clear instructions that present students options for execution.

Performance scholar Sarah Bay-Cheng identified the virtual capacities of *Mr. Burns* as early as 2015 in her *Theatre Journal* review "Virtual Realisms: Dramatic Forays into the Future." Reading Washburn's play alongside Jennifer Haley's *The Nether* (2014), Bay-Cheng develops a concept of virtual realism by reading both playtexts' use of digital media and culture against their more traditional dramatic structures. If *The Nether* is a world too immersed in the virtual, *Mr. Burns* is a world wrought through technological impoverishment. Defined by the societal possession and loss of electricity, Washburn's America is a country in freefall where the characters grasp at lines, images, and memories from television stories to stabilize themselves and build identities anew. The result, Bay-Cheng compellingly argues, is that *Mr. Burns* remediates the "silliness of *The Simpsons* to suggest that the layers of seemingly meaningless popular culture might cumulatively be the primary source of meaning and relief in a hostile world" (2015, 698).

Washburn's "hostile world" exists in reaction to an unarticulated "Event" in *Mr. Burns*. Although this event is never detailed, it feels sympatico with the post-apocalyptic world of Emily St. John Mandel's novel *Station Eleven* (2014), in which a flu pandemic with a 99% mortality rate shudders global civilization. Given that both debuted in 2014 and trace a small band of travelers who perform recovered iterations of the Western canon (*The Simpsons*, for Washburn, and Shakespeare, for Mandel), in early 2020 it was not difficult to imagine *Mr. Burns* as post-Covid future. Indeed, in March 2020, as Covid-19 scaled into a full-fledged pandemic, Lauren Halvorsen, dramaturg and author of the theatre newsletter Nothing for the Group, observed that "It feels like we're all like a week away from living in the first act of Mr. Burns" (2020).

By spring the following year, university faculty, staff, and students were well-accustomed to the hyper-immersive inversion of life into the digital: Zoom University. With nearly all aspects of one's social life playing out in rowed boxes on the screen, daily life was increasingly remediated in similar ways to Mr. Burns. Conversations cited, linked, or screen shared to digital cultures, which then informed face-to-face conversations that fed back into online life. I used this observation to generate three strands of conversation around Mr. Burns, a play we spent three weeks with during a 16-week term.[1]

Storytelling

- Texts: "Cape Feare" (The Simpsons Season 5, Episode 2); Selections from H.M.S. Pinafore, Act I of *Mr. Burns, a Post-Electric Play*
- Time: Two class sessions, 75-minutes each

The premise of *Mr. Burns* begins with storytelling – strangers sitting around a campfire, reminiscing over an old episode of *The Simpsons*. That *Simpsons* episode, however, is a nesting doll of other stories. Season 5, Episode 2, "Cape Feare," is a parody of the 1991 film *Cape Fear* (dir. Martin Scorsese), during which there is an extended sequence during which Sideshow Bob and Bart perform the entire score of Gilbert and Sullivan's *H.M.S. Pinafore*. Washburn's play mimics this layered storytelling through a series of time jumps that subsume the previous act's action while continuing the narrative throughline of the "Cape Feare" episode. Introductory students often have difficulty with this play because they either do not know or understand the script's range of cultural references. Dramaturgically, they do not need to. Focusing on storytelling as *action* helps students follow the throughline of the play, even if the time jumps or ironic parody passes them by during their first readings.

Before students begin reading *Mr. Burns*, assign "Cape Feare" as viewing homework.[2] Students mustn't read Washburn's script before watching the episode, or they may try to shape the class activity based on the play's action. During the next class meeting, send students into breakout rooms and ask them to take turns recounting *everything* that they can recall from the episode (plot, dialogue, costumes, specific action). Have students in each group record each telling into a shared group Google doc. Students should have at least 40 minutes, although you must stress that students should not Google or search for any material from the episode.

After the discussion ends, bring each group back into the primary room and facilitate a conversation on storytelling itself:

- What went well? What was difficult? Were specific details easy to remember or more challenging than you suspected?
- Did a group structure or rhythm emerge? If so, characterize the workflow and describe its impact on the results.
- What is storytelling? What makes for a good storyteller? What makes for a good story?
- Do you think your recounting was inherently theatrical? Why or why not?

Depending on your curriculum sequence, this conversation is an area where students tend to thread in knowledge about play structure or motivation, or information on the origins of theatre from their Theatre History and Historiography courses; use this to supplement the class's understanding of theatrical performance as art that traditionally requires an audience. Finally, turn the class's attention back towards the shared document, which should now be full of iterations of "Cape Feare," and use this document to end your discussion.

- Which version seems the most complete?
- Does any iteration seem particularly effective at getting to the humor of the original? How does it achieve this effect?
- If you had to use one as the basis for a theatrical production, which would you use? Why? If "completion" is not your primary criterion, what criteria are you using to judge?

Assign Act I of *Mr. Burns* for the following class. When students return to the next lesson, you can choose a variety of approaches to begin unpacking the text: asking a student to summarize the act, others to detail the given circumstances of this strange new world the characters find themselves in, and mechanical observations about story, structure, character, dialogue. Given that the first act of *Mr. Burns* begins with campfire storytelling, make sure you ask students to identify these characters' superobjectives – are they telling a story just for entertainment or for a greater purpose? Cumulatively, these questions help reinforce a central question that undergirds all PA courses: how do we tell stories, and what makes compelling drama?

Students interested in pursuing this question further were invited to compose a two-page "playbill note" that reflects on Act I or create an imageboard that draws on the text for design inspiration. For students who thrive with firmer instructions, I suggest focusing on Maria's story about the man she encounters in Walmart during Act I,[3] but this assignment does not have a specific prompt. Instead, it asks a series of open-ended questions, such as: What connections can they draw between her story – and its moral – and "Cape Feare"? Does her story seem like a distillation of the entire act? By asking students who submitted these materials to offer their thoughts at the beginning of the class period scheduled for Act II, you can begin to thread the metatheatrical connections between the play's disparate acts.

Text Analysis

- Text: *Acts I-III* of *Mr. Burns*, Play Reader Reports
- Time: Open Discussion time or None; End-of-play assignments

One learning outcome of my PA course is to bridge artistic production with rigorous attention to a playtext as a text. I am often frustrated by iterations of script analysis courses that use traditional paper models to demonstrate textual analysis skills when conventional academic papers are not the format many student-artists will work with during their professional careers post-graduation. To achieve a course sequence that patterns assignments directly connected to students' artistic work, I reached out to theatre companies that use reader reports to assess plays for inclusion in upcoming seasons and asked them if they would share their reports for educational use. After collecting a set of eight reader reports, I anonymized these reports and assigned one report to each play.

My set of reader reports are from companies in the United States, England, Scotland, and Ireland – ranging from new play development workshops and National Theatres to smaller regional theatre companies. Look at your professional connections and regional theatres to curate your own set of reports.[4] Using reports that students may encounter during internships or work in the immediate area is one professional advantage. Still, it also enables you to openly discuss with students how these reports are structured. What kinds of information do they value? How are they inviting readers to assess a playwright's work? Are they anonymous? Named? Do they seem equitable, or is there a company bias towards certain forms of art inlaid in its architecture? A sample of questions in these reports include:

- What is your assessment of the playwright's voice (writing style, genre, POV, intention, and any unique qualities)?
- How did the story appeal to you? Was it well-written? Did it grab you or leave you flat? Did the story have something to say?
- Wild Genre-ization (Be creative! Is the play a psychedelic romance or a twisted vaudevillian family drama?):
- What questions would you like to see explored in development? Please include both positive and negative responses.

Many offer direct questions; they ask for genre identifications, mechanical aspects of production, and plot summaries. Most, however, contain areas for open-ended analysis on the mechanics of character, pacing, structure, and dialogue. These spaces challenge students to demonstrate dramaturgical analysis through close readings, though these reader reports help students frame this work as a necessary and transferable skill.

With *Mr. Burns*, students had the opportunity to compose one of two variations of the reader report. They could write a reader report only on the Act III play-within-a-play *or* they could respond to all of Washburn's text. This split facilitated classroom discussions about the Act III pageant and interrogated our expectations of contemporary style while making space for more holistic responses to the play. Ideally, these reports capture a reader's initial reactions. In PA, I allow students to complete these at any time before the turn-in checkpoint discussed in the introduction. I find that students are open to suggested submission dates that sync with course discussion. Still, the flexibility of submission time may mean that you receive a reader report *after* discussing that work as a class. And that is okay! A student still must synthesize that conversation in the completion of the report, and it is unlikely that they will outright copy another student's ideas if they are explicitly discussed in class. The critical thing to remember is that students in PA are still learning to read plays and only beginning to write about them: reader reports are a guide that helps them work through the parts of analysis without having to formulate an "original" thesis just yet.

If you are unable to curate play response forms or wish to de-center traditional written forms of text analysis, you can alternately curate a "production meeting" day where each student has 5–7 minutes to present a "dream design" for an element of the playscript in production. This activity gives your design and production students' opportunities to hone their close reading skills in a class where their work sometimes feels sidelined. Your non-design students a chance to learn early in their course sequence how designers attend to the script differently from actors and directors. I model this "Dream Designs" activity on a similar event in the play development process during the National Play Conference at the Eugene O'Neill Theatre. In that meeting, designers present their fantasy design of the play, based solely on their reading, and converse with other designers and the playwright. The goal is not to "set" the world but to explore the palimpsestic worlds a script holds unencumbered by a specific directorial vision.

When explaining the activity in course instructions, you might suggest students create a costume rendering, a photo collage of lighting and color, a playlist of music, an original musical composition or specific sound cue, or a demo projection sketch. Students should present their design by explaining their choices through a close reading of the play text: the public presentation simultaneously reinforces dramaturgical thinking as processual work and demonstrates differential approaches to the reader. Finally, set students into small groups to their individual choices. Using *Mr. Burns*, you can curate your groups by separating the class into thirds and having each take a different act, but this is not necessary – grouping across the time jumps of each act break can be just as generative. This creative activity is easy to mark through presentation rubrics passively, but I would encourage you to be an active interlocutor throughout this process. Allow this to count as a "present and participatory" assignment. Use the class time to ask questions, affirm and praise decisions, challenge ideas, and orchestrate conversation between students who have contradictory or complementary readings of the playtext. Modeling critical conversations, grounded in specific choices with textual support, teaches students to disagree about collaboratively realizing a play in a supportive environment.

Conclusion

Given how contemporary language derivatives of the Greek word *charis*, the root for grace, are charity and charitable, it is not difficult to imagine how most institutional citations of academic grace reaffirm unequal relationships or conferrals of power. However, throughout this essay, I have attempted to model a more equitable form of academic grace in digital classrooms that is a more appropriate match for the methodologically open field of theatre and performance studies. By creating more flexible course structures, we acknowledge that our window into a student's life is limited by the zoom frame or text box and accordingly hold space for their accessibility and care needs. We also divest ourselves of some power by enabling students to choose their own pathway through an assignment sequence. Scaffolding an open set of assignments in Play Analysis that use texts to create clearer connections between "academic assignments" and "professional work" contextualizes the course materials and helps instructors signpost the rationale for coursework.

Organizationally, practicing a more flexible syllabus contact yielded three takeaways that I should acknowledge. First, by allowing students to submit a variety of assignments to achieve their grades, there is a significantly higher amount of preparatory labor and instructional writing. Between discussion boards, short paper prompts, collecting and anonymizing reader reports, and final collaborative projects, this iteration of PA averaged about ten more hours in overall course prep time. This is because you must write enough material so that students have multiple pathways to their desired grade. A student who writes only one reader report but composes robust replies to every discussion board might still do well in this course structure. Second, this structure yielded a more manageable amount of grading. Due to students' ability to choose their assignments, it was rare that I would have material from the entire class to grade – dramatically shortening my grading time throughout the semester even though students technically have more options to submit work for feedback. Third, and most significantly, the variation in assignments and assignment completion greatly improved student discussion. Giving students the ability to choose which formats work best in their schedule, with their available technologies, accessibility needs, and artistic interests generated more course investment while negating the tendency towards Zoom fatigue and digital burnout.

When I began this pedagogical experiment, I did not have a clear sense of how (or if) I would continue this flexible syllabus forward during in-person semesters. Candidly, since I changed universities mid-pandemic, I will have to rerun this test with a new student body and departmental culture before deciding how much of the course structure I will maintain, alter, or divest. What remains, however, are the student successes under this model. By shifting towards a more flexible model, students reveled in their ownership and seemed to enjoy the combinatory levels of course completion and accountability because the course was a negotiation between student access needs and my desired outcomes as the instructor. In every course, we deliver instructional content – but we are also teaching students how to be effective student learners. It is a trial-and-error process, full of fits and starts, that requires successes and failures and a bit of grace, too.

Notes

1 In online courses I err towards more time with fewer texts–partly because facilitating conversations and lectures on digital platforms like Zoom, Skype, Google Hangouts, or Microsoft Teams inevitably takes longer than during face-to-face instruction.
2 I found this was a particularly welcome assignment following the submission of material for their previous play, and during the mid-term season. It offered students a respite from "conventional" expectations of dramatic literature homework, and earned a bit of goodwill too.
3 Maria tells her story on pages 147–152 in the version of *Mr. Burns* published in *Mr. Burns and Other Plays* (Washburn, 2017). Pagination will vary in other editions.
4 For this project, I emailed literary managers at theatres who specialized in new play development or regularly hold open submissions, explaining my desire to curate new forms of reading in Play Analysis and asking for their own play response forms. I made sure to mention that all forms used would be anonymized so that students could not readily back-trace forms to specific companies. To preserve their anonymity, I will not list the theatres here since I give examples of questions. Still; I want to express my gratitude to the literary managers and dramaturgs who responded; all were overwhelmingly positive about the project.

References

Bay-Cheng, Sarah. 2015. "Virtual Realisms: Dramatic Forays into the Future." *Theatre Survey* 67, no. 4 (December): 687–698.

Blum, Susan D. 2020. "Introduction." In *Ungrading: Teaching and Learning in Higher Education*. Edited by Susan D. Blum. Morgantown: West Virginia University Press. 1–22.

Böhler, Michael J. 1998. "*PMLA* Abroad." *PMLA* 113, no. 5 (1998): 1128–1129. Accessed June 6, 2021. doi:10.2307/463246.

Cueva, Bert María. 2014 "Institutional Academic Violence: Racial and Gendered Microaggressions in Higher Education." *Chicana/Latina Studies* 13, no. 2 (Spring): 216–241.

Dolmage, Jay T. 2017. *Academic Ableism: Disability and Higher Education*. Ann Arbor: University of Michigan Press.

Halvorsen, Lauren (@halvorsen). 2020. "It Feels Like We're All Like a Week away from Living in the First act of Mr. Burns." *Twitter*, March 12, 2020, 1:35 p.m. https://twitter.com/halvorsen/status/1238171779253841927.

Halvorsen, Lauren (@halvorsen). 2021. "The Mr. Burns Revivals Are Coming Earlier Than I Expected (Please Note That in This House It Is Never the Wrong Time for Anne Washburn)." *Twitter*, June 1, 2021, 3:29 p.m. https://twitter.com/halvorsen/status/1399825475501973510.

Kohn, Alfie. 2020. "Forward." In *Ungrading: Teaching and Learning in Higher Education*. Edited by Susan D. Blum. Morgantown: West Virginia University Press. xiii–xx.

Melzer, Dan, D.J. Quinn, Lisa Sperber, and Sarah Faye. n.d. "So Your Instructor Is Using Contract Grading." *Writing Commons*. https://writingcommons.org/article/so-your-instructor-is-using-contract-grading/.

OED Online. 2021. "grace, n." Oxford University Press. Last modified June 2021. https://www-oed-com.proxyau.wrlc.org/view/Entry/80373?rskey=DrDzUF&result=1.

OED Online. 2021. "grace, v." Oxford University Press. Last modified June 2021. https://www-oed-com.proxyau.wrlc.org/view/Entry/80374?rskey=DrDzUF&result=2.

Piepzna-Samarasinha, Leah Lakshmi. 2018. *Care Work: Dreaming Disability Justice.* Vancouver, BC: Arsenal Pulp Press.

Schechner, Richard. 2013. *Performance Studies: An Introduction.* Third Edition. Media Edited by Sara Brady. London: Routledge.

Washburn, Anne. 2017. *Mr. Burns and Other Plays.* New York: Theatre Communications Group.

Yale University. n.d. "Year Four–Dissertation and Teaching." Accessed May 22, 2021. https://religiousstudies.yale.edu/graduate-program/graduate-student-handbook/year-4-dissertation-teaching.

Chapter 4

I Hope This Email Finds You (Well)
Teaching in Traumatic Spaces during the COVID-19 Pandemic

Les Gray

There is an ancient phrase that dates back well before 2020, though this was a year in which we saw it reach its heights in Twitter: "Fuck around and find out." In less vulgar terms, it is perhaps to reap what one sows. In Spring of 2020, I taught a class at the University of Maryland in College Park titled, "'A Giant Trigger Warning:' Performances of Trauma and Terror." When the semester began, I was wrapping up my dissertation and my bodymind was attuned to a pedagogy informed by trauma and disability more than ever. Our lives were upturned by a pandemic and instructors of record were given two weeks of Spring "Break" to migrate their courses online. Unknowingly, after proposing and designing a course about trauma and terror, my students and I were met with lives saturated with trauma and terror. Despite all the care I imagined myself to intentionally offer on a day-to-day basis, this would be the semester I undoubtedly fucked around and consequently found out.

This essay attempts to articulate how I utilized the hybrid physical/virtual classroom as trauma-informed and disability-informed space. Treating the faces and dark squares on the screen not as student avatars, but as real students, I learned to approach the folks in my course motivated by a pedagogy of care,[1] using what we were learning to inform *how* we were learning it. How could we answer questions about how cultural producers have performed in states of terror while also being in a state of perpetual trauma ourselves?

> *Just so you know, when I designed the course, this was not the scenario of terror I would have imagined. I possibly have a lot of work to do and will definitely keep you updated about what online THET408P is going to be.*[2]

Designed as a seminar course for upper-level undergraduate students in the Department of Theatre, I organized plays into subsections considering the nature of trauma and terror in the broadly or global political, the intimately personal, and those that appeared at the slippery intersection of both. This included plays such as *Ruined* (Nottage 2010), *4:48 Psychosis* (Kane 2000), *Dear Evan Hansen* (Levenson et al. 2017), with a semester ending on the note of the Aleshea Harris' Black ritual *What to Send Up When It Goes Down* (2019). Throughout the

DOI: 10.4324/9781003229056-6

semester, plays were paired with accompanying texts designed to nuance a definition of trauma and terror informed by these performance texts, history, and theory, encourage each student to develop an ethic of engagement with works, and be able to identify how cultural products such as these can reify or undermine our social hierarchies with dominant and marginalized identities. I have taught my students to be suspicious of grand narratives and to interrogate those "Royal We's" that frequently appear in discourse. However, I quickly learned that I was not an outside neutral party. *We* would all in some way or another be touched by the tendrils of trauma and terror. I will meditate on what transpired in my course during the Spring of 2020 and how a careful relationship to trauma and terror empowered me (and my students) to name and hold spaces that eschewed executing and doubling down on neoliberal ideas of rigor and production. Instead, we worked to replace these harmful notions with sustained, relentless empathy.

How do I balance centering theory, my experience, my students, and the work (in the class)? The answer is: I don't. That's not how trauma works and why should this writing? Traditionally, I might structure a chronology-informed and somewhat formulaic, "In this essay, I will" statement. However, in this particular case study, a time schema is an imposition that does reflect my exposure to teaching in the midst of a global pandemic. This is not to put an undue burden on you, the reader, to "make it make sense," but rather to offer up a space of engagement that is showing rather than telling, as theatre practitioners are often inclined to do.

The structure of this essay echoes and reflects the traumatic circumstances in which it was experienced and is being re-experienced. This is informed by a praxis of foregrounding my bodymind while performing what Andrew Sofer terms traumatic involuntary "rehearsal machines" (Sofer 2013). While I suggest some structure, this object lesson presents itself in flashpoints, glimpsing into The Darkest Timeline,[3] wherein a pandemic invited me to teach a class on trauma and terror in a way that was itself informed by trauma and disability. Consequently, the objects of study are overlapping interpretations of teaching traumatic theory through traumatic praxis in the context of hybrid pedagogical spaces. This is a site (with all its multiple valences) wherein students sometimes registered as disembodied black boxes and emails but were asked to reassert the value of and privilege real and fictionalized traumatic bodyminds.

Trauma-informed Practices

I want to begin by discussing the area of trauma-informed work and sharing how my course found itself situated into this idea as practice. Trauma work is spread across multiple disciplines with iterations of it appearing in both clinical work and various sites in the humanities. In their work as clinical practitioners, researchers, and educators, Janice Carello and Lisa D. Butler explain:

> To be *trauma-informed*, in any context, is to understand the ways in which violence, victimization, and other traumatic experiences may have impacted

the lives of the individuals involved and to apply that understanding to the design of systems and provision of services so they accommodate trauma survivors' needs and are consonant with healing and recovery.

(Carello and Butler 2015, 264)

The area of trauma-informed work is frequently oriented around specific principles with a strong emphasis on safety and the avoidance of (re)traumatization. This re(traumatization) is often shorthanded as "triggering" students with the course material itself or the way that it is taught. For me, engaging trauma-informed and disability-informed pedagogy in hybrid and changing spaces meant challenging expectations and assumptions about how and when folks show up, a process that is undergirded by trauma-informed care.

In order to sit with the degree to which trauma-informed work appeared in my theatre and performance course, it is necessary to first identify the foundations of what constitutes trauma-informed. Carello and Butler discuss the contributions of Roger Fallot and Maxine Harris, summarizing the core of trauma informed work consisting of: "ensuring safety, establishing trustworthiness, maximizing choice, maximizing collaboration, and prioritizing empowerment" (Carello and Butler 2013, 264). To illuminate this concept, I will make note of some evidence of these practices as they played out in my classroom. As I gestured to earlier, I would like to fully lean into the messiness of teaching traumatic material and the precarious condition of trauma that surrounded us. At times, the needed principles of trauma-informed work were clearly signaled by and to the socio-political moment and to the content of the course.

For me, safety and trustworthiness are intimately connected. At one point in my life, I might have said that I can only imagine the pitfalls of existing in a classroom that circulates trauma surrounded by folks you deem unsafe and untrustworthy. Then, I went to graduate school as a Black femme student and the painful realities of a trauma-saturated, unsafe classroom came into clear focus, a fact that I will expand upon later on in this essay. It no longer falls under speculative pedagogical fiction; I saw the consequences of this unfold around me as the pandemic set in. For example, on Twitter @emArbelo tweeted on April 7, 2020:

> My TA fully said her friend died and began to cry on zoom and the professor responded by saying that's why we still have assignments, to get our mind off tragedy. Sir what?[4]

I want to reassert, echo, and name that "Sir what?" @emArbelo tweeted. I think this points to the directly related unsafe, untrustworthy, and unforgiving nature of neoliberal infatuations with productivity, labor, and patriarchal values. I witnessed countless professors, frequently more senior and much more established than I, fiercely attempt to hold onto the ways of the Before Time and onto the concurrent and complicating notions of compulsory linearity and rigor. Instead, I let go. I breathed into a time where breath was pathologically being stolen from us, trusting that if I continued to show up for my students, they would absorb the knowledge that was of the utmost importance; I held them and their survival in far higher regard than any grade or deadline.

> *I cannot overstate this: I care about you. Your wellness. I care about your learning and your absorbing something new that will make you more thoughtful, ethical, creative producers and human beings and anything else is basically for the birds.*[5]

In endeavoring to teach a class on trauma and terror, I had set myself up well to utilize safe practices as scaffolding for the course and the other mentioned principles seemed to follow suit. Under a section of my syllabus titled "Trigger Warning-ish?," I gave some instruction to my students as to how to proceed with troubling material. I told them: "Constantly practice care for others. Just because something is not landing hard on you doesn't mean it isn't landing hard on your peers." This was a starting place to model my empathy, something I would unconditionally extend to them and expect them to extend to others around them. I also encouraged them to sit with discomfort but to also step away as they needed. I point-blank told my students my situatedness as their instructor's and while:

> *I am not a trauma specialist or a therapist, I can answer some of your questions regarding the work, hold space for you to sit with some of your reactions, and direct you to resources if your feelings potentially become too overwhelming.*[6]

The original purpose of these statements was to open myself, the instructor, up to unique human realities and anticipate catching some of the complex reactions of my students. As an original way of orienting them to the course material, these instructions also became useful guides for responses to the emotional and physical fallout associated with the pandemic. Widening the possibilities of what it means to "show up" in such a hybrid site, I was intentional and attentive to the space that I held for students. Holding space at times meant greeting silences with a kind of radical acceptance; rather than assuming students were unprepared, I held them spaces to contemplate, meditate, regroup, and sometimes collectively think through. In response, I have had students explicitly articulate their appreciation of what they perceived to be my comfort with silences. Once, a student excitedly volunteered that they had recently learned teachers should wait a significant number of seconds before following up in the synchronous virtual classroom.[7] When they extended their gratitude that I actually followed through on this, I was a bit taken aback as I had honestly no idea that this was a suggested practice.

In this same vein, I want to be as transparent in my writings here as I tried to be in my syllabus and pedagogy. These principles are integral but simultaneously pose challenges for a course that was literally titled "A Giant Trigger Warning." How does one go about incorporating trauma-informed practices into a course that is designed to foreground traumatic theatrical narratives?

This is a question that Carello and Butler team up to answer in response to "Potentially Perilous Pedagogies," by urging educators to consider separating the idea of *teaching* trauma and trauma work *as pedagogy*. They are alarmed by the practices of college professors who seem to approach trauma without care. Among other effects, the authors are troubled by the fact that "educators appear to interpret symptoms [of traumatization] as evidence of effective teaching and learning rather than as potentially harmful or undesirable" (Carello and Butler 2013, 159). Trauma-informed work is less a noun than a verb; it is a set of precise practices put into action to serve the well-being of others. This work is deeply suspicious of the traumatic/traumatizing pedagogies of educators that can prove harmful. Instructors teaching and grading around traumatic experiences can unintentionally privilege traumatic disclosure essays, assignments, or trauma-adjacent actions that lead to a lack of nuanced boundaries between the roles of students and educators. For this reason, I was quick to listen to my students, their anxieties and responses to the work and their lives around them, but also maintained diligence around directing them to trained folks with more tools than I could offer them.

Trauma-informed scholarship also emphasizes the need to understand the emotional needs and pulls of the students. We

> ...instructors should assume that in virtually every classroom some unknown subset of students will be at a heightened risk for re-traumatization or vicarious traumatization as a result of personal trauma histories, mental illness experiences, and current challenges or difficult life transitions.
> (Carello and Butler 2015, 269)

In the beginning of teaching this course, I anticipated the first mentioned suppositions but later found myself along with my students grappling more with the latter two in our post-Spring Break transition to pandemic semester life. We experienced, to varying degrees, elements of debilitation brought on by the pandemic with the threat of sickness and death becoming pervasive specters of terror. These factors necessitated the application of disability-informed care alongside the trauma-informed.

Disability-Informed Pedagogy Practices

To discuss the implications of disability studies, an area that has been deeply connected to my scholarship and bodymind, I want to center scholars such as Sami Schalk and Margaret Price who deploy the term bodymind. In doing so, they are perpetually gesturing to the intersections of material raced, gendered, and (dis)abled bodies over time. Bodyminds, according to Schalk, pull at the thread of Cartesian dualist understandings of bodies and minds pointing us to how it

> insists on the inextricability of mind and body and highlights how processes within our being impact one another in such a way that the notion of a physical versus mental process is difficult, if not impossible to clearly discern in most cases.
>
> (Schalk 2018, 5)

She proposes that this term is tied to disability studies in its existence as "a socially constructed phenomenon and systemic social discourse which determines how bodyminds and behaviors are labeled, valued, represented, and treated" (Schalk 2018, 2). Thus, I would be remiss if I did not mention how tied trauma and disability are in discourse and in reality. This is not to say that the traumatic body is always already disabled or to suggest that the lived reality of a disabled bodymind is always traumatic. However, there are clear links that became more evident to me in my class. In an anonymous survey I sent to my students, I asked them questions regarding their safety, their access to food, access to healthcare, their access to reliable internet/technology, and provided a section to disclose any potential barriers to their education as we proceeded online. The results were surprising, with multiple students revealing the disabilities that they felt were unnecessary to mention earlier in the semester but they feared would have an impact on their learning online.

In response, I found myself trying to be more diligent in considering how I could best accommodate and support my students. I also discovered that the combination of the course material, the traumatic circumstances, my own investment in disability, and my students' disclosures resulted in me reconceiving my approach to the work I was doing in the virtual classroom. Cripping the classroom, for me, meant laying bare the insidious intricacies of compulsory able bodiedness that often hold us captive. I put in place elements of universal design practices meant to acknowledge and remove as many pedagogical stumbling blocks as possible for my students.

My disability-informed work and practices of care effectively became a way that I was able to crip my own pedagogical models and better serve the intellectual and emotional needs of my students. The shifts were represented in my treatment of my students but also manifested in how they understood their relationship to the work and each other. This can perhaps most be clearly illustrated in our collective relationship to disabled or crip time.

My course centrally operated on "crip time," which hinges upon the concept that trauma and disability do not necessarily function on the linear timeline of compulsory able-bodiedness. This at first might seem like a vaguely applicable theoretical analytic, but I found that there were many ways to put this into meaningful practice, whether it was encouraging asynchronous coursework or not penalizing late work. I explicitly told students that I prioritized meaningful engagement over deadlines, bestowing to them a perhaps gratuitous flexibility. Obviously, I presented the class with a structure and understood that it was possible to program the learning management system (LMS) to automatically deduct points for late work. Despite this, I struggled to see pedagogical merit to such a practice during a time when our grasp on what day it was presented as precarious at best.

In retrospect, for many, the circumstances of the pandemic and its willy-nilly relationship to constructs of time reinforced a concept some students had struggled with in the course. As I introduced them to dramatic works that played dangerously with the assumed rigid structure of linear time, I asked them to consider how that might reflect the traumatic circumstances the characters were dealing with. As trauma theorists such as Cathy Caruth argue, trauma often re-asserts itself in its disruption of life, with traumatic moments being perpetually revisited or narratives being told non-linearly seemingly without rationale to back up such manifestations.

> *Productivity is a trap. Do what you can to survive right now. That is really the only important thing. If there is anything you think of in the future that I can do to support you and help you get through this semester let me know. If you need me to Amazon Prime you some tea for you to slow down and practice some self care, I will do it.*[8]

When I look back at my emails from this course, it is awash in a sea of apologies. Most of them were about time. There were so many: "I will try to do my best and get things in on time." "So sorry this is late." "Apologies for my delayed response." Looking back, I (perhaps too often) refused to accept their apologies, deflecting them as if they were compliments I found inappropriately awarded.

During a talk, a scholar once stated emphatically that scholars were in no way rewarded for making their work accessible. This is not to suggest that they *should* be, but it probably wouldn't hurt. I put this forward to build upon the notion that the pandemic collectively forced our hand toward (perhaps temporarily) accessibility and accommodation. Imani Barbarin generously gave the advice:

> If you are tired of prefacing your emails with 'I hope you're staying safe' or 'I hope you're alright.' Might I suggest 'I hope this email finds you safe at home enjoying the many accessibility features disabled people fought for and still don't get' as an alternative.
>
> (Barbarin 2020)

Central to my argument is this idea that trauma-informed and disability-informed practices are necessary in the pursuit of higher education. As the reality of the pandemic set in, disabled people who had been long-acquainted with regular disenfranchisement and institutional lacks, watched as able-bodied folk scrambled to reinvent the debilitation wheel, so to speak. Ableds struggled to find ways individually to deal with (gestures vaguely)... everything. The truth of being home-bound, while not alone. Walking around with a lot of baggage but rarely traveling. These things were neither new nor revelatory to people inhabiting disabled bodyminds prior to pandemic life, though those less familiar with such notions worked quickly and often haphazardly to create mutual aid and systems of survival despite the fact that disabled folks had been nailing this for decades.

Trauma and (sometimes simply the threat of) debilitation led to some students in my course becoming undone. The binding circumstances further limited their imagination of how a theatre and performance course could help them survive. Why did this course/this semester/their education even matter?

To answer this, I needed to revisit my own education and worldview as it greatly informs my practices of care. Beginning as soon as my first year of Ph.D. coursework, some tropes developed around my existence as a graduate student. If there was a guest presenting research, I usually had some standard go-to questions that I desperately wanted (nay needed?) answered. I found myself clinging to them to propel myself through my own work: (1) Why this object of study now? (2) How do you orient yourself as a subject in your work? At times, in the midst of sorting through my own struggles (such as reoccurring traumas of Black folks being assassinated in this country) sometimes the question posed would aggressively begin, "Given that people are dying..."

I did not realize at the time how much that question would inform my "pedagogy of care" alongside trauma and disability-informed practices in my classroom. It was always in my brain, this supposition: "given that people are dying, how do I grade this assignment?" "Given that people are dying, how do I respond to this student's email?" Because the reality was, at some point, we were all liable to be debilitated by this pandemic, whether it touched our bodies or those around us. While the rumination "given that" may register as an exaggerated trauma response, it enabled my hybrid pedagogy to morph, for better or for worse, into one that anticipated the catastrophic failure of bodyminds in and outside of my classroom—even, in some ways, welcomed its arrival. My orientation toward trauma as an educator and as a human provided me with the opportunity to exercise a radical empathy that one might associate with weakness or just being a straight-up sucker.

But, truly, I am okay with my sucker pedagogy as it is. Long before COVID, I had done away with such ableist and classist notions such as doctor's notes for illness or obituaries for deaths in the family, or rewarding perfect attendance. I was horrified when, as a part of a theatre teaching online/hybrid education group, multiple theatre teachers recommended an educator force a student's hand by asking them to get a doctor's note for their alleged condition after the student resisted a specific type of participation in a theatrical makeup class. Rage. What kind of sociopath would suggest that you demand your student see a doctor for something so incredibly superficial during a global pandemic? When I was a child I taught as a child but as we become educators, I truly believe we should do away with such ableist things.

In some ways, I hope that this essay by the time it is published will have written itself into a sort of irrelevance. But I doubt it. Holding the materialities that I do in this bodymind, there is no normal to return to. I can already see progress being undone as disabled employees are terminated after demanding continuance of the remote work that was so recently a viable way of doing labor. I believe that it behooves us to realize that our collective cultural memory is abhorrently short and that we often quickly forget all we have lost. Almost as quickly as we forget all that we have gained.

It is my hope that this essay has, through the lenses of trauma, disability, and accommodation, allowed some space for us to acknowledge those realities. We have lost so many people and simultaneously gained so many tools to survive such devastating loss. What we, as performance practitioners, scholars, and educators do with this knowledge, I argue, can be a site of revolution and liberation from those events and moments that alienate us. This essay itself provides a necessary trauma and disability-informed space to hold binaries and dialectics together with care: bodies and minds, isolation, and gathering. Ultimately, my course on performances of trauma and terror during a time of trauma and terror endeavored to answer and encapsulate the simple question that is this: how can we find ways to be alone, together?

I believe academic rigor and challenge can be achieved in hybrid or online spaces. But what if, rather than centering stumbling blocks to acquiring knowledge, we emphasize those things that are deeply embedded in the practice of theatre and performance? Rather than trafficking in neoliberal informed configurations of often empty production, what would it mean to shift our gaze toward those things we excel in such as empathy, collaboration, and general practices of care?

In my course, we revisited central questions: why would someone write or perform this? Why this play, now? As we settled into the depths of that pandemic, sometimes these questions emerged and simply answered themselves. We share stories of trauma because trauma and terror frequently happen around us. To us. We share so that, when we find ourselves quarantined, eyes vaguely glazed over and locked on a Zoom screen with our peers' bodies curled up on their childhood beds, swaddled in blankets with their family pets briefly entering the frame, we can remind ourselves that we are not completely and utterly alone and without support. And if, by chance, you didn't come into my class that semester with a sense of that fact, it is impossible that you left without it.

Notes

1 "Pedagogy of care" is, to me, an educational praxis that deploys an ethic of care (hooks 1994; Goralnik et al. 2012; Zygmunt et al. 2018).
2 Announcement on my Canvas March 13, 2020.
3 This is a reference to the television show *Community* which focuses on a motley crew of non-traditional/traditional community college students. The show features multiple episodes wherein time is reconstructed or re-experienced, sometimes based on the

mere rolling of the die. What emerges is what comes to be known as "The Darkest Timeline" where characters are forced to confront the worst versions of themselves in the worst of circumstances.
4 Tweet from @emArbelo on April 7, 2020.
5 Announcement on Canvas on March 31, 2020.
6 Quotations from my initial in-person and revised online syllabus.
7 It should be said though that the concepts of "wait time" and "think time" studied by Robert J. Stahl far predate online courses. See R. J. Stahl, 1994 "Using 'Think-Time' and 'Wait-Time' Skillfully in the Classroom," *ERIC Digest, ED370885*, 1–6.
8 Email to student, April 12, 2020.

References

Barbarin, Imani. 2020. "If You Are Tired of Prefacing Your Emails." *Twitter*, 30 April 2020. https://twitter.com/Imani_Barbarin/status/1255870744984248325?s=20.
Carello, Janice, and Lisa D. Butler. 2013. "Potentially Perilous Pedagogies: Teaching Trauma Is Not the Same as Trauma-Informed Teaching." *Journal of Trauma and Dissociation* 15, no. 2: 153–168.
Carello, Janice, and Lisa D. Butler. 2015. "Practicing What We Teach: Trauma-Informed Educational Practice." *Journal of Teaching in Social Work* 35, no. 3: 262–278.
Em. 2020. "My TA fully said her friend died." *Twitter*, 7 April 2020. https://twitter.com/EmArbelo_/status/1247545903482839042.
Goralnik, Lissy, Kelly F. Millenbah, Michael P. Nelson, and Laurie Thorp. 2012. "An Environmental Pedagogy of Care: Emotion, Relationships, and Experience in Higher Education Ethics Learning." *Journal of Experiential Education* 35, no. 3 (October): 412–428. doi:10.1177/105382591203500303.
Harris, Aleshea. 2019. *What to Send Up When It Goes Down*. New York: Samuel French.
hooks, bell. 1994. *Teaching to Transgress: Education as a Practice of Freedom*. New York: Routledge.
Kane, Sarah. 2000. *4.48 Psychosis*. London: Methuen.
Levenson, Steven, James Lapine, Benj Pasek, and Justin Paul. 2017. *Dear Evan Hansen*. New York: Theatre Communications Group.
Nottage, Lynn. 2010. *Ruined*. New York: Dramatist's Play Service.
Schalk, Sami. 2018. *Bodyminds Reimagined: (Dis)ability, Race, and Gender in Black Women's Speculative Fiction*. Durham, NC: Duke University Press.
Sofer, Andrew. 2013. *Dark Matter: Invisibility in Drama, Theatre, and Performance*. Ann Arbor, MI: University of Michigan Press.
Zygmunt, Eva, Kristin Cipollone, Susan Tancock, Jon Clausen, Patricia Clark, and Winnie Mucherah. 2018. "Loving Out Loud: Community Mentors, Teacher Candidates, and Transformational Learning Through a Pedagogy of Care and Connection." *Journal of Teacher Education* 69, no. 2: 127–139.

Part II

Dance and Movement

Chapter 5

Imaginative Deixis and Distributed Fictions in the Suzuki Method of Actor Training

Christopher J. Staley

This chapter focuses on the challenges and opportunities in remote instruction of the Suzuki Method of Actor Training. I mostly base this on participation in online programming with the Saratoga International Theatre Institute. SITI Company officially offered virtual public training with their "Day One" meeting in June 2020. At that pilot event, one hundred artists around the world convened to practice the Suzuki Method, Viewpoints, and attend symposium. SITI soon began weekly drop-in classes to bridge together a roster of one-off and serial intensives made available for artists not able to participate in situ. These included their Boise Intensive in August 2020; a series of Beginner, Intermediate, and Advanced Intensives in January 2021; a joint Alexander Technique/Suzuki Method Workshop in March; all leading to the virtual Skidmore Summer Intensive.[1]

The current chapter incorporates research into deixis, or the ability to point. Due to the overt speech-acts, gestures, and perspective-taking practiced in the Suzuki Method, I argue a psycholinguistic reading of its deictic components can benefit a broad field of practitioners and scholars. I suggest the deeper technique developed in these Suzuki Cultures is the performer's ability to simultaneously enact specificity and polysemy in their bodies: that is, to point at something and nothing at the same time. I offer an autoethnographic perspective of these online environments and possible lessons to remember as we all "return to normal." Comparing virtual templates with whatever presumptive standards or ideals might be in place for teaching the Suzuki Method in person, I resist the idea that virtual or remote options are less effective than in-person pedagogy and argue they may sometimes be more useful. I hope to inspire readers that even and especially over Zoom, teachers and students may still access deeply imaginative relationships to their surroundings and remote scene partners, not despite the hurdle of distance, but because of it.

This is not idealism. The Suzuki Method is undoubtedly rigorous, athletic, and martial, and there are definite limitations to what one can do with the exercises and sequencing based on technology and physical environment. From the ground up, these immediately include problems with the floor. Many of the exercises showcase a stomping action with the feet, along with specific vocabularies

DOI: 10.4324/9781003229056-8

of locomotion (i.e., walking or marching) across the stage. An ideal studio for Suzuki training has sprung surfaces to protect the body's joints but also the architecture. Actors who go for "full stomps" at home will find feedback from furniture, shelving, and the bones of their buildings resonating as feet hit the floor. In comparison to the austere and empty training studios on most campuses, at home, objects can be jostled out of place, giving actors clear lessons on how the impact of their stomps reveals a gravitational relationship between earth, performer, and sky which radiates to the rest of their environment.

The volume of space itself becomes an issue in the sense that the range of motion that the actor explores in the Suzuki Method varies from the most inner and proximal (invisible micromovements inside the pelvis) to the most distal, reaching towards the edges of one's kinesphere (such as pointing or slicing with the hands). In larger studios, there are obviously larger paths for the actor to explore continuous movement or actually travel a real distance, but only to a degree; the edge of the stage still means something concrete. Likewise though, actors at home are also exploring this illusion of continuity just as much as they are traveling a real distance, however small, to achieve the illusion of traveling somewhere beyond their living room. Here, the non-volumetric virtuality of theatrical fiction rubs up against the very real issues of volume in and around the actor's body.[2] Actors at home may have to extend themselves farther and work harder to achieve the same level of theatricality as their counterparts in a "legit" theatre space.

This extensible reach – through the feet to the floor, to their walls, and neighbors – immediately raises issues of aural space. In most dedicated studios with soundproofing or schedules, there are no concerns about making noise at the expense of privacy or politeness. Actors at home might worry about disturbing roommates, parents, children, landlords, or pets, or about being intruded upon themselves. These obstacles demand actors handle their performances with dignity – to stay in it – and maintain intention toward their image, while being safe and practical. Complicating this is the strained distribution of the ensemble's sense of timing, wherein the impossibility to stay in-sync is more pronounced over Zoom. Understandably and excitingly, cohesion soon falls apart. At any time, the actor's center cannot juggle everything, and something has to give, whether it be their speed, stability, form, or image. The actor must make a choice of what to hold onto and of what to let go.

Actors have always required their own agency to elevate the Method (or any role) above dogma and sports. It is not enough for an actor to achieve mechanical precision in the forms for this to function *as an actor training*. This is what sets the Suzuki Method apart from "Movement Training" in that the point is to engender the actor's communicative potential onstage, not to develop marionettes. This is a training in failure. In witnessing everyone seek and yet never achieve a contrived ideal of perfection, students are given the chance to "fail again" and "fail better" as Beckett said famously in "Worstword Ho" (Beckett, 2006, 471). The actors' requisite absurdity in persevering reveals the existential philosophy undergirding Suzuki's desire to train the actor's sense of autonomy. This stems from his deep studies of Sartre and Merleau-Ponty, and also his many years as a political activist. The humanity of the training lies in the fact that each member of the ensemble can only ever be responsible for themselves and their own actions despite high social dependency. The transindividualistic potential of the training is therefore its limitation: that we can only teach and train the individual through understanding how the individual reflects and is reflected in society.[3]

Without the benefit of proximity, remote settings may exacerbate this myopia and egocentric individualism. Proximity in the room creates the illusion of being really in sync, but the existential plank under the training insists that we are always forever alone onstage, even when surrounded by others. Still, it is easier to feel more connected when one is actually feeling the vibrations, heat, and sweat of another actor in the room. Over Zoom, it is just harder to feel the intensity of the other bodies and to perceive the feeling of a shared fictional moment, either when students are working onstage or watching their colleagues from the audience. The flipside is that virtual instruction can increase appreciation for how much freedom actors have always had in their individual contributions to a wider group fiction and extended learning environment, no matter the size or set-up or play. By whittling away at the material extraneities we think are required of our training environments, we can follow a similar *via negativa* as Jerzy Grotowski in *Towards a Poor Theatre* or Peter Brook's *The Empty Space*.[4]

Such reminders – that we've already been down this road before – productively trouble the mindset that virtual instruction is inherently a deficit model. Instead, remote pedagogy proves to be robust for increasing the proxemic reach and scope of these "Suzuki Cultures" in safe and effective ways. In these (post)quarantine ecologies, Zoom's glitches, a fragile kitchen floor, intruding families, or daily changes in one's physicality are no longer impediments to acting. Instead, actors remember that training only really begins by recognizing these real-life hurdles as theatrical obstacles that they must mindfully attend and imaginatively address rather than automatically ignore or to admit defeat.

This leads to a rhetorical question: if significant modifications are required for virtual training, does this mean actors in domestic settings are achieving/receiving something less than those training in-person or in theatres? The answer would seem to be yes, if one over-prioritizes the importance of the vocabulary, or *kata*. Yes, the physicality of the training is paramount. However, by dogmatically clinging to forms over principles, there is more risk to conceptualize this training as only a violent type of calisthenics, or as stylized voice and speech classes. To do so overlooks the main tenets of the Suzuki Method – control of energy production, center of gravity, and breath – which ultimately serve the actor's intention toward an imaginative or "divine fiction" (Suzuki, 2015, 29). These acting lessons lie not in the rigor of the movements, but rather in the rigor of really imbuing them with fictive stakes. The stomps, walks, cuts, points, or statues are ultimately artistic "mummies," silly theatre games, or gymnastic parlor tricks, unless they are given meaning through the actor's ostension.[5]

What Is the Suzuki Method?

The Suzuki Method is a set of acting theories and ethics articulated by Tadashi Suzuki and the Suzuki Company of Toga into a series of disciplines. Most students now encounter the training distilled into six Basics which are used to harness vital "animal energy" onstage (Suzuki, 2015, *passim*).[6] The Method has been in development since the 1960s when Suzuki began defining his "grammar of the feet." He was not then setting out to create an eponymous acting system. Instead, Suzuki focused on exploring *kata* that would help his actor-colleagues achieve the type of vessels he found necessary to meet the circumstances of his plays, especially with the meteoric trajectory of *Toroia no Onna (Trojan Women,* 1973). SCOT's rehearsal methods evolved into oral trainings to onboard actors and maintain continuity through an aggressive repertory and touring schedule. Demonstrations of their regimen began to accompany Suzuki's establishment of a variety of his own festivals (e.g., the 1982 Toga Summer Arts Festival or Theatre Olympics). These efforts aligned with co-founding of satellite training companies like SITI in 1992. Through the tandem labors of SCOT and SITI primarily, the Method has become one of the most widespread global acting systems.

It is common in Euro-American studios to misunderstand the training as a stylized and aggressive form of eurythmics. These misunderstandings often track along Orientalist biases, which exoticize it as patently Japanese and contradict Suzuki's truly syncretic nature: as a global amalgam drawing from Noh, Kabuki, and more native martial arts (*kendo*) and walking traditions (*namba aruki*), yes, along with other transnational practices such as ballet, Martha Graham technique, Kathakali, et al. Suzuki incorporated principles of Japanese traditional theatre into a globalist avant-garde aesthetic because ultimately he "want[ed] to have [his] own particular forms and words" (Goto, 1998). To reduce the training to Orientalized athleticism or to instrumentalize it as just a means to feign classical virtuosity is to cheapen the central pillars of the pedagogy: these involve creating awareness of the actor's "invisible body" in relationship to a fictional image (Lauren, 2011). Urgency around the fictive body is not unique to Suzuki's philosophy, and with that, the widespread misunderstanding of its importance is not unique to his training either. Suzuki describes similar confusion around Stanislavski's legacy. He esteems the "revolutionary hypothesis" of Active Analysis before bemoaning its limits as seen in Americanized, capitalized Method Acting:

> this mutant form of the Stanislavski method skips a critical stage in the creation of a role… the step where the actor must use his or her imaginative work to create a fictional space and experience emotions unique to the act of being onstage.
>
> (Suzuki, 2015, 36)

There have been many mutations of the Suzuki Method which misunderstand this fictional basis. With an acute period of evolution and proliferation now at

Imaginative Deixis and Distributed Fiction 61

hand given the Method's forced migration to Zoom, it is important to ask, by process of *via negativa*, which common denominations remain unchanged?

What distinguishes solipsistic and violent encounters with the Suzuki Method versus more sociable and sustaining approaches lies in how actors use it to generate "stage awareness" or "performative consciousness" (Suzuki, 2015, 37–38, 59–61). Suzuki describes such awareness as a nuanced ability to "cozen" the audience into a fictional belief, though importantly, this is not anything like the proverbial suspension of disbelief.[7] In these cases, "spontaneous… stage awareness" makes actors aware of their ability to embody multiple meanings while simultaneously chasing a singular target in every moment (Suzuki, 2015, 47). Actors-in-training are thus performers-as-researchers, investigating what Baz Kershaw called the paradox of "boundless specificity" (2008, 26). In the Suzuki Method, there are no concrete boundaries marking entrances and exits, so actors practice dilating their bodies between a spontaneous instance of arrival/disappearance as well as sustained durations of presence/absence. Audiences then attend to what actors actually do in the *kata* as it blends with the fictive reality seeming to motivate such actions. Put another way, as Anne Bogart says in her 2019 blog, "Ways of Seeing," we must remember that spectators attend theatre not just to see for themselves, but more so to "see the actors see." This manipulation of the deictic frame, for the audience's benefit, is exactly what the Suzuki Method sensitizes.

What Is Deixis?

Patrice Pavis opined that "deixis plays such an important part in theatre as to be one of its specific characteristics…" (Pavis, 1998, 91–92). It derives from ancient Greek, meaning to reference, indicate, display, or point. Linguistically, pronouns like *I, you, here, now, there, then, yesterday, or tomorrow* are deictics that only carry meaning in relation to their performative function. Deictics coextend with non-verbal grammars like glances, gestures, or poses – known as "manual deictics" – and literally point out the context-bounded nature of language and reality (Kita, 2003). Acts-of-pointing are fundamental to communication, and manual/verbal deixis is universal to human speech as well as some primate and hominid "proto" languages (Bejarano, 2011).

Deictic analyses yield new understandings of what we colloquially refer to as "grounding down" or "being grounded" when speaking. As SITI actor, Stephen Webber, and others echo in practice, "The foot is the voice" (training notes, March 2021). But how? This exploration of grounded diction is clearly important for Suzuki, who writes, "acting, in the broad sense, is not only an expression of inner life, but an ongoing experimentation with the language of performance as it has evolved throughout human history" (Suzuki, 2015, 12). I believe this experimentality that Suzuki refers to is his unstated but innate sense of the power of sensing one's "Deictic Ground." For deixis, as cognitive theatre scholar Eve Sweetser defines it, "refers to the conventional use of linguistic forms whose meaning depends on the (implicit) Ground." Sweetser notes this in her opening to *Viewpoint in Language: A Multimodal Perspective*, explaining that she chose her title "Introduction: viewpoint and perspective in language and gesture, from the Ground down" because it "articulates something that the rest of the book confirms: cognitive perspective starts with bodily viewpoint within a real physical Ground of experience" (Dancygier and Sweetser, 2012, 3). This Ground is made explicit for Suzuki, as he offers a diagnostic through which actors increase cognizance of their social settings by texturizing intelligence of surroundings from underfoot.

In theatrical media, deixis involves such multimodal ostension when actors project real or imaginary images on the landscape through the "material anchor" of their bodies (Dancygier, 2016). The late Jerzy Limon extensively analyzed actors' supreme (metatheatrical) abilities to interweave and untangle multiple deictic axes into a unified event-stream, seen clearly in Stoppard's *Arcadia* (2010) or the Mousetrap in *Hamlet*. Applying this to an ancient example, Euripides' *The Bacchae* opens with the line "Here I am [now], Dionysus," in which the actuality of the actor saying "Here I am now" is re-contextualized through a semantic Character trait, in this case the name, Dionysus. This anaphora creates two Deictic Fields through which the actor-character appears to move in a linear fashion: the actor speaks now, as seems to Dionysus, and they both illusively traverse a kind of theatrical hamster-wheel or treadmill-like narrative convention throughout the play. This kinespheric surf-simulator is pinned to the actor's "deictic center" or "Origo" wherefrom they enunciate themselves as themself and as character (see Figure 5.1).

Cognitive linguist Ellen Fricke has studied how deictic centers can be moveable, or "allocable," seen easily when a person recounts a story by taking on two or more scenic perspectives, such as changing facial profile and directions along with their voices (2014). The ability to track an unfixed, "non-volumetric" center requires listeners attune themselves to other people's environmental affordances and goal-orientations in relationship to their own, which likely underlies the deeply innate faculties central to Theory of Mind. Fricke built upon Karl Bühler's foundational connection of the "tactile body image" and, most applicably, his idea of the *origo*, which is a notion of self as the zero-point in a kind of Cartesian grid system (Bühler, 1982). For my purposes, I equate the origo/deictic center with Suzuki's conception of the *hara*, also referred to as the *koshi*. Without getting much farther into technical language, it is helpful to highlight Fricke's extensive research in this area, as she parses two main traditions of deictic theory, namely the Anglo-American and Bühlerian schools.[8] The distinction she makes is at the heart of my argument into the actor's imaginative priorities in the Suzuki Method. Per Fricke's account, Anglo-American semioticians were too "limited to perceptual deixis, or *demonstratio ad oculos*" (1806). However, Bühlerian schools understood deixis not as bound by material environments, but rather as boundless due to one's imaginative capacities of projection (*deixis am phantasma*). The projection of multiple non-volumetric entities (or origos) in

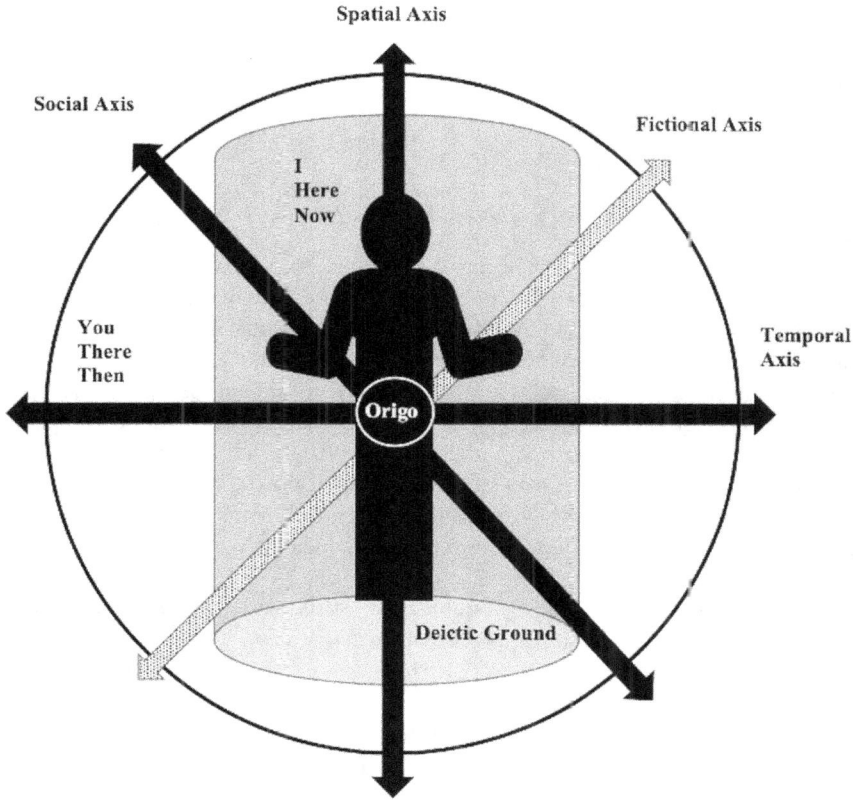

Figure 5.1 A schematic of deictic axes originating from the Deictic Ground through the actor's Origo, or Deictic Center.

the process of recounting narrative constitutes a type of performative that Fricke calls "origo-allocating acts" (1818). This resonates with the actor's enactment of fictional space and time with the stomps, points, or other *kata* in Suzuki training.

I am struck by the repeated use of this term "allocation" in my fieldnotes from Ellen Lauren's virtual classes. Paraphrasing slightly, Lauren asked students over Zoom: "how do you allocate your energy?" She then suggested that they use the training to "generate sensation…in [their] body and allocate it in relationship to [their] scene partner" (training notes, June 2021). The Method is not about meaningful movement, then, but about meaningful *stillness* in order to craft more time for these moments of allocating one's energy. As Suzuki instructed students in Toga Mura, it is not a "movement training" but instead it is a "training to stop movement" (training notes, August 2018). In the process of negotiating the stops, the actor manipulates an illusion – spontaneous and/or sustained – of their character's body/origo as it overlays onto the material reality of what the actor is doing with their own "real" body/origo. In our classical example from *The Bacchae*, the actor doubles the capacity of their deictic center when they invoke the name Dionysus and speak from such a blended space, or al-location.

Imaginary Deixis: Who Am I Now? Now? Now?

In real life, the entire body is a pointing machine. Manual deictics, like pointing with a finger, head turn, or glance, become significantly more charged onstage. The technique behind the Suzuki Method is remembering the actor's full-bodied capacities to fictionalize space and time, beginning with the deictic ground. Actors constantly stomp in place or locomotion, testing their sense of *here, here, here* and *now, now, now*. Focusing on the here and now immediately begets a corollary task, which is to not anticipate the next beat happening over there and then. To stay present, actors seek out a "classical axis," a grid-like, frontally oriented schema of the body's sagittal, coronal, and transverse planes. Suzuki describes the performer's alignment in terms of a deictic mapping of their image:

> When a clear central focus is established in this way, the actor and his body must maintain a relationship with it, *moving along a sort of axis...* Even when the actor turns his back on the audience, he is still intensely aware of his relationship to it. In such a context, the purpose of speech is not to express [a] psychological state... but to prove the distinct and absolute presence of the object to which the actor speaks and shows his body...
>
> (23–24)

Especially on Zoom, when actors may give up all sense of a proscenium frame or visibility for the camera, the onus is on them to teach themselves by clarifying what exactly they are facing off against.

Examples from some primary disciplines, Basics Three and Four, may help demonstrate the legibility of these theories and geometries in training. Basic Three comprises three movement series, lettered 3A, 3B, and 3C. In each, the challenge of holding a fictional reality is challenged along horizontal, vertical, and rotational paths, and each form targets the problem of directionality from a different angle. Basic 3A is made of gestures which highlight mobility and stillness across horizontal and vertical planes, while Basic 3B is more frontally oriented with vertical *relevés* onto tiptoes. While the same ideas are at play for each, Basic 3C clearly evidences Suzuki's point about the relationship of body to target, especially when the actor turns away. To start, the actor squats upstage, back facing their target. They will pivot downstage on their left and right feet along 180-degree arcs while their center corkscrews upwards to stillness in respectively opened and closed stances.

In each form, a crucial aspect of the system is how to engender the impulses for action. Usually, instructors yell out cues or hit the floor with a long bamboo implement. In 3C, the sound propels the body into a state of rotational velocity and movement, which must then be *instantaneously* stopped in relation to the fictional target. In purpose-built rooms, actors are dared to safely test their limits, which means for 3C, tracing bigger arcs on the floor, tempting momentum within the spirals, and risking a fall as their speeds increase. Many at home practitioners rightly diminish their diameters on the floor and cut back on velocity to prevent injury, especially if on carpet. Are those actors who limit their speed or range-of-motion any less "spontaneous" or "aware" of their fictional image than those who might seem to be going full throttle?

Though intensity of speed and directionality are crucial factors in the Suzuki Method, the increased sensitivity toward individual lag time brought on by Zoom has revealed these technical questions of fiction to be no less profound. The vividness of one's image within the Basics is certainly enlivened by the actor's ability to stop quickly, but its veracity is not reducible to velocity. While avoiding prescription, this reveals the importance of my pedagogical stance in terms of why there may be *better curiosities* to explore in these studio spaces, especially those at home. Focusing on curiosity rather than virtuosity allows the former to serve the latter in training and onstage.[9] It is the idea of creating replicable conditions for emotions to emerge onstage by chasing after action rather than affect or sense memory. Each stop is not a stop for stopping's sake, but rather a chance to refresh one's sense of presence, working "moment to moment" in a way reminiscent of what practitioners doggedly chase in Meisner technique or in Practical Aesthetics.

The potential of these stops to explore deictic enunciation is also very apparent in Basic Four, or Standing/Sitting Statues. In Standing Statues, from a similar neutral position as 3C, actors rise to variably high, medium, and low levels on their toes, adopting either a set- or free-form shape with the upper body. The structure of the arms, head, and torso depends on the quality of relationship between the actor's core and their external target, whether that focus be near, far, or infinite in scale. In these abrupt stops, the next movement is isometrically held, and the actor uses this inhibition to deepen their imaginative circumstances. When attending to external fiction, actors can re-hypothesize their ideas of Performance-as-Research by monitoring their image and fictionalizing each *kata* with greater "boundless specificity" (per Kershaw) moment to moment. As they become more competent with sequencing, actors require less cognitive load to remember the next form and instead can utilize the *kata* to mindfully practice expressing their inner life without resorting to solipsism.

Conclusion

Suzuki writes that each movement and stop onstage creates "a gesture that can lead to the creation of a fictional space, perhaps even a ritual space, in which the actor's body can achieve a transformation from the personal to the universal" (2015, 71). So too, the actor's pedestrian home can be imbued with a sense of the heroic and fantastical, and the sensibility of this larger endeavor is shareable amongst the ensemble. In these moments of spontaneous world-building, the actor gets feedback from an aggressively fed-forward impulse (e.g., a stomp); this information comes from somatic responses of the body-schema struggling in the form. Voice then manifests as material expression of the body's futile efforts to contain itself, creating new feedback loops. These loops are always doubled since the actor must remain aware of their own origo and their character's origo in relationship to an ever-shifting external target. The impossibility of the actors' attempts to isometrically stabilize their center of gravity reflects their "asymptotic" effort to manage the unstable allocation of their personal origo as it im-possibly blends with that of the character (Suzuki, 2015, *xiii*).

While outside the bounds of this chapter to expand fully, it is worth clarifying my stance relative to the practicability of exploring deixis in these studio spaces. How do any of these theories help actors? One obvious perk that comes from using the Suzuki Method over Zoom is that we can deal with the issues of "talking heads" in real time, especially on a platform that cuts away so much of the body's expressive potential in its heterotopic rectangles. On screen, I speculate that we use many more of these traditionally conceived manual deictics; our fingers, thumbs, and faces do a lot more of the talking. In any Suzuki setting, but especially over Zoom, the actor is given the opportunity to showcase their ability to make their manual deictics more full-bodied and footlike, or "podal."[10] A larger benefit therefore comes from developing the actor's curiosity and empathy in extending their imaginative conception of the other person – to remember that while the embodied realities of another person are not actually accessible, they are imaginatively available.

To conclude, I share a personal reflection from a Process module in SITI's Virtual Skidmore curriculum. The seminar, led by Anne Bogart, revolved around "the many issues that arise in the process of collaboration… in relation to the current cultural and political shifts, Covid recovery, and personal trajectories" (2021 Participant Packet). The first question Bogart posed to participants was "What adjustments will you make to return to the theatre world?" We were given time to free-write our answers before sharing them with the group in wider discussions. I thank my colleagues and teachers from this most recent training, and by way of ending, I copy my written response here:

> I don't think I ever turned away from theatre nor did it turn away from me during the pandemic. I left theatre spaces, but I never left the thing I was doing before, which was training. So I want to remember that my work as an actor, director, or audience member is never really any different than what it has been on Zoom. My work is not deadened by dealing with remote distance, but instead is enlivened by it. I have to work harder to achieve the same thing – so really I just need to adjust the level of how much I care when I 'return' to the theatre world.

As more training circles joyously revert to in person set ups, I aim to remind my colleagues and myself of all the rich insights provided by this extended interval of remote practice. I hope to recuperate this period of experimentation, frustration, and successful failings. Ultimately, that so many diverse participants were able to access these trainings solely because of their online formatting is itself a great blessing and opportunity to celebrate, one to which we cannot become jaded.

Notes

1. I have been fortunate to attend SITI's virtual trainings in 2020 and 2021, and Skidmore Intensives in 2009, 2017, and 2019. I leverage this alongside fieldwork with the Pacific Performance Project in 2016 and 2013 and the Suzuki Company of Toga in Toga Mura, Japan in 2018 and 2019.
2. The idea of "non-volumetric" performance is highly germane to analyses of deixis; see following section, especially vis-à-vis Fricke (2014).
3. My ideas here are highly indebted to Eve Kosofsky Sedgwick's writing on "Pedagogy of Buddhism" in her book *Touching Feeling: Affect, Pedagogy, Performativity* (2003). She writes, "In this world, it is as though relation *could only be* pedagogical – and for *that* reason, radically transindividualistic" (*160*).
4. Suzuki addresses Grotowski and Brook and theories of "The Theatre's Essential Element" in his chapter "On Acting", (2015, 31).
5. Suzuki draws ire from some in the Noh community for his comments on the "mummification" of traditional theatre forms in Japan. For example, see Harper (1985).
6. There is a vast amount of vocabulary beyond these Six Basics. In symposia over recent decades with members of the iSCOT (International Suzuki Company of Toga), Suzuki re-codified and sequenced the essential disciplines forming old/legacy and new "schools" of practitioners.
7. He writes,

    > My training, therefore, is not a forum for the actor to show off [their] abilities, but rather something that allows the actor, as a specialist on the use of the body and voice, to cultivate flexibility and sensitivity in identifying and playing with the myriad of sensations of being onstage. It could be described as a strategy for cozening the audience in an infinite variety of ways.
    >
    > (Suzuki, 2015, 60)

8. Bühler's idea of the tactile body image and origo-relative language was an "early predecessor" (Fricke, 1811–1821) for George Lakoff and Mark Johnson's seminal conceptions of mental space theory and embodied metaphor, along with Gilles Fauconnier and Mark Turner's Conceptual Blending Theory. This has been critical for cognitive theatre scholars, as Amy Cook (2018) explains.
9. Many thanks to the editorial team for highlighting that the cognitive practicability of these ideas lies in the attentional processes they serve; put more simply, creating more *curious* humans onstage is the goal of all actor training.
10. I am currently writing about "podal deixis" in my dissertation project, titled "'What's the Point?': Multipodal Orbits in the Suzuki Method of Actor Training."

References

Beckett, Samuel. 2006. "Worstword Ho." In *Samuel Beckett: The Grove Centenary Edition. Volume IV; Poems, Short Fiction, Criticism*, edited by Paul Auster. New York: Grove Press, pp. 471–485.

Bejarano, Teresa. 2011. *Becoming Human: From Pointing Gestures to Syntax*. Amsterdam: John Benjamins Publishing.
Bogart, Anne. 2019. "Ways of Seeing." Accessed July 6, 2021. http://siti.org/ways-of seeing.
Bühler, Karl. 1982. "The Deictic Field of Language and Deictic Words." In *Speech, Place, and Action*, edited by R.J. Jarvella and Wolfgang Klein. New York: John Wiley and Sons, Ltd., pp. 9-30.
Cook, Amy. 2018. *Building Character: The Art and Science of Casting*. Ann Arbor: University of Michigan Press.
Dancygier, Barbara. 2016. "Multimodality and Theatre: Material Objects, Bodies, and Language." In *Theatre, Performance, and Cognition: Languages, Bodies, and Ecologies*, edited by Rhonda Blair and Amy Cook. New York: Bloomsbury.
Dancygier, Barbara and Eve Sweetser. 2005. *Mental Spaces in Grammar*. Cambridge: Cambridge University Press.
Fricke, Ellen. 2014. "Deixis, Gesture and Embodiment from a Linguistic Point of View." In *Body, Language, Communication*, edited by Cornelia Muller and others. Berlin: de Gruyter, pp. 1803–1823.
Goto, Yukihiro. 1998. "Suzuki Tadashi: Innovator of Contemporary Japanese Theatre." Doctoral thesis, University of Hawaii.
Harper, Hilliard. 1985. "Suzuki Acting Method: Focus is on the Body." *LA Times*. Accessed July 6, 2021. https://www.latimes.com/archives/la-xpm-1985-01-23-ca-14665-story.html.
Kershaw, Baz. 2008. "Performance as Research: Live Events and Documents." In *The Cambridge Companion to Performance Studies*, edited by Tracy Davis. Cambridge: Cambridge University Press, pp. 23–35.
Kita, Sotaro. 2003. *Pointing: Where Language, Culture, and Cognition Meet*. Mahwah, NJ: Taylor and Francis Group.
Lauren, Ellen. 2011. "In Search of Stillness: Capturing the Purity and Energy of Not Moving is the Roof of the Invisible Body." In *American Theatre Magazine*.
Limon, Jerzy. 2010. *The Chemistry of the Theatre: Performativity of Time*. New York: Palgrave Macmillan.
Pavis, Patrice. 1998. *Dictionary of the Theatre: Terms, Concepts, and Analysis*. Toronto: University of Toronto Press.
Sedgwick, Eve Kosofsky. 2003. *Touching Feeling: Affect, Pedagogy, Performativity*. Durham, NC: Duke University Press.
Suzuki, Tadashi. 2015. *Culture Is the Body*. Translated by Kameron Steele. New York: TCG.

Chapter 6

New Geographies of Space in Virtual and Hybrid Performance Classrooms

Kelley Holley

Nadjie slowly performs contemporary choreography between two kitchen trash cans. A lone flip flop lies next to her on the floor. Her roommate opens the front door just at the edge of the screen, but Nadjie takes no notice. Her focus is on the precision of her movement; she is fully in the dance despite the peculiarity of her setting. With a punch, Bruce Springsteen's "Dancing in the Dark" starts playing and other Zoom boxes are revealed, each containing a dancer. Like Nadjie, each dancer is alone, but now, they're dancing with each other. As digital performances have become increasingly common throughout COVID-19, the question of liveness has become familiar, with practitioners and scholars alike trying to find ways to preserve theatre's essential qualities in virtual space. In *Keep Moving*, a virtual dance performance by way of a visual podcast produced in 2021 by Monica Bill Barnes & Company and danced by students at Hunter College, dancers evidence a new geography of performance spaces. While each dancer is in their own unusual performance space, the spectator regularly sees them as linked, merging the geographical distance in favor of their technological proximity. The spaces are connected by the (un)synchronized choreography of the dancers' bodies, received as a mosaic of videos. The new spaces of performance give additional meaning to each performance and additional meaning in relation to each other. The spectator is invited into their lives by glimpsing their personal spaces. The performance's spatial configuration operates topologically to connect the performers and spectators across distance so that while they are physically divided, they are virtually united.

Theatre is an art form largely concerned with the *here* and *now*, qualities inherent in the condition of liveness. However, as liveness has been theorized, its temporal qualities have been privileged over a shared spatiality. Philip Auslander's influential *Liveness: Performance in a Mediatized Culture* (1999) argues that liveness correlates to temporality rather than in physical proximity. It is through this lens that theatre is often situated, as a time-based art. Consequently, as social distancing eliminated the possibility of shared performance spaces, the privileging of a shared temporality continued as a key condition of many theatrical endeavors. Significantly less attention has been played to the role of space, a concern only returned to in efforts to debunk digital theatre as "theatre." The

DOI: 10.4324/9781003229056-9

subservient position of space to time mimics its position historically throughout social theory. Edward Soja remarks, "Space still tends to be treated as fixed, dead, undialectical; time as richness, life, dialectic, the revealing context for critical social theorizations" (1989, 11). Soja saw an opportunity to reassert space as a valuable feature of critical thought, not as a neutral container to the materiality of time but a rich vertical of consideration in itself. Rather than foregoing "space" as a vital feature of performance, the pandemic provides the occasion to reinvest and transform how space and place are conceived on stage and in our classrooms.

Though space, as we have long been accustomed, is no longer shared, hybrid and virtual learning offer new points of intervention. In particular, this chapter will consider two core elements: how performance spaces are experienced as connected through virtual proximity, and how distance learning can center space as a primary pedagogical concern. Using *Keep Moving* as a central case study, I examine how Monica Bills Barnes & Company transforms distance into an intimate portrait of dance through new spatial dramaturgy. In this capacity, the relationships between spaces are not rendered by their geographic distance, but through the proximity of their shared activity. To this, rather than an obstacle that must be overcome, space becomes a primary consideration: How is the meaning of our performance practices shaped and altered by our familiar surroundings? How can we create spatial intimacy across distance?

Building on my site-specific performance course, this chapter considers site-specificity and virtual performance as a means of reimagining the role space as a central feature within our classrooms, as both a pedagogical approach and performance practice. The chapter offers a means of integrating cultural geography into the performance classroom, considering specific interventions and practices for practitioners and instructors in asynchronous and synchronous learning environments.

The Specificity of Place: Working within the Limits of Space

I first taught site-specific performance in the spring of 2019, building off my dissertation research on an audience's experience of place in site-specific work.[1] Toward the end of the semester, Monica Bill Barnes and Robbie Saenz De Viteri visited to host a one-day master class, in which they workshopped material for their upcoming site-specific dance *Days Go By*, performed at Brookfield Place in Manhattan in October 2019. Beginning in a rehearsal room, before visiting two other sites, Barnes and Saenz De Viteri taught my students simple choreography to "Dreamin'" by the Cascades. With triumphant fists, the choreography was representative of the company's style: intense jubilation in the form of athletic dancing that is simultaneously precise and unrestrained. Barnes and Saenz De Viteri emphasized the transformed performer and spectator experience that occurred when "dance [is brought to] where it doesn't belong" (Kourlas 2017).

It is this spirit that they carried into *Keep Moving*, under a new formulation in which dance could now *only* be performed where it "didn't belong."

While many digital performances look to mask their new "non-neutral" backgrounds, others, like *Keep Moving*, have embraced these contexts as an added dimension of the performance. In this capacity, these performances best resemble site-specific performance, creating an intimate connection between the performance and place. Mike Pearson and Michael Shanks define "site-specific" as performances that "are inseparable from their sites, the only contexts within which they are intelligible" (2001, 23). Anything but empty, site-specific performances pull from the rich particularity and familiarity of spaces, often directly engaging their histories and cultural practices. Significantly, performance recontextualizes space as much as space transforms the performance.

Though *Keep Moving* was performed in locations of convenience rather than design, the space becomes integral to the performance itself. It is no longer a coincidental backdrop, but a central point of rumination. The unique conditions of the site, such as its architecture, its typical uses, and its familiarity to the performer or spectator, impact both the practical logistics and the interpretative possibilities of the performance. The commingling of performance and mundane spaces spectacularizes the ordinary, offering a model of theatrical space that suggests meaning emerges through juxtaposition. In this capacity, we illuminate a key pedagogical theme: space is not a neutral nor secondary condition, but a primary means of meaning-making in performance. While we, as spectators, are more accustomed to public sites of performance, performances like *Keep Moving* make use of the personal space as a rich site of dramaturgical impact.

Consider Kai, a student who removed their mattress so they could have more performance space. COVID-19 forced Kai to figure out how to dance at home, a two-floor building in Brooklyn filled with 11 family members. When they got rid of their mattress in the bedroom they now share with their sister, they have a 6'×4' space to dance in. The narrative of their experience is featured in Chapters 4 and 5 of *Keep Moving*, as they speak in conversation with Saenz De Viteri. The intimacy of the personal narrative is inherently entwined with the space, building meaning together. The context of where they dance is never forgotten by the spectator. It's never forgotten by Kai while performing either. They bring performance into everyday spaces, as they simultaneously throw the act of dancing into extraordinary times. Room is made for each in the other, while a lingering strangeness persists: the peculiarity of dancing at home, the peculiarity of dancing while one's family is sick.

Students grapple with a new configuration of theatrical space in which the public is invited to the private. As Kai narrates, they recall how previously, dance was something they kept separate from their parents. Now, that would be impossible. Kai's space is far more than the 6'×4' rectangle. For many students involved with *Keep Moving*, their family or roommates are just behind a door. For Reagan, it's not always necessarily *behind* the door her mom making a quick cameo appearance before realizing her daughter was filming. Anakeiry asks her family to stay in their rooms while she dances. She only has space to dance in her living room, a tight corner between a staircase and a couch. While students may contend with these "obstacles," they also develop creative solutions that shape the dance. The physicality of their movement responds to both the social and material contexts of the performance.

It is not simply the lack of privacy, but also the physical features of their new performance spaces that challenge students. In many cases, they are part and parcel of the same matter, in which the need for privacy from those in the immediate vicinity necessities a move into more restrictive spaces. Kai needs to dance against the wall to stay in frame, because of their limited space. Another student dances with her boyfriend asleep behind a tri-fold room divider. To achieve a level of privacy from those around them, the dancers invite the public audience into their intimate spaces. This shift demonstrates the selection of a purposeful audience for the performance and points toward intimacy as a strategy for bridging the distance.

Personal intimacy substitutes for physical intimacy; a personal connection is formed where there cannot be a proximal one. The spectator can see open closets, clothing on the floor, personal decorations. The vehicle of the performance gives the public access to spaces in which life is "in progress," an intimate portrait of the personal space of the performer. Here, we can situate Nadjie's roommate's flip flop left haphazardly in the kitchen or Kai's personal account of their family's struggles during COVID-19. In her discussion of shared spaces in performance, Erika Fischer-Lichte suggests that sight offers a form of "closeness and intimacy that is similar to physical contact" (2008, 62). In virtual performance, the sight of a performer's private space offers a form of intimacy that is like sharing a physical space. Personal narratives and glimpses of private spatial practices collude to create intimacy between the spectator and the performer, despite the distance between their geographical locations.

The Multiplicity of Place: Sharing Space through Virtual Means

In addition to being "neutral," theatrical space is assumed to be singular. Birgit Wiens calls this the "spatial exclusiveness" of theatre (2010, 93). The assumption fights the common trope in which "space" is imagined as empty. While technologies have allowed access to other spaces vis-à-vis telecommunication software for some time, this has been rejected through a belief that the technological reproductions were incongruent with the material realness of theatre, as experienced in a shared space. It becomes apparent that for many the spatial dynamic of theatre is viewed as a limitation, a factor that relies on immediacy and perhaps intimacy, but unable to expand beyond its proximal confines.

The problem, however, is that space nor place, in neither geography nor theatre, is singular or empty. As famously argued by Henri Lefebvre, space is socially constructed and never a neutral container, as one might imagine it to be in mathematics (1991, 26). Similarly, no place is singular but instead constructed through its dealings with other places (Gupta and Ferguson 1992). Gupta and Ferguson illustrate that place, as a social construct that is continuously being produced, is an experienced condition that is connected to but separate from physical space. Seeing place as an interconnected phenomenon allows for a diverse set of spatial logics in which place only has meaning relationally.

The interconnected dancers on Zoom perhaps articulate a new meaning to Foucault's comments on space: "We are in the age of the simultaneous, of juxtaposition, the near and the far, the side by side and the scattered" (1997, 350). The dancers create a network of geographical locations that are simultaneously distanced and proximal. They feel connected even when they are far away. Juxtaposing the locations builds new geographies that do not contour to the physical world, but instead extend our spatial imaginings through intermedial technologies. As Wiens argues, "The intermedial stage affords the exploration of performative configurations between here and other spaces, and experiments with simultaneous actions at different (locally or geographically separated) locations" (2010, 94). Technology has allowed for spaces to be weaved together against the restrictions of geographic proximity. Where Wiens identifies this as the intermedial stage, others might call it a product of "glocalization," a process by which technology has "compressed" the world that reconfigures the spatial relations of the local and global into the other (Robertson 1992). In our classrooms, or in performances like *Keep Moving*, technology operates in a similar capacity, to draw close what is now far, and replicate as best as possible the experience of shared space.

While intermedial space efforts to replicate proximity, it also invites the possibility of heterogeneous space coexisting, and asks the spectator to navigate a new map. Spaces are playfully connected, despite their geographical distance. Imagine a patchwork quilt as a map, in which the arrangement of the patches became a new geography. In this way, the intermedial space approaches what Bertie Ferdman (2018) has referred to as "off site" performances. In her terminology, Ferdman pushes back at site-specific performances, instead arguing that performance spaces have long been relational. Off site signals a connection between spaces, and situates it as the primary concern of its dramaturgical spatial practice: "An off-site is not so much about the specific space where it *is*, as much as it is about where and when it *is not*" (25). In this capacity, off site creates a "betweenness" that operates to connect absent locations in performance.

In *Keep Moving*, a Zoom gallery sutures the various performance locations together. Contained in a single image, 17 video boxes hold 17 dancers and 17 snippets of their worlds. They move synchronously to "Mama Tried" by Merle Haggard, or as synchronously as they can with the inevitable video lags. Together, looking up, they use one arm to perform a quick series of rhythmic snaps across their body, with their other arm tucked behind. A dancer does not realize until much later that she has been performing everything backward, unaware that her camera was mirrored. As we become accustomed to the composed image, Saenz De Viteri, in his role as the narrator, instructs the spectator to pick one box, any box, and focus on the dancer, a reminder of the unique spaces each dancer inhabits. Their shared choreography highlights the connection between the spaces, while never erasing the distinct qualities of each.

When the spaces are not joined via Zoom gallery, they are through the sequential editing. The choreography passes from body to body, space to space: where one person began a movement, another will finish it. The sequence joins the spaces while highlighting the stark differences between them. One woman dances in front of the Bronx-Whitestone Bridge in a Chicago Bulls jersey. Seconds later she's replaced by a woman dancing in front of family photos and a painting of a ballerina. And Monica Bill Barnes dances in her physical therapist's office. The dancers pass kinetic energy through the choreography as if they once again shared the stage. The shared movement causes new spatial configurations to manifest through the sequential temporality. This strategy aims not to replicate the effect of a shared space but to offer an alternative form of dancing in unison so familiar to dance performances. Space, here, is capacious, illustrating the ways in which the dancers' bodies are connected in space while occupying their own. *Here* and *there* aren't quite as far apart as they seem.

Keep Moving joins the performance space with the space of the audience, remembering that shared theatrical space is not just between the performers. The performance extends the kinetic possibility of dance to the spectator: you, too, are part of the dance, the performance space. When "Dancing in the Dark" plays, Saenz De Viteri comments,

> This is the moment where Bruce and you and anyone you're watching are pushing for the biggest, jumpiest dance to take over your screen. ...But if you're a modern dancer who gets up in the middle of the night, it probably looks more like [what the spectator is seeing on screen]. If you want the other thing, maybe just get up and do it yourself.
>
> (2021)

I know I did.

Spatial Dramaturgy as Pedagogy: A Critical Exercise

Emphasizing these "new geographies" understands that theatre is always space-based as well as time-based. In digital and hybrid classrooms, it might be tempting to forgo any analysis of theatrical space. However, such classes are primed to consider the complexities of cultural geography through a performance lens. While the bulk of this chapter has looked at the ways in which digital performance can create spatial intimacy for students, the remainder will directly consider how distance learning can center space.

Pedagogy that is attentive to the student's space, in many ways, resembles a pedagogy of care: it is attuned and responsive to the individual conditions each student learns in, investigating their environments and building the performance from these contexts. In this capacity, there is no assumption that students have safe, spacious, or neutral areas to perform in at home. Instead, performances are beholden to the student's ability under any physical or social restrictions. Space is elevated through an understanding of its significance as the student's lived environment. Similarly, networking together the spaces of performance can combat isolation, by placing students (and their spaces) as one node within a constellation.

Centering space in the classroom can begin by integrating readings from cultural geographers.[2] In a similar vein, one should include works by theatre theorists and performance studies scholars who directly take up the question of space.[3] Reimagining space in the virtual classroom can take the form of a number of assignments that provide creative means to reassess our assumptions about spatial relations, but also their dramaturgical impact. Here, I provide samples of pedagogical exercises in which the concepts of space and place are creatively and critically applied.

Workshopping Space and Place: In this assignment, students identify and communicate the qualities of a place to their classmates. Students investigate the features of spaces that they inhabit and those that they do not have access to, to gain a deeper understanding of the complexities of space. Students do so by communicating their experience of a space to a partner. In some ways, it's like a space-based game of "Telephone." This assignment can be completed synchronously or asynchronously in online or hybrid classes. At the end of the assignment, students will be able to analyze the essential features of a place and apply key concepts from cultural geography.

To begin, students select a local place. This might be a spot in their neighborhood, a special place in their city, or even their own bedroom. Students then write their answers to the following questions:

- What is this place?
- What is this place to you?
- Who uses this place?
- How is this place commonly used?
- What does this place smell like? Sound like? Look like? Feel like? (Taste like?)
- What is the place's shape?
- What are the special rules of this place?
- What is your first memory of this place?

Next, students use images and drawings to describe the place. Students are asked to submit a map, and then draw one. The two images may not be the same type of map. I provide students with creative cartographic examples. Students then share three artifacts from the space. These could be recordings of the soundscape, photos, or even food or tactile objects. Lastly, students move in the space and map their movement for another student to replicate.

After the documentation process, students share their places with a partner via this report. For most, they have never been to their partner's space. Once they have swapped documentation, partners compile their understanding of the place, retracing the steps from a distance: they mark the same movements remotely, they listen to the sounds, and they touch the materials. Each then writes a one-page response about their experience understanding the other's space. Then, they write a joint paper applying two concepts from cultural geography as one means of understanding their reconfigured spatial arrangements.

Performing Space and Place: Building off the foundation of the workshop exercise, students work with their partners to create site-specific performances that operate *between* their two spaces. Working collaboratively, students devise a performance that utilizes both locations and connects them. This is intentionally open-ended. For example, one pair created a performance with a tasting menu that was designed to capture Washington D.C.'s particular cuisine. Other students utilized simultaneous movement in their respective locations, like in *Keep Moving*. At the end of this project, students are able to analyze the unique qualities of their spaces and apply the key concepts from the course through creative performance. Spatial dramaturgy offers a means of recentering and reimagining the role space plays in performance, even in digital and hybrid learning environments.

Notes

1 Thank you to Fraser Stevens for his help in the original development of this course.
2 See Doreen Massey (2005) and Tim Cresswell (2014), who along with more prominent theorists like Lefebvre, Soja, and Foucault, have become staples of the spatial turn.
3 See Joanne Tompkins (2014), Fiona Wilkie (2015), and Gay McAuley (1999), among others. Additionally, Kim Solga's *Theory for Theatre Studies: Space* (2019) is comprehensive and exceptionally accessible for undergraduate students.

References

Auslander, Philip. 1999. *Liveness: Performance in a Mediatized Culture*. New York: Routledge.
Cresswell, Tim. 2013. *Geographic Thought: A Critical Introduction*. Chichester: Wiley-Blackwell.
Cresswell, Tim. 2015. *Place: An Introduction*. Second edition. Chichester, West Sussex; Malden, MA: J. Wiley & Sons.
Ferdman, Bertie. 2018. *Off Sites: Contemporary Performance beyond Site-Specific*. Theater in the Americas. Carbondale: Southern Illinois University Press.
Fischer-Lichte, Erika. 2008. *The Transformative Power of Performance: A New Aesthetics*. New York: Routledge.

Foucault, Michel. 1997. "Of Other Spaces: Utopias and Heterotopias." In *Rethinking Architecture: A Reader in Cultural Theory*, edited by Neil Leach. New York: Routledge, pp. 350–356.
Gupta, Akhil, and James Ferguson. 1992. "Beyond 'Culture': Space, Identity, and the Politics of Difference." *Cultural Anthropology* 7 (1): 6–23.
Kourlas, Gia. 2017. "Is There a Date-Stamp on the Moving Body?" *The New York Times*, September 1, 2017, sec. Arts.
Lefebvre, Henri. 1991. *The Production of Space*. Translated by Donald Nicholson-Smith. 33. Print. Malden, MA: Blackwell Publishing.
Massey, Doreen B. 2005. *For Space*. London; Thousand Oaks, CA: SAGE.
Pearson, Mike, and Michael Shanks. 2001. *Theatre/Archaeology*. London; New York: Routledge.
Robertson, Roland. 1992. *Globalization: Social Theory and Global Culture*. London: Sage Publications.
Soja, Edward W. 2011. *Postmodern Geographies: The Reassertion of Space in Critical Social Theory*. Radical Thinkers. London: Verso.
Solga, Kim. 2019. *Theory for Theatre Studies: Space*. Theory for Theatre Studies. London; New York: Methuen Drama.
Tompkins, Joanne. 2014. *Theatre's Heterotopias: Performance and the Cultural Politics of Space*. Contemporary Performance InterActions. Houndmills, Basingstoke, Hampshire New York: Palgrave Macmillan.
Wiens, Birgit. 2017. "Spatiality." In *Mapping Intermediality in Performance*, edited by Sarah Bay-Cheng, Chiel Kattenbelt, Andy Lavender, and Robin Nelson. Amsterdam: Amsterdam University Press. pp 91–96.
Wilkie, Fiona. 2015. *Performance, Transport and Mobility: Making Passage*. Houndmills, Basingstoke, Hampshire: Palgrave Macmillian.

Chapter 7

Dramaturgy and Social Media
New Tools for Composition

Elisha Clark Halpin

With the onset of COVID and the closing of studios and stages, we saw an explosion of dance on social media and streaming platforms. From mini-line dances to spontaneous bursts of movement, to dance challenges, to professional pieces re-imagined for online viewing, it seems as though people are dancing and more interested in dance than ever before. And it seems that people enjoy accessing dance in many online formats. For many, dance has been a highlight of joy and fun in exceedingly challenging times. Social media has always been an excellent way to bring connection and fun through movement. Before the pandemic, for professional dancers and choreographers, it was mainly used to invite followers to shows, give updates on projects, and take the "audience" behind the scenes. Pandemic performance life has resulted in new ways of thinking about and engaging with social media as a performance platform.

And even as we continue to look to a post-pandemic performance life, there are aspects of continuing and further developing our use of online dance spaces that have arisen in these unprecedented times. Rather than waiting for an established production arm to take notice in the traditional application-audition process, with the explosion of streaming and online dance performances, many young artists can have greater reach and develop an audience for their work. This chapter illuminates how applying a dramaturgical and curatorial approach to compositional teachings can lead young choreographers to leverage their social media space more effectively, thus impacting their connection to audiences and future presenters.

Context

From its onset, modern dance has often operated with the dancer serving in multiple roles. The dancer is the choreographer. The dancer is often the musical director or arranger, sometimes even the composer. The dancer is the costumer. The dancer is the stage technician. This mindset, which began at the inception of modern dance, has stayed the modus operandi for most modern dancers. As the form grew over the 20th century, so did notions of the dancer as entrepreneurial creator and theoretical practitioner. Serving multiple roles can be

DOI: 10.4324/9781003229056-10

limiting to creative development, as dancers often carry a large workload and get lost in the multitasking nature of the work. But it can also be an opportunity for artists to flex their creativity in many ways.

If the dancer is the composer, choreographer, and lighting designer, they are often also the dramaturg. Dance dramaturgy and performance curation are not always part of the standard teachings of dance composition and choreography. But by not exposing young artists to these two practices, we miss the opportunity to help young creators see their work in a larger context and to begin taking part in the cultural "conversation" that is presenting work from the beginning of their making/performing career. Inviting students to engage the full scope of their work, including identifying audiences for their chosen style or genre of dance, invites them to amplify their voice from early days, as it also invites them to see themselves as part of the larger community of dance. This awareness of the relationship between themselves, their audiences, and other dancers invites an awareness of the tapestry of the lexicon they are building. The need for exploring dramaturgical and curation practices earlier in the performance/choreography career brings a more active element in the creation and dissemination of work. It requires young artists to be more responsible for the process of who has access to their work and how it is presented.

Social Media as Stage and Gallery

Each tiny window of an Instagram post is a free stage for a performer. And though there are sometimes constraints around the performance, most of the power of presentation lies in the account holder's hands. Their "page" is essentially a living archive or gallery. This is fertile ground for the young artist to practice self-dramaturgy and curation. As Austin Kleon lays out in *Keep Going: 10 Ways to Stay Creative in Good Times and Bad*, it is in the artist paying attention to what they pay attention to that they can learn about themselves and identify the patterns within their work (114). Social media provides a ripe landscape for young artists to pay attention to their work. In this process, the dancer as creator/performer can also act as dramaturg and curator to present their work, pay attention, and create a contextualized conversation around the process.

The "whats" of choreography training proceed from the trends of the larger dance world, which are influenced by larger cultural and artistic trends. But for most academic dance programs, the legacy of "hows" put in place by early master teachers such as Louis Horst and Doris Humphrey has continued to be passed down implicitly and explicitly through the generations. When choreography students begin training, they are assigned studies or short compositions. Each study explores an aspect or two, and when woven together, the studies become larger pieces. The studies are comparable to compositional studies created in many genres of visual art. But choreographers don't tend to look at their compositional studies as an opportunity to curate a body of work or craft dialogue with their audience. (This sentiment is not new; in 16 years of teaching up-and-coming choreographers, I am quite familiar with it.) Now more than ever, there is the need for a new framework for choreographers to claim their artistic real estate and step into the process of curating their work in a dynamic and specified way. In this chapter, I advocate creating a new framework inside compositional courses that provides a structure to this process. The academic dance curriculum often ignores online platforms as a fruitful ground for networking, exposure, or viable performance opportunities.

What began as a reaction to studios closing and stages going dark now looks like an opportunity to cultivate a new relationship with the compositional study. Armed with personal digital studios, dancers capitalized on what they already knew and created work from the spaces (inner and outer) they were inhabiting. They took ownership of that itch to perform, create, and share, pouring work out into the strange new world. For many young artists who could not be in the studio through 2020 and into 2021, social media became the only stage to present their creations. And while the outpouring of reactionary raw art was appropriate, there is an ongoing lack of contextualization of the presented work, perhaps because social media dance is ignored as a viable form of performance. This lack of contextualization and conversation is a loss for artists, critics, and audiences alike. Social media, YouTube, and other online platforms have not been treated as performance outlets for the "serious" artists. They were and are used for promotional materials and process shares. What is the potential for these platforms if they were viewed as free performance spaces with value by young and mid-career artists looking to craft their voice and engage with an audience?

Dance Dramaturgy, a Brief History

Dance dramaturgy came to be in 1979 when Raimund Hoghe became the first dance dramaturg, at least in title, working with Pina Bausch. He "shared with Bausch the conviction that one always has to seek a form: a form" that takes the personal beyond the private and prevents mere self-presentation or self-exposure" (Profeta, 8). His work to shape and edit the mammoth theatrical spectacles Bausch created set a standard that has often kept dance dramaturgy, at least in the United States, relegated to big-budget theatrical productions. Professional dramaturgy is not a standard or even a norm in most of the dance world; it has lived in the "high-art" arena of modern/post-modern dance and ballet and in the trenches of devised performance art. The idea of having a dramaturg in the studio is often a luxury that choreographers cannot afford. Others fear the disruption of having another voice or vision in the room. And the "dance for dance's sake" choreographers have not taken up the mantle of the dramaturgical process, preferring to continue as Balanchine did with the notion that the dance speaks for itself. In her work as a dance dramaturg, Katherine Profeta works with Mark Bly's (1997) dramaturgical tenet, "I question." Profeta, a collaborator of choreographer Ralph Lemon, has had a great impact on dance dramaturgy beyond the pieces she's worked on. Her book, *Dramaturgy in Motion*, explores five areas for the dramaturg's attention: text/language, research, audience, movement, and interculturalism. While this book is a great accompanying text in composition courses, even the premise of guiding students into the process of questioning from curiosity can have a great impact. Profeta's metaphor of a dramaturg dancing between the "inside(s)" and "outside(s)" of the process and the performance, and being a "collaborative witness' is most easily seen when choreographer and dramaturg are separate roles, but the metaphor holds even when they are not.

The Rub of Curiosity as Artistic Rigor

> Because of it I attend carefully to what might come first and what next, what might establish a code or break one, how patterns form, whether causal links between events are suggested, encouraged, or discouraged. I have no particular agenda to create or enhance narratives, my conviction is that they are always already present, as engaged through the act of perception. My agenda, insofar as I have one, is notice them, or their potential, and fold that awareness into our conversations.
>
> (Profeta, 55)

Profeta acknowledges the complexity of defining a dramaturg, and alludes to the messiness it can create, complicating the need for theatrical roles to be efficient and defined. But in her words, "the rise of the dramaturg (and the dramaturgical) over the last 40 years suggests that something more interesting than a wasteful redundancy is going on" (12). This notion of "dramaturgical process" is most helpful and advantageous for inviting young creators into artistic rigor. Profeta concludes that dance does not need a dramaturg but a dramaturgical process (11–12). This notion has found its way into the processes of several key contemporary dance artists, including Tere O'Connor, Camille A. Brown, Kyle Abraham, and Bebe Miller. Miller, a well-established choreographer and composition teacher, uses the dramaturgical process cohesively with other choreographic processes. Miller, who began teaching online workshops and compositional salons during the pandemic, lets the questions that arise from the framework of the dramaturgical process be "the rub" (as she calls it) that she works up into and against. She has said, dramaturgy "opened for me that there is another way of standing back from your own process and looking at what you're doing" (Miller). The flexible and adaptable nature of dance dramaturgy has allowed these choreographers, directors, and instructors to apply various dramaturgy methods to large-scale or ongoing projects. Miller states that working from this place of dramaturgy in the choreographic process invites the choreography to play with and claim a point of view. "What is involved in that gesture you're making right now, not only this sensation and in place and time, but what does it look like, what does it remind you of?" She says that the movement must be viewed from how it looks in various ways, framings, and perspectives. "I mean, it's a way of asking questions to drive interrogating work. You can go to town on that all by yourself" (Miller).

Self-Dramaturgy as a Tool

Some Dance or Choreography MFA programs and undergraduate programs include instruction in the dramaturgical process alongside their writing and choreography courses, usually part of the critique or group response process. In a composition class, the dramaturgical process could be an informal or formal part of the critique process as students present their choreographic studies. Whether formal or informal, the class serves as the dramaturg, offering insights about what is referenced, aiding in clarifying content, and interrogating intention to assist in developing kinesthetic clarity. This process provides the choreographic student with the opportunity to investigate and consider their work through multiple lenses. This process implies that the refinement of intention and expression creates a more discriminating and cultivated work.

The conversation changes when a choreographer works alone and does not have a group to respond to work in progress. While there have always been differing pedagogical approaches to choreography, I argue that introducing dramaturgy as an element of the process at an earlier stage of creation can provide artists with more meaningful choices in perspective, lexicon, and conceptualization of their work. This is incredibly potent when working with their own body as both generator and crafter of movement and the performer. Many compositional sequences start with the requirement of solo work. And of course, during the pandemic shutdown, a lack of space or ability to gather often meant that there was only one body available. Regardless of how it comes about, at some point in every choreographer's training, they are tasked with tackling the question: *What happens when I am the only body generating and responding inside this process? How do I see?* The dancer as dramaturg approach is necessary for young artists to have a framework to pay attention to their work, the rub, and ignite the sparks that the rub might create.

To move to a dramaturgical process that makes space for the self to stand outside and create inside the process, essential aspects of dramaturgy include collaborating with an outside eye. There must be space and place for dancers to develop (inside), present/perform/share, and then exercise the dramaturgical framework. This self-dramaturgy process is valid as an ongoing part of the process and also when the process is considered complete.

Miller provides examples of what this can look like in the professional workshops and classes she teaches that intertwine composition and dramaturgy to allow for "the rub" to host a more profound conversation within the work. For Miller, the process of choreography is not separate from the dramaturgical process. And while she works with award-winning dramaturg Talvin Wilkes, she also relies on the performers to collaborate in the dramaturgical process.

Another example of the dancer as dramaturg comes from Montclair State University's Danceaturgy archive and course. As taught by Neil Baldwin, Danceaturgy is a pedagogical process where students/writers examine the works in which they are performing and "are given the task to develop a critical analysis of the works by 'stepping out' and looking at pieces objectively." According to the statement on Montclair's website, this work trains the performer who is inside (creating) the work to also look at and think as a spectator outside the work. Students in the course share that this helps them to "conceptualize what [they] physicalize" and to "analyze the whys of [they] we do" (Baldwin, 2017).

Curation to Strengthen and Enliven the Choreographic Voice

As the dancer dramaturg moves from creation into producing/presenting, the concept and practice of curation can have a powerful impact on the development of the artistic voice and connection to an audience. Curation is a practice most associated with the visual arts and museums. In the dance world, the curatorial process happens in the work of presenters curating a season. This aspect of curation is tied to the values, goals, or mission of the presenting institution. Occasionally highly esteemed choreographers will have a retrospective, especially in conjunction with awards. Only sometimes is the artist involved in the curatorial process of their work. I believe dancers would benefit from taking a more active approach to curation in the age of social media. According to the Tate, the network of significant art museums in the United Kingdom, the primary goal of a curator is to "interpret the collection to inform, educate, and inspire the public" (Richman-Abdou). This explanation is so apt for how young artists can use their social media platforms as performance real estate that lets them make an impact with their choreographic voices. As someone who selects and interprets works of art, the definition of curator sounds strikingly close to dance professor Neil Baldwin's definition of the danceaturg. And since curation is about showcasing the alignment of voice, values, and engagement of the works, curation as part of the self-dramaturgy process makes space for the dancer to reflect on their work as if they are outside of it, looking in. Young choreographers often lack a detachment from their work that allows for the discerning eye of editing. This is even more true when they are "inside" (performing) the dance. The ability to use the dramaturgical and curatorial process to ask questions about what they are paying attention to, and to contextualize their work through their chosen alignment, then invites them to move the study from what Anne Lamott calls the "shitty first draft" into a form that stands with a clear choreographic voice (Lamott 20). While not working through social media, Miller does give us an example of the power of an artist using curation in performance. Her project History is a "piece of active memory and generative process, a 'Living Archive' to create something new"(Gordon). Through this piece, she worked with "the body" as the curatorial landscape allowing the alignment to arise from what the body was paying attention to as it saw and heard snippets from previous performances. The performer was in the role of dramaturg by creating and editing in the moment of performance.

Conclusion

The pandemic allowed many educators and artists to explore new tools that had not been considered before. Prior to the pandemic I was exploring dramaturgy as part of composition and devising classes but would not have used social media as part of the presentational platform. In returning to teaching I am left with the understanding that I want to continue to empower the students to take ownership of the presenting of their work so even as they pursue traditional channels of presentation they are staying in agency. I want to invite more rigor while lowering the stakes on the production side while we navigate issues with spaces and live audiences. Social media and live streaming performances fit well with that intention. I also appreciate the access to work that comes with this delivery. My goal is to have students find new ways of exploring the larger cultural tapestry and be clearer in participating in the cultural dialogue as student creators. But most importantly it is to invite students to not wait for a future time to see their work as potent and important. This pandemic has shown me that we cannot wait and that art is indeed an essential aspect for the wellbeing of society. Young artists are just the energy and outlook we need in these ever-challenging times.

References

Baldwin, Neil. "Danceworks Pre-show At Montclair State University, April 7, 2017." *YouTube video*, 20:58. April 12, 2017. https://www.youtube.com/watch?v=vLtzjBAbyi4.

Bly, Mark. 1997. "Bristling with Multiple Possibilities." In *Dramaturgy in American Theater: A Source Book*, edited by Susan Jonas, Geoff Proehl, and Michael Lupu. Fort Worth: Harcourt Brace College Publishers, pp. 48–55.

Gordon, Ain. "A History." 2015. Video. https://vimeo.com/113528957.

Kleon, Austin. 2019. *Keep Going: 10 Ways to Stay Creative in Good Times and Bad*. New York: Workman Publishing Co., Inc.

Lamott, Anne. 2019. *Bird by Bird: Some Instructions on Writing and Life*. 25th Anniversary ed. New York: Anchor Books.

Miller, Bebe. Interview by author. *Zoom Recording*. State College, PA, July 2, 2021.

Montclair State University. "The Danceaturgy Archive." Accessed July 7, 2021. https://www.montclair.edu/creative-research-center/the-danceaturgy-archive/.

Profeta, Katherine. 2015. *Dramaturgy in Motion: At Work on Dance and Movement Performance*. Madison, WI: University of Wisconsin Press.

Richman-Abdou, Kelly. "What Is Curating? See Why More and More People Are Interested in Becoming Curators." *My Modern Met*, August 1, 2019. https://mymodernmet.com/what-is-curating/.

Chapter 8

Teaching Alexander Technique (without Hands) Online

A Study of Kindness

Gwendolyn Walker

Alexander Technique (AT) is about letting go of harmful habits that you may have learned in your life. It teaches you to release tension and move through the world in a more easeful and energized way. For me, learning and teaching AT has been more about changing the way I respond to stimuli than it has been about changing the way I move. The way I describe it to students is that how you think determines the quality of your container (your body) and the quality of your container determines the quality of your life. I believe that AT is about practicing radical kindness towards yourself. In every moment, you have a choice of how to react, of whether to add tension to your body and mind or not. If you begin with kindness, you have a better chance of succeeding not only in releasing tension, but in learning to not add tension in the first place.

Traditionally, teaching AT demands a substantial in-person—and often silent—component. The teacher places hands on the student's body to locate places where the student may be stopping the flow of energy through their body through learned patterns of misuse. At the start of the 2020 pandemic, I very suddenly had to learn how to teach AT online. I had never taught AT online and very few people I knew ever had. Would it be possible to teach AT principles without my hands while I and my students were in separate spaces? The answer was, yes.

Further, online teaching provides an exceptional opportunity. AT teachers have long struggled to get this important work to a larger audience, and online teaching removes geography as a barrier. Moreover, when the entire world is in crisis, this work could not be more useful. Our nervous systems are in a state of high alert due to the pandemic, and AT offers unique solutions to coping with stress so that the trauma we experience does not turn into misuse, pain, or disease.

Although I direct this chapter as if to a teacher of AT, these principles are useful to anyone who teaches performance.

It is exciting to imagine a world where AT and anatomy is taught to students in elementary schools before their young bodies begin to absorb the stress of sitting in uncomfortable chairs for hours and before they are asked to do things beyond their current abilities and so they compress and disintegrate their natural coordination. It is exciting to imagine a world where people think about their bodies and how to use them. It is my hope that online AT classes can begin an exploration of teaching this important work on a larger scale to a larger audience.

What follows is an exploration of exercises that through trial and error I found communicated AT principles with clarity and simplicity. I believe that what I discovered is important for the entire field of teaching performance because by learning to pause and be kind to ourselves as we educate, our bodies and our minds are more agile and the information that we impart will be more deeply received due to the lack of tension in the body and voice of the teacher.

What Is the Alexander Technique?

In order to make this chapter useful to a wide variety of practitioners, it is necessary to introduce a brief history of AT. The founder of AT, Frederick Mathias Alexander (1869–1955), was a Tasmanian actor who lost his voice when he performed. His doctors said they could not help him, so he took matters into his own hands. After spending years watching and analyzing himself speaking to the mirror, he discovered the cause of his voice loss: it was how he used his body. For example, he found that he contracted and shortened the back of his neck when he thought of speaking to a crowd. He also pushed his larynx down, which caused an audible gasping sound when he inhaled. Most distressingly, the more he tried to change the way he used his body when he spoke, the more things stayed the same. Eventually, he discovered that he did these same things not only on stage, but when he spoke in everyday life, just to a smaller degree (Alexander 2001, 32–33). This important revelation led him to finally discover a way to change these habits, and a new way of thinking about the mind-body connection (what he called "psychophysical") emerged. The technique he created was so revolutionary, thousands of teachers around the world now teach his work, and scientists are just now catching up to some of his discoveries one hundred years later.

Mind-Body Unity

Prior to his studies, Alexander, like most of us, considered the mind and body separate entities. The first principle we explore in AT class is how to begin to integrate mind and body – a principle Alexander called "psychophysical unity." After years of trying to separate the two using one to control the other, he finally discovered they are interdependent: the way we think affects the way we move and the way we move affects the way we think (Gelb 1994, 38). If a person's thinking is tense, their body will be, too. People justify their bodies' difficulties in all sorts of ways: we just move the way we move, or we hurt because people in our family have bad backs, weak knees, etc. In every activity we engage in, we can choose to accept the tensions we have learned over a lifetime as innate and immutable, or we can reconnect to the organized system we were born with that moves with organized, natural grace. If we learn how to think of our bodies and our minds as one thing, everything we do becomes easier – as a performer, but also as a human being. Mindfulness about mind-body unity has the power to change the quality of your life.

Interoception and Exteroception

To begin this work in person or online, students must learn how their thoughts affect their bodies. They must therefore become interoceptive, defined as "sensitivity to stimuli originating inside of the body,[1]" to notice how their bodies respond automatically when they are involved in everyday activities. Throughout our work, I use a variety of cues to prompt thoughts that may lead to a better understanding of how our bodies react to mental and physical stimuli. For example, the cue might be to imagine they are late and are going to lose their only chance at an opportunity. Then I ask them what they noticed about their body when they had the thought. At first, their comments are always localized: "My jaw tightened!" "My shoulders lifted!" "I held my breath!" "I tightened my neck!" I am encouraging about these observations but then ask them to pay attention to their entire body for the next go around. I cue them to think of the stressful situation again. Students notice their bodies more broadly and may notice that they curl up their toes, tighten their gluteus muscles, or pull in their abdominal muscles. In fact, they notice that their whole body gets involved when they merely think of the stressful situation. They are noticing the connections between parts of their bodies and beginning to think of themselves as whole beings. Now, they start asking the relevant questions: "Why did I tighten my hip flexors?" "Why did I grip my quadriceps?" "Why did I clench my jaw muscles?" Why indeed. Now the students have begun to glimpse that we all have patterns of use that we employ in response to stress. This is the beginning of becoming consciously interoceptive.

Exteroception is the perception of the world outside our bodies. Having begun to think about their bodies from the inside, the next step is for students to notice the world around them as a means of finding more easeful movement. I tell my students to place a cell phone across the room from them and use the cue that they are expecting big news. I tell them it is urgent that they pick up the phone as quickly as possible. "Go! Go! Go!" I say. The students retrieve the phone, and I ask, "What did you notice?" "Nothing," is a common response. Another is "I wasn't breathing," or "I didn't see anything but my phone!" In short, they did not notice much of the room or of their own physical sensations. Next, I tell them to pick one more thing in the room and to notice that also when they do the exercise. They may choose anything – a chair, a bed, a plant, etc. "Now go, go, go!" I say. When asked what they notice this time, students commonly say, "I felt calmer," or "That was a little easier," or "I was breathing." Most people who do this exercise report feeling more ease when they expand their focus to include an additional item in the room. We are getting somewhere.

Before the next go-around, I ask the students to begin expanding their awareness of their surroundings. I lead them through a visualization exercise with a series of cues:

There is ground under your feet.
There is a wall to your right.
There is a wall to your left.
There is a wall in front of you.
There is a wall behind you.
Now imagine that because you have all the space that you have, that you can expand like a dry sponge absorbing water. Your back can soften and widen. You can be taller.
Next, we focus on the eyes.
How much of the room can you see from where you are standing?
Soften the muscles around your eyes and try to expand your peripheral vision as far as you comfortably can from side to side and up as high and down as low as you can do so comfortably.
Now, while you see the whole room, notice your back. Feel how wide and long it is. Incorporate the back half of you into your kinesthetic awareness including the back of your legs, head, and arms.

Now, I cue the students to do the phone exercise again, saying, "While noticing these things, answer your phone. It's important" I say. Alexander called this interoception and exteroception "one after the other and all at once (Jones 1976, 17)." This time the feedback is different. "I felt calmer!" "I was breathing!" "I didn't tense my neck!" "I had the same physical responses, but they were much smaller this time!" or "I felt bigger." "I felt taller." This is the integration of interoception and exteroception. Once students have had this experience, I find I can cue them to simply check into what they are currently noticing. If they are being overly interoceptive, I cue them to notice the world. If they are being overly exteroceptive, I cue them to notice their bodies. As with most things, practice makes this easier. This exercise gives students an experience of a "unified field of awareness."[2] At this point, this unified field of awareness is still just an isolated feeling, but that taste of lightness and ease they have just experienced is powerful and can be translated into everyday life. Additionally, that moment where the student simultaneously considers their interoception and exteroception is an act of radical self kindness. It is not necessary to add all that physical and mental tension to simply answer the phone!

Downward Pull

The second principle I explore with online students is what Alexander called "downward pull." This is what Alexander discovered when he learned he shortened and tightened the back of his neck when he thought of public speaking. I like Barbara Conable's words about this important discovery in her foundational book "*How to Learn the Alexander Technique:*"

> Habituated tensing of the muscles of the neck results in a predictable and inevitable tensing of the whole body. Releasing out of the tension in the whole must begin with the muscles in the neck.
>
> (Conable and Conable 1994, 2)

The average adult head weighs approximately ten to eleven pounds and it is meant to be supported by the bones of the spine.[3] When the head is pulled off its bony scaffolding, a series of compensations ensue, the most important of these is that pulling the base of the skull down and back prevents the equal distribution of weight throughout the skeleton. Learning to inhibit downward pull can reset your body to a sense of sensory lightness and ease.

To teach this online, I ask the students to exaggerate this downward pull. I show them a picture of a person in an extreme version of downward pull, as in Figure 8.1.

I ask them to imitate this posture or to imitate someone they know who uses their body like this. Then I ask them to walk around the room in this posture

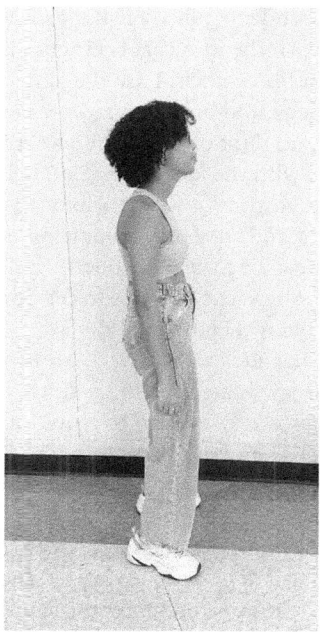

Figure 8.1 Person in downward pull.

and notice how it affects their emotions, their movement, and their breathing. What other parts of their bodies react to this compressed neck? How is their breathing? When they lift their arms directly out in front of themselves, is it easy or hard? Are there places where they feel restricted in their movement? I prompt them to lift their knees and try to march and to note how easy or difficult it is. Because my students are singers and dancers, I ask them to sing in this position or try a pirouette. When asked how it feels, some report that it feels "Awful" or "Weird," but others may say that it: "Feels normal" or "Totally comfortable." If the student is habitually in a smaller version of downward pull, they may not notice new sensations by exaggerating the pattern that they already habitually carry. So if a student already shortens and tightens the back of their neck and tucks their pelvis under, they may not feel much difference from their normal posture when it is exaggerated in this fashion. Chances are that they will notice more differences when we use cues to do something that is more unfamiliar.

Here, I employ the body mapping work of AT teachers Bill and Barbara Conable. The Conables discovered that understanding your anatomy substantially speeds the learning of AT (1995, 30). Knowing anatomy provides the student with a map in their mind that they can use as a guide to how the body operates optimally, thereby facilitating greater ease of movement. To better understand downward pull, I ask my students to show me where they believe the bottom of their head to be in the back. This is something most people know. It is where they can feel the base of their skull with their fingertips. Then I ask them where the bottom of their head is in the front. Most students put their hands under their chin. I ask them to walk around the room with the idea that their chin is the bottom of their head and then I ask them to report how it felt. I ask the same questions as I asked before about their feelings, arms, legs, and breathing. Many say that it feels normal. Some say that they feel awkward and tight or that their jaws feel tight and their head feels heavy. One of the problems with the idea of the chin being the bottom of the head is that it causes the student to think there is a joint in the middle of the cervical spine where there is no joint and they may be putting undue pressure there to try to create a bend in the spine where there is none.

Next, I show photos of where the top of the cervical spine meets the bottom of their skull like the one below (Figure 8.2).

I ask them to change their idea of where the bottom of their head is in the front. I tell them that their jaw is an appendage to their head just like their arms are appendages to their torsos. I cue them to think of the bottom of their head as the roof of their mouth.[4] Then I ask them to put their hand under their cheekbones (Figure 8.3) and walk around the room thinking that this is the bottom of their head.

This time the feedback is quite different: "I feel so light!" "I can see a lot more!" "I'm breathing!" "My legs are moving by themselves!" By connecting the students to their true anatomy and helping them discover where the joint is at the base of their skull/top of their spine, their use has significantly improved. Body mapping really works.

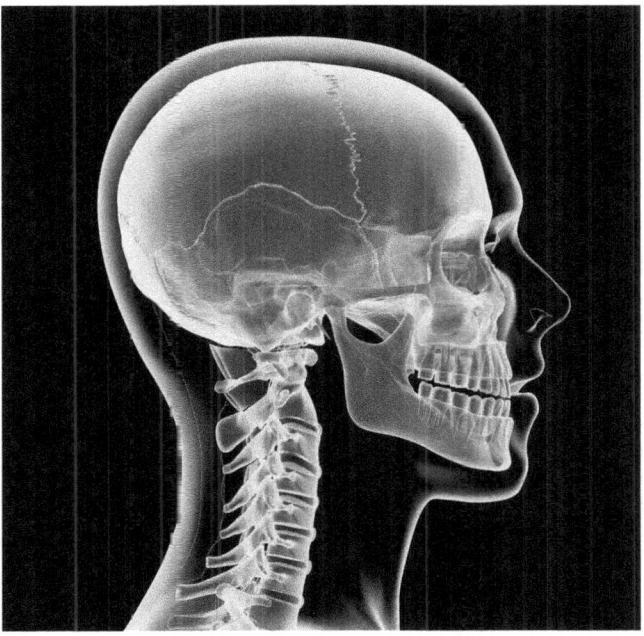

Figure 8.2 Side view of head and neck skeleton illustrating where the top of the spine meets the bottom of the head (superior facets of the atlas meet the occipital condyles of the skull).

An important concept to teach when releasing downward pull is connecting the idea that a free neck leads to a free spine, which leads to free joints. The head leads the body in movement and the spine follows in sequence. A good online exercise to teach this is to get down on our hands and knees and let our eyes find something, have our head move toward the object, and then attempt to have the spine follow in sequence. If you can locate videos of babies crawling, these are good case studies to watch.

End-Gaining vs. Means-Whereby, the Orders, Inhibition, New Direction

As noted, Alexander noticed that the more he tried to improve, the more things stayed the same due to the power of habit. He discovered that this was true if he was thinking of achieving an end. For example, if he thought of speaking publicly, even if he tried not to shorten and tighten the back of his neck, it still happened when he introduced the thought of doing the task. Even when he thought he was not shortening the back of his neck, he noticed in the mirror that he was in fact doing exactly that, so he concluded that his senses were unreliable.

Figure 8.3 Person illustrating where the bottom of their head is by placing their hand underneath their cheekbones.

He discovered that he could not simply will his faulty habit away. He called thinking of the activity he wanted to perform "end-gaining," instead of thinking about the process, which he called the "means-whereby" (2001, 41).

When, however, he gave himself the option of doing or not doing the activity, or simply of doing something else entirely, he began to make progress. But simultaneously, he had to stay out of his old, faulty habit of shortening and tightening the back of his neck. He had to refuse to respond in his habitual way to the stimulus. He called this refusal "inhibition" and by inhibiting his habitual response, he was better able to do something new (Jones 1979, 25).

He further found that giving himself directions (or what he called "the orders") while inhibiting his habit allowed for more success. His primary orders are as follows: "(1) Allow the neck to be free, (2) Allow the head to go forward and upward. (3) Allow the back to lengthen and widen" (Brennan 1991, 24).

Finally, he found that a clear direction about a new activity in addition to restriction of the old one helped to break his habits and allow for something new. For example, he might say to himself, "While inhibiting my habitual response, I will consciously give myself the orders and then I will direct myself to either do or not do the activity based on whether I am able to inhibit my habitual response."

The word inhibition would later take on a negative connotation because of Freud's definition of the word, but Alexander insisted that this word was the best for describing the process that he intended. To Alexander, inhibition meant "delaying the instantaneous response to a stimulus" (Jones 1979, 25). In my AT work, I use the word "pause" instead of "inhibit." I teach that AT is all about choice. In any moment, in any activity, you always have a choice in how you physically and mentally respond in that moment or activity. You can learn to pause or inhibit your body's natural response to any situation. For example, you can hear shocking news and pause, inhibit your habitual response, and remain in your body and in the world (interoceptive and exteroceptive), and choose to lengthen and widen. You can simply add a habit of taking a deep breath when you hear startling news. You may find that you add less tension to your mind and to your body this way.

I like to add the additional step of celebrating the act of noticing, of becoming aware of automatic physical habits. I developed this step because many of my students practice negative thinking. Typically, they notice a habit they are trying to release, and their response is to be unkind to themselves. They may think things like, "Why am I still doing that?!" or "Oh my gosh I'm so stupid!" or "Why am I so slow?!" Instead, I cue them to celebrate what they noticed. I tell them to celebrate because noticing is the beginning of your ability to change a habit that is no longer useful to you and you cannot change what you do not notice. Please notice that I used the words "no longer useful" and not "bad" when speaking of habits. You have all of your habits for a reason. They were once useful. Value judgments about your body use only add more physical and mental tension.

For example, Let us say the student lifts their chin when they sing high notes. In this scenario, when they notice that they have lifted their chin, they would celebrate the noticing of that habit ("Yay, I noticed!"). Then I ask them to pause. In this pause, the student may let go of what they noticed (lifting the chin). The next step is to give themselves a positive new direction. Not using a negative direction is vital. Telling yourself not to do something simply does not work, as Alexander discovered. In this scenario, I might cue them to lift the back of their head slightly as a positive direction. So, the steps to changing a habit that I teach my students are:

1 Notice
2 Celebrate
3 Pause (inhibition)
4 New Direction

To teach these principles online, we build on what we have learned previously. While noticing our bodies and the world (using our interoception and exteroception), I work with the students one on one in any activity. A common activity we practice is getting out of a chair. First I ask them to not get out of the chair, but to simply think of getting out of the chair and see what they notice in their bodies. Often, students will jut out their chins or lift their chests. This is vital information. Then we can proceed with the steps above. We celebrate noticing! Then we pause and let go of what we noticed, then give a new direction. If the student lifts their chin, I direct them to lengthen the back of their neck.

I prompt them to think of their feet pressing gently into the floor while lengthening the back of the neck. While asking them to press their feet into the floor and lengthen the back of the neck, we reintroduce the thought of getting out of the chair. Students can spend a long time in this space, but the important thing is that they are learning the principles. What is the "means-whereby?" In this case it is lengthening the back of the neck. Are they learning to notice? Are they beginning to understand how to give themselves an opportunity to either do or not do the activity? Are they learning to inhibit/pause? Are they being equally intero- and extero-ceptive?

Here is another way to think of this process:

1. Have an idea that you are going to do something.
2. Notice a habit that you have that is not helpful around doing the thing (unnecessary tension that you added in your body somewhere).
3. Release what you notice.
4. Give yourself a strong new direction that is an opposite direction from your habit (no negative directions!).
5. Re-introduce the thought of the activity and see if you can inhibit your habit.
6. If you manage to not add the habit that you initially noticed, proceed to the activity.
7. If you notice that the same tension pattern occurred, return to step #3.

Semi-Supine as a Means to Primary Control

Alexander discovered that the optimal position of the head is what he called "forward and up" in relation to the torso and spine. However, when he tried to "put" his head forward and up in relation to his torso and spine, it did not have the desired effect. Only when he did not interfere (what he called nondoing) and when he used the process of conscious intention (direction) did the proper relationship between head and spine come into place (Alexander 2001, 30). Because this relationship had such a profound effect on the whole-body mechanism, he thought of this as the primary relationship, and coined the phrase "primary control" in his later work to describe it (2001, 49). We are born with primary control. The relationship between our heads and spines remains balanced long into toddlerhood, but this relationship often significantly changes throughout our youth as we try to do things that are more difficult like sitting at an uncomfortable desk for most of the day or learning to write our letters properly. However, that innate coordination is always there for us to return to, we simply need to take away what we are doing to get in the way of our natural grace. Importantly, there is no "right" position for the head.

The relationship is dynamic and fluid, and changes in activity. Students must understand, however, that though there are no "right" positions, some positions are more advantageous – what Alexander called "positions of mechanical advantage." In an online class, teachers must notice when the students are in a more advantageous position and point it out when it occurs. Infants and some exemplary adults provide good examples of the "primary control." I show my class videos of Michael Jackson, Gene Kelly, and Abby Wombach and also of animals who move with great primary control. Big cats hunting are great video examples to show.

Primary Control is perhaps the most difficult concept to teach online, but also, by far, the most important piece to understand after a semester of AT lessons. If this relationship can be balanced, the student will find more ease in all their physical endeavors.

To work online, we start with a position that Alexander called semi-supine. Semi-supine is a position of lying on the floor with your knees up and your hands on your abdomen and a few books beneath your head. As we go through our day, we lose height from the loss of fluid in the discs between our vertebrae (Malko, Hutton, and Faiman, 2002, 158–159). This compression may result in fatigue, misuse, or ultimately, pain and possibly injury. Instituting a 20-minute semi-supine routine in our late afternoon may therefore be important for performers, who work at night, to provide the necessary energy to be productive into the evening.

When the student first lies down in semi-supine, they may be tempted to adjust themselves to what they believe to be "correct posture" in this position. Ask them to inhibit this response to allow the body to settle. Here are some minor adjustments to give students as they lie in semi-supine.

- If you notice that your knees want to fall outwards, separate your feet a little more so that they fall inward or you may tie a scarf around your knees to keep them from falling out.
- If you notice that your shoulders want to curl upwards, direct the shoulder blades to release down the back.
- If you notice that your chest wants to lift off the ground, direct your back to widen and flatten against the floor.
- If you notice that one of your feet feels lighter on the ground than the other, direct it to have more weight.
- If you notice that your chin is lifted towards the ceiling, direct the base of your skull to have more contact with the floor.
- If you notice that your chin is tucked, direct your head to go forward and up from your spine.

I often lead the students through exercises I have learned from other Alexander teachers as well as some of my own while the students are on their mats.

From Jane Ruby Heirich:

Recite lines from poetry or a song or monologue and make the phrases as long as possible. Focusing on extending breath in semi-supine is helpful to the mind as well as to the body.

(Heirich 2005, 50)

From Robyn Avalon:

Imagine that you are filling the inside of your skin, your body sack, with whipped cream. Start at your head and go in circles starting at the inside of the top of your head going slowly down. At the neck, make the choice to go down one arm in circles, then to the top of the other arm and down. Then your torso, then one leg and foot at a time. Go slowly making sure not to miss any corners. Imagine that your whole container is full of whipped cream.

My own:

Breathe in through your nose and imagine a yellow light entering from the top of your skull. With each inhalation, light slowly fills your body. Slowly fill your head, then your arms, then torso, hips, one leg and foot and then the other leg and foot with this brilliant, bright light.

These exercises can help the student get out of their perceived "right" or forced way of thinking about what "should" be happening, instead of what might happen if they had no forced idea of correct posture. Additionally, it causes them to consider their entire body rather than a collection of parts.

To get out of the semi-supine position: tell your students to come onto their hands and knees, and put one foot out in front of them at a 90-degree angle. While directing their heads up and forward, and the heel of your bent leg into the floor, rise.

After the students come out of semi-supine, ask them what they notice. Have them do the same examination that they did before with respect to their breath and the movement of their knees and arms. How much of the room can they see? The time just after getting up from semi-supine offers the chance to learn another necessary concept while learning this work: sitting in the unfamiliar. Students must get used to not trying to "fix" something, when it doesn't feel habitual or "comfortable." If their bodies are currently disorganized, the process of becoming more organized will at first feel "wrong" or "weird." They must learn to sit inside of that unfamiliarity and try not to adjust themselves to their more familiar, habitual physical patterns. The only way to learn to do something new with the body is to allow ourselves to sit in the not knowing what is right, and thereby experience new feelings and a new physical organization.

I avoid the word "posture" in Alexander teaching altogether because everyone has an idea of what "correct" posture is, and it tends to involve rigidity and holding. The idea of "standing up straight" is responsible for so many physical ills in our society. Your spine is not straight. It is a series of curves. Similarly, I avoid using the word "relax" primarily because it causes people to collapse and also because it can be a triggering word for some higher-energy folks who have been told to relax often in their lives. Instead, I use the phrases, "Be in this room." "Release into your curvy, neutral spine." "What do you notice that you can let go of right now?"

Conclusion

To be clear, this is just an overview of some of Alexander's main principles that we explored in my online class. There are a lot more principles and discoveries that need exploration, but for the purposes of this chapter, I have covered what I think are the tools an AT student needs to begin.

I believe that AT can be taught skillfully online. The principles applied are the same, but the teaching techniques need to be imaginative and explorational. I cannot overstate the importance of being kind to myself as we explored this unfamiliar territory. Being kind to myself allowed me to be playful and discover valuable new online teaching techniques. Additionally, teaching my students to be kind to themselves as a core principle of AT quickens their understanding of the material, and improves the quality of their bodies in their daily lives. At the end of the course, I was thrilled to discover that the student feedback was immensely positive. The students revealed the concerns they had had about the effectiveness of moving the course online but were pleased to find that they continued to learn valuable information and deepened their knowledge and skill in the online class.

Notes

1 The Free Dictionary, accessed 11.16.21 https://www.thefreedictionary.com/interoception.
2 It is not certain who coined this term, but it is often attributed to one of Alexander's first pupils, Frank Pierce Jones.
3 https://whatthingswe.gh.com/how-much-does-a-human-head-weigh/,%20accessed%2011-16-21.
4 I learned these cues from the coordinator of the Contemporary Alexander School in America, Robyn Avalon, who has a particularly playful and fun way to teach Alexander's principles.

References

Alexander, F. M. 2001. *The Use of the Self.* London: Orion Books Ltd.
Brennan, Richard. 1991. *The Alexander Technique: Natural Poise for Health.* London: Element Books Limited.
Conable, Barbara and William Conable. 1995. *How to Learn the Alexander Technique: A Manual for Students.* Oregon: Andover Press.

Gelb, Michael J. 1994. *Body Learning*. New York: Holt Publishing.
Heirich, Jane Ruby. 2005. *Voice and the Alexander Technique*. California: Autumn Press.
Jones, Frank Pierce. 1979. *Body Awareness in Action: A Study of The Alexander Technique*. New York: Schocken Books.
Malko, John, Hutton, William & Fajman, William. (2002). An In Vivo MRI Study of the Changes in Volume (and Fluid Content) of the Lumbar Intervertebral Disc After Overnight Bed Rest and During an 8-Hour Walking Protocol. *Journal of Spinal Disorders & Techniques*, 15(2), 158–159. Retrieved from http://ovidsp.ovid.com/ovidweb.cgi?T=-JS&PAGE=reference&D=ovfte&NEWS=N&AN=00024720-200204000-00012 June 30, 2021.

Chapter 9

Turn on Original Sound

Releasing Expectations in the Digital Dance Studio

Michele Dunleavy

Yeah, it's on the lower left-hand corner. Uh-huh, on the bottom. No, on the left. Yeah, it looks like a microphone. Uh-huh, see the carrot? Yep. Click on that, and a menu should pop up. See it? Ok, scroll to the bottom and click on audio settings. In the next window, scroll down and click the box next to, "show in-meeting option to 'Turn On Original Sound' from the microphone" Ok. Close that window and when you return to the main screen, you'll see a dropdown menu in the upper left-hand corner – make sure it says "Turn On Original Sound." Ok, great. Yep, I can hear you now. Start again from the top ….

This scenario played out repeatedly over the last 15 months as my students and I attempted to navigate the challenges of teaching and learning tap dance during periods of remote instruction. Like so many of the educators I know, switching to remote instruction was neither easy nor satisfactory from a pedagogical standpoint. We ended up doubling or tripling our workload with little to no idea if anything we were doing was even making an impact. I changed plans, created assignments, canceled assignments, then added new assignments, as I tried, again and again, to put a round peg in a square hole. I was nimble! I pivoted! I pivoted nimbly!

This essay is not a tutorial on how to successfully teach tap dance on zoom. I have no magic bullets for that. It is an accounting of my experience teaching a beginning level tap class during the seven weeks of remote learning at the beginning of the Covid-19 pandemic and how the limitations of Zoom, while incredibly frustrating, afforded an opportunity to lead with empathy and compassion in my classroom. I share some strategies I employed for maintaining community in an online environment, reducing student stress, and facilitating access and engagement with the course content.

Context and Timeline

The course I've selected for analysis, DANCE 252, is a requirement for second year students in Penn State's top ranked Musical Theatre program. Though we are currently in the process of renaming our dance courses and removing descriptors such as "beginning" and "advanced," this course has traditionally been

DOI: 10.4324/9781003229056-12

called "Beginning Tap II." The "II" merely references the fact that it is the second semester of a two-semester sequence. Despite the beginning label, this class, like most of our dance classes, is mixed level. Typically, this class comprises a handful of true beginners, a solid percentage with some previous training, and a few with extensive experience. My priority in the first semester is to simply get everyone on the same page by focusing on building vocabulary, good mechanics, musicality, tap history, and teaching a few classic tap routines. By the start of the second semester, the class is usually in a place where everyone can approach learning specific musical theatre repertoire, albeit with varying degrees of success. In addition to the musical theatre students, I often have a small number of students from other disciplines. I had two dance majors, one stage manager, one non-theatre student, and twelve musical theatre students in this class. At the start of the remote period, we had just completed the mid-term (the title number from *Anything Goes*) and were preparing to start the opening number from *42nd St.*

The period of remote instruction began immediately after spring break in March 2020 and lasted through the end of the semester in May. The announcement came when the students were already off-campus; meaning most of them did not have any school supplies with them when classes resumed, which meant no tap shoes in the case of my course. Even for those students who managed to retrieve their shoes (I actually mailed a pair to a student in Georgia), many did not have an adequate place to dance at home. Most found themselves in garages and basements, on patios and balconies, and without the appropriate flooring to absorb the impact of their movements. Additionally, they often endured the well-meaning but nevertheless intrusive eyes and ears of parents, siblings, and in some instances, neighbors during their practice.

The course met Monday/Wednesday mornings at 9:30, making it the inaugural Zoom of the remote period for most. That first Monday was a little chaotic but also fun in an odd way as we worked together to figure out how to use Zoom. We infused our "room" with a sense of possibility and, quite frankly, genuine gratitude for this technology that allowed us to meet at all – even if the circumstances were less than ideal. Our relatively easy acceptance of the situation was in no small part due to the fact there was a three-week time limit on the remote period. The general feeling was – "we got this." Two days later, after our university announced that we would be remote for the remainder of the semester, student morale dropped significantly. I began to rethink the course to accommodate this new paradigm.

Limitations of Zoom

Though it is a relatively new phenomenon, much has been written about the rise and potential causes of "Zoom fatigue." A simple Google search yields 2,040,000 results ranging from scholarly articles written by researchers at Stanford and Rutgers to more accessible articles in the *Washington Post* and *USA*

Today, which mostly reference the aforementioned scholarly articles. At the start of the remote instruction period, Zoom fatigue was hardly a concern for me, but the latency cited as a contributing factor became my nemesis. It's no secret that video conferencing platforms like Zoom have a certain amount of audio and video latency, and that the technology is only as good as your internet service. Even in the best of circumstances, there remains a slight audio delay of approximately "150 milliseconds – quicker than the blink of an eye" (Johnson 2020). This poses an array of challenges for participants of virtual meetings, including increased cognitive load as a result of processing latency in images and audio (Bailenson 2021).

Tap dance sits squarely at the intersection of sound and movement. This defining trait is the heart and soul of the dance. It also makes it incredibly challenging to transfer effectively to a remote learning environment. The impact of latency on teaching tap dance via Zoom cannot be overstated. Potential cognitive overload aside, Zoom eliminates the customary practice of dancing together as a group with music – a practice that fosters community while teaching musicality, cooperation, and listening. There is simply no possibility for synchrony in sound or movement on Zoom. Students remain muted in their individual spaces and listen to the sound of my feet and music through their computer speakers. When they dance "with" me, not only are we not synchronized, but *I can't hear them because they're all muted*. If I actually want to hear the students dance, the only way to do that is one at a time, which after accounting for unmuting, turning on original sound, receiving feedback, and quite possibly repeating the exercise, can take an enormous amount of time. Much more than it would in a face to face setting. Multiply that times 16, and you can imagine how this navigation of technology might kill any momentum generated during a given class. Add to that the likelihood that one or more students would experience internet dysfunction on any given day and it was a recipe for disaster. At the very least, the situation was less than ideal. The need to adjust my content, delivery, and expectations was clear. Time to pivot. Again.

Maintaining Community and Stress Reduction

I started to consider possible strategies to accommodate the limitations of Zoom while simultaneously striving to minimize the anxiety and stress of the students. I thought a lot about what it might mean to truly "meet the moment." I read articles about dance education in the virtual space and received countless invitations to join faculty support groups via social media. I reached out to colleagues in the tap community to see how others managed the latency issue. Many responded with valuable information about adjusting audio settings that helped immensely (Hilary-Marie 2020). But it wasn't enough. It became clear that the only way forward was to cease trying to make the class function remotely as it had when it was face to face.

In an effort to help ground and focus the students, I changed the way I began my classes. On most days, I provided space at the top of the class for students to share what was on their minds: to give voice to the frustration, fear, isolation, and anger they were feeling. Following that I would read what I hoped was an inspirational quote or poem. Then we would breathe. I led the class in a variation on a technique designed to lower stress called square breathing. We all kept time by patting our hands on our thighs while breathing in for four counts, holding for four counts, exhaling for four counts, and then resting four counts before beginning the cycle again. This would go on for anywhere from 1 to 3 minutes. At this point we might be 20 minutes into our 75-minute class period without having made a sound with our feet. The pressure to prepare students to succeed in the highly competitive field of musical theatre promotes a culture of toxic productivity both inside and outside of the academy. Though I fully understood the negative impacts of working within this paradigm, I was also reluctant to confront this mentality for fear of "not doing enough" to help ensure my students' success. Without realizing it at the time, I began prioritizing the mental and emotional health of the students over skill acquisition as a way of meeting the moment.

Facilitating Access and Engagement

Despite all the previously identified challenges, we danced "together"– and by that, I mean simultaneously. Still, the ten minutes of warm-up exercises we performed as a group did serve to build community. The students would follow along with my feet (adjusting the camera to aim directly at my feet was a huge boon for the students) and I would watch their disembodied feet repeat my actions 1 to 3 beats after me; silently, out of sync, and quite possibly on the opposite foot. My goal was not precision but simply to get warm enough to attempt choreography, which brings me to my first strategy: pre-recorded videos.

I started creating pre-recorded video content because the students struggled to learn anything beyond basic choreography over Zoom. These instructional videos broke down the steps and timing slowly and came with an added benefit: students could move at their own pace through the content. In the context of our class period, after completing the warm-up, students would pull up the instructional videos in a separate window on their computers and work through the content while I watched and provided feedback. Given the circumstances, this proved to be an effective method of content delivery until I realized that I would unintentionally disrupt the entire group every time I unmuted myself to give feedback to an individual student. The need to provide individual attention generated my second strategy: breakout rooms.

I discovered that by placing the students in individual breakout rooms, I could give specific feedback without disrupting the rest of the class, but I could also listen to them dance one at a time without making the rest of the class wait their turn. Likewise, students had the opportunity to ask pertinent questions specific to their needs. This was the closest I came to replicating the classroom experience on Zoom. I was able to give the type of personalized feedback and attention that I am accustomed to providing in the studio and, even though it meant isolating the students, it was worth it. After roughly 20 minutes in the breakout rooms, I'd bring the students back to the main room and see if there were any questions for the good of the group. At that point, if there was any time left, we would improvise. I'd play a song and everyone would dance at the same time in whatever fashion they chose. I couldn't hear them but watching them release their bodies and express themselves without inhibition brought me joy. And hope.

As I stated previously – zoom fatigue was not on the radar in these early days of what my students had taken to calling Zoom University. Nevertheless, I had concerns over the amount of screen time the students were accumulating over the day, so I prioritized creating assignments that got them away from the computer and out of the house. Two of these assignments were predicated on the act of taking a walk with prompts intended to promote both external listening and internal rhythmic awareness. An opportunity for students to turn on their own original sound, if you will. The first was called *Foli*, named after the video the students were instructed to watch prior to completing the assignment. Created by filmmaker Thomas Roebers, *Foli* chronicles the daily actions of the Malinke people in West Africa. The film includes making a djembe (a type of African drum) and underscores how rhythm imbues every aspect of daily life. After viewing the ten-minute film, students were given the following prompt:

> *Go take a walk. See if you can begin to notice the rhythms all around you. Perhaps it is the rhythm of your own feet, the chirping of birds, sounds of vehicle traffic, etc. Document your experience through one of the following methods:*

- *Written reflection (1 page double spaced)*
- *Create, record, and upload a rhythm inspired by your experience (audio or video)*

This assignment required the student to connect with the external world and attend to the environment. I hoped that not only would it get them out of the house but that it might also serve to distract them from their current situation. There was no rubric for grading this or any of the assignments during the remote period. If a student turned in the assignment, they received full credit. This took the onus off having to be "right" and created space for the student's creativity to flourish.

The follow-up assignment was called *Walking/Rhythmic Gait Analysis*. This assignment also required that the student go outside and take a walk but utilized a different prompt:

> *Instead of focusing on the sounds and rhythms around you, focus on your gait. Notice the underlying tempo and feel. Is your walk straight? Swung? If each footstep was a downbeat, how would you subdivide your walk? What is the*

"feel" or "groove" of your walk? Could you create a secondary rhythm with your hands to play while walking? Record your discoveries and submit your audio recording with a brief description (this can be written or spoken as part of the recording).

This assignment required the student to focus inwardly, to "listen" to, then analyze, their internal rhythm using musical terms and concepts introduced earlier in the semester. It offers a challenge to those so inclined by posing the question: Could you create a secondary rhythm with your hands to play while walking? This open-ended invitation leaves it to the student to choose whether or not to accept this challenge. Once again, students received full credit regardless of whether or not they took on the extra challenge.

The submissions for both of these assignments were wildly creative and varied. I received poems, original musical compositions, stream of consciousness ramblings, essays, shoebox drumming, duets with pets, and everything in between. It was clear that the students were responding positively to the adjustments in course content. Although we weren't getting through all the choreography initially planned for the second half of the semester, they continued to grow as young artists. Perhaps more importantly, they were beginning to connect course concepts to their everyday lives.

Unintended Consequences/Student Reflections

Earlier I mentioned that when we entered the remote period, the class was preparing to work on the opening number from *42nd St*. Perhaps you're wondering, "what happened to that?" Well, it still happened – sort of. I determined that we were never going to be able to get as granular and detailed as the choreography requires using Zoom, so I recorded the content and let students work on it at their own pace without a specific outcome attached.[1] Previously, in the "before times," students would perform this choreography for their final exam as part of their overall assessment, but since synchronized group performances were off the table, I let go of that expectation. It's funny how amid a global pandemic, practices, and conventions that once seemed crucial can lose their meaning completely. When the time came for the students to access the pre-recorded videos, I let them choose their own adventure. Most of them decided to work on some part of *42nd St*, many completed learning the choreography entirely, and others worked on totally different drills and exercises. Ultimately, I concluded that it really didn't matter what they were working on as long as they engaged with the content, given their individual limitations in shoes and flooring.

The act of releasing expectations was unfamiliar to me. Not in concept, but in practice. I had always leaned into rigor before empathy; not that I was a cruel taskmaster, but I definitely subscribed to a disciplined pedagogical approach with limited exceptions made for mental and emotional health. I trained in a culture that taught young artists to leave their personal lives at the door and not let it interfere with "the work." That has proven to be a very hard lesson to unlearn. It took this period of remote instruction predicated on a global health crisis for me to fully comprehend the falsity of that notion in both theoretical and practical terms. That the admonishment to leave our personal lives at the door is not only impossible but actually counterintuitive to the work of a performing artist. Somewhere along the line, I had conflated humanity with leniency and needed to be reminded that they are not the same. Perhaps it was the shift from the clinical, public, space of the studio to the privacy of our homes that jolted me firmly into this awareness. I suspect that this knowledge was already lurking, half-formed in the shallows of my subconscious, just waiting for a trigger to set it in motion. I also firmly believe that the limitations of Zoom – as much as I hated it (and I *REALLY* hated it) – afforded the opportunity to radically rethink my class content, delivery, and assessment methods.

It's exciting and revealing to reflect upon the hybrid instruction period that came later and notice what lessons I have carried forward, which epiphanies were easiest to hold onto as things returned to some semblance of normalcy, and where I still struggle to find balance. To give one example: students have continued to request pre-recorded videos as a way to facilitate their practice outside of class, and I have complied in some but not all instances. I worry that they will come to rely too heavily on the videos rather than build the necessary skills required to quickly learn and accurately reproduce choreography, a key to successful auditioning. The fact remains that I am charged with training young artists to enter a highly competitive field where they will need every advantage and a field where success often comes at the expense of mental, emotional, and physical health. The global pandemic combined with the reigniting of the Black Lives Matter movement has made this glaringly obvious. Conversations that previously lived at the margins of the arts community are suddenly center stage. Conversations that propose a new paradigm based on models of abundance, not scarcity, security instead of precarity, and collaboration rather than competition. Invariably these topics have leaked into my classroom, and my pedagogy moving forward must create the space to address them. I don't have all the answers. I spent most of those first seven weeks throwing the proverbial spaghetti at the wall to see what would stick, but I do know that the path forward begins with empathy, and that for me, the process of reimagining my pedagogy for remote learning provided an early roadmap.

Note

1 In their final reflections, a third of the students commented that one positive aspect of remote learning was how the use of pre-recorded videos allowed them to work at their own pace, something that is difficult to do in a group studio setting.

References

Bailenson, Jeremy N. 2021. "Volume 2, Issue 1 Invited Articles Published on Feb 23, 2021 Nonverbal Overload: A Theoretical Argument for the Causes of Zoom Fatigue." *Technology, Mind, and Behavior* 2, no. 1 (February): n/a. DOI: 10.1037/tmb0000030.

Johnson. 2020. "Why Zoom meetings are so dissatisfying." *The Economist*. https://www.economist.com/books-and-arts/2020/05/16/why-zoom-meetings-are-so-dissatisfying.

Marie, Hillary. 2020. "Here's the Solution to Your Sound Problems in Zoom." iTapOnline Community Is a Private Facebook Group Serving Tap Dance Practitioners and Educators. This post by administrator, Hilary-Marie offered specific strategies for dealing with sound issues in Zoom. iTapOnline Community. *Facebook*. https://www.facebook.com/groups/138234976827857.

Part III

Doing Theatre Online
Research, Rehearsal, Production

Chapter 10

An Archive by Any Other Name

The Historiographic, the Digital, the Hybrid

Daniel Ciba

What's in an Archive?

There was a moment in April when I realized that the pandemic was going to last much longer than I had initially hoped. Suddenly, my current book project with the working title *Blue Roses: Tennessee Williams, Memory, and the Queer Archive* was in indefinite limbo; could I do anything substantial without the remaining trips I had planned to in-person archives such as the Harry Ransom Center and the Harvard Theatre Collection? I certainly had research and writing tasks I could accomplish—cataloging the expanse of digital photographs from my initial research trips; looking heavily into and culling citations from my secondary sources about Williams, memory studies, and queer archival methodologies; and even throwing together some messy drafts. All these tasks were possible, but suddenly seemed fruitless given the uncertainty of when and how in-person archives would reopen. More onerous for me than the switch to virtual teaching, the closing of institutional archives brought my book project to a halt.

When I began to write this reflection during the summer of 2021, none of the archives that I will analyze in my book were open; as I revised it several had reopened but with reduced hours and waiting lists to gain entry. This friendly manifesto documents where I am at—rather than what is supposed to be done with—archives. I quote from other sources because my thoughts on the archive come from many conflicting voices circulating in my head that accompany me when I approach an archive. What does a scholar whose work lives primarily in the use of in-person archives do during a time when there is no access to the materials they need to make their arguments? How might my experiences with digital archives during the pandemic encourage me to rethink how I teach and create theatre historiography?

I teach archival practice as part of my undergraduate theatre history and general education courses because I aim to demystify the archival process as a means of decentering existing power structures. I encourage my students to think about the interconnected nature of archival research, historiography, and performance, a triad explored by Terry Cook and Joan M. Schwartz: "the practice of archives is the ritualized implementation of theory, the acting out of the script that

DOI: 10.4324/9781003229056-14

archivists have set for themselves" (2002, 173). I also acknowledge that I bring my own agendas into the archive as I warn my students to never assume that any history is truth merely because it emanates from archival sources. I remind them of these discussions when they craft their own papers, referencing Randall C. Jimerson's advice that applies to both archival research and historiography in general: "The first step is to abandon our pretense of neutrality" (2006, 28).

Weaving my research and my teaching together, as I do in my classroom, this reflection begins with the question "What is an archive?" because non-theatre scholars apply the term to a wide variety of systems; two extreme examples of many being video games and rocks.[1] Theatre and performance scholars seem just as interested in reading various concepts as archives. Andre Lepecki's exploration of dance as embodied actualizations[2] and Suk-Young Kim's archival lens for ethnographic interviews[3] further suggest the spectrum of potentials for archival methodologies to do much more than scour in-person archives. Saidiya Hartman calls her most recent book *Wayward Lives, Beautiful Experiments* its own archive.[4] Not having an interest in categorizing what should or should not be categorized as an archive, when asked I quickly reframe the question: does labeling something an archive change how it can be read?

I skip Jacques Derrida's *Archive Fever* because I agree with Eric Colleary of the Harry Ransom Center, who tweeted as I was preparing to write this essay that Derrida's infamous piece "really has very little to do with archives and I never fail to be surprised how often it comes up as recommended reading for archival theory" (2021).[5] Instead, I start with Diana Taylor's *The Archive and the Repertoire* in which she advocates for a balance between archival and performative sources:

> Embodied performances have always played a central role in conserving memory and consolidating identities in literate, semiliterate, and digital societies … It is difficult to think about embodied practice within the epistemic systems developed in Western thought, where writing has become the guarantor of existence itself.
>
> (2003, xviii–xix)

I consistently apply embodiment as part of my archival practice as a queer scholar in all my theatre history and dramatic literature courses. Emphasizing embodiment helps me unsettle the way Western and straight assumptions exclude lived experiences that do not fit traditionally conceived cultural norms.

I integrate archival methodologies throughout the semester, teaching my students how there are many ways to approach each dramatic and theoretical text because there is no single way to approach an archive. Queering the archive is nothing new for performance scholars. In *In A Queer Time and Place*, Jack Halberstam considers the boundaries of temporal and spatial dimensions of queer identity in the process of rethinking what constitutes an archive.[6] In *An Archive of Feelings*, Ann Cvetkovich theorizes a new methodology that connects trauma and sexuality to emphasize emotional aspects of queer archival practice.[7] In "Ephemera as Evidence," José Esteban Muñoz calls out archives that exclude identities that do not fit the pattern of official histories:

> The presentation of this sort of anecdotal and ephemeral evidence grants entrance and access to those who have been locked out of official histories and, for that matter, 'material reality.' Evidence's limit becomes clearly visible when we attempt to describe and imagine contemporary identities that do not fit into a single pre-established archive of evidence.
>
> (2008, 9)

Halberstam, Cvetkovich, and Muñoz are not alone in, but serve as a good introduction to, the naming of queer impulses that resist the normalizing mythologies of the archive as a place that collects and legitimizes knowledge.

My theatre history classroom requires students to grapple with how Western, white, and male scholars created archives as a means of consolidating power; what Rebecca Schneider sees as a limitation when performance is "predetermined by a cultural habituation to the patrilineal, West-identified (arguably white-cultural) logic of the Archive" (2001, 100). I introduce this ongoing concern because it allows me to include my queer research as part of my classroom, but also to be honest with my students about my suspicious attitude toward several of the theoretical and historiographical texts we read. Over five years of teaching undergraduates at three different institutions, I have become significantly less concerned about prescribing what facts my students *must* be able to recite about each historical period. This queer approach to archival historiography encourages my students to be much more thoughtful about how they select and integrate evidence into their papers. We collectively question how we know what we think we know.

I argue in this essay that each archive might need its own methodology. The researcher must adjust and adapt their methods every time they encounter new materials presented in new configurations. I take for granted that my readers accept that there are obvious differences between in-person and digital archives. Theatre historians can use a hybrid approach to the archives, blending in-person and digital formats to teach their students how to evaluate what sources they use and how they use them.

In-person Archives

I think about my first few trips to archives when it seemed so strange to lock up my belongings in the provided locker, have a gatekeeper open my laptop to check I was not bringing in any outside materials/smuggling anything out, and use the institutional pencil and scrap paper (usually brightly colored) to make my notes. I have yet to encounter an archive that made me wear gloves, except when touching photographs to protect materials from the oil on my hands. I very clearly remember the decision to choose Tennessee Williams as my main research project (which evolved into my dissertation and expanded into my book project) during a field trip arranged by Heather S. Nathans at the American Antiquarian Society for her "Introduction to Graduate Research Methods" course.

One of the readings for that course was Thomas Postlewait's *The Cambridge Introduction to Theatre Historiography*, which I viewed, at the time, as a foundational reading—the how-to book that would train me to be a historiographer. When I returned to my notes for this essay, I found this passage highlighted:

> If the archive does not deliver a unified event, the historian connects the parts until they deliver a whole—an action that can be described and explained in terms of its internal logic, as understood by the historian. A process of mediation occurs in the making of historical understanding …The historian is always attempting to be true to what the documentation reveals, but that revealing process is itself a kind of action, a kind of event.
>
> (2009, 226)

As I revisit this passage, which I most certainly took for granted as a rule when I first encountered it, I struggle. The training that I (and the other historiographers whose practices were directly or indirectly influenced by Postlewait's notable contributions to the field of theatre historiography) received is to deliver a unified event—to polish history so as not to see the mechanics—but my internal impulse, my usual queer questioning of all advice about how to make history, is to resist the very notion that such unification is possible. I never see a unified event in the kind of histories I seek. I am currently more fascinated by the messiness and chaos that are part of every archive; inspired by Martin F. Manalansan IV's mapping of queer immigrant households as archives: "Mess is a way into a queering of the archive that involves not a cleaning up but rather a spoiling and cluttering of the neat normative configurations and patterns that seek to calcify lives and experiences" (2014, 99). But, if I am honest with myself, my actual process falls somewhere in the middle of Postlewait's and Manalansan's differing perspectives on straightening/queering the archive. And I need both sides of the process—order and chaos—to make the archive as visible as possible in the histories I craft inside and outside the classroom.

I have no fear that in-person archival research will vanish. As no archival categorization system functions like a digital search engine, part of the process is finding materials in unexpected places. For example, I rely heavily on experimenting with what I request to find materials that, because of their description or placement in the finding aid, other researchers might overlook. Of course, sometimes this doesn't work out. I remember the day I requested six boxes of "Box Office Statements" for *A Streetcar Named Desire* located in the Audrey Wood collection at the Harry Ransom Center by mistake and felt ashamed having requested something not particularly useful for me. Instead of admitting my mistake, I pretended to spend what I thought was a decent amount of time looking at documents that I knew I was never going to use, before moving on to my next request. Admitting these statements might offer some valuable insights to another historian, I have come to find that I sift through a lot of materials to isolate a comparatively small percentage of items on which I focus.

But when you find something good in the archive there is a magic that accompanies it. Robin Bernstein's "Dances with Things" includes a focused contextualization of one piece of archival evidence. As Bernstein addresses the unanswerable questions that she places around an archival photograph of "a light-skinned woman ... behind a larger-than-life caricature of an African American eating a slice of watermelon," she explores how archival evidence invites scholars to consider archival items as "scriptive":

> A scholar understands a thing's script both by locating the gestures it cites in its historical location and by physically interacting with the evidence in the present moment. One gains performance competence not only by accruing contextualizing knowledge but also, crucially, by holding a thing, manipulating it, shaking it to see what meaningful gestures tumble forth ... The archive then becomes a ghostly discotheque where things of the past leap up to ask scholars to dance, and we listen, accept the invitation, and, hearts pounding, step onto the floor.
>
> (2009, 90)

I have shaken many a thing to find its script. Similarly, Carolyn Steedman describes how dust is a magical component of the archive, how archival materials gain significance because of the dust they accumulate: "But the Historian who goes to the Archive must always be an unintended reader, will always read that which was never intended for his or her eyes" (2009, 75).[8] While neither archival evidence nor the individuals reading should proclaim objectivity, part of the appeal of archives are assumptions related to the claims of authority, definitiveness, and order that accompanies the mythic and capitalized Archive—a place where the historian can interact with the past.

Over time, my comfortability with archives has turned my process into a scavenger hunt, during which I enjoy seeing how much material I can sift through in the limited time I have, time based on funding more than anything else. When I surveyed the 46 uncategorized boxes in the Esther Merle Jackson collection at the Stuart A. Rose Manuscript, Archives, and Rare Book Library, I knew I would only have one chance, so I made a personal quota of six boxes a day. Although I spent (wasted?) a full day taking digital photographs of her second unpublished 797-page manuscript, I was able to dance, albeit quickly, with materials from every box.

Over the past eight years that I have been conducting archival research, digital cameras and laptops have become more common and more accepted as a valuable part of the archival research process. I cannot imagine doing research without hurriedly attempting to take as many pictures as possible, while making sure to handle fragile materials with care. Of course, sometimes I find entire folders with already damaged materials like the time I informed the Harry Ransom Center that the drafts of Tennessee Williams's mother's autobiography *Remember Me To Tom* were getting ruined by decaying tape sticking the pages together. Part of my ritual now is to slightly straighten each box as I go.

Over time, I realize that what I currently do, most often, is make my own personal digital archive of contents that may not be interesting to anyone else but me (taking 220 photographs of assorted *Suddenly Last Summer* drafts that will occupy a single anecdote for the Epilogue of my book or making a database of all 670 pieces of uncategorized fan mail for an article for the *Tennessee Williams Annual Review*). I could not entrust many of these in-person archival tasks to anyone else, because another person would make different decisions: when my interest will be in the 71 used checks in Box 16 of the Esther Merle Jackson collection rather than the manuscript atop which they sit. In-person archival research is not for everyone, but I find magic in holding the past in your hands and hoping that your current find has been overlooked by other historians.

The excitement of the in-person archive—which I use instead of "traditional" or "conventional" because that would delegitimize the digital systems in the following section—also comes with a history of exclusion. Many scholars acknowledge how archivists have made archives based on the solidification of power to mandate what types of knowledge get preserved and who has access to it. As part of exploring Tibet and Shangri-La in *The Imperial Archive*, Thomas Richards frames the archive as a "collectively imagined junction of all that was known or knowable, a fantastic representation of an epistemological master pattern, a virtual focal point for the heterogeneous local knowledge of metropolis and empire" (1993, 11). Roberto González Echevarria equates archives in Latin America to modern novels:

> The Archive, then, is not so much an accumulation of texts as the process whereby texts are written; a process of repeated combinations, of shufflings, and reshufflings ruled by heterogeneity and difference. It is not strictly linear, as both continuity and discontinuity are held together in uneasy allegiance
>
> (1990, 24)

Lorraine Daston argues that the authority of archival research in tandem with the preserving of scientific records: "Early modern archives were bastions of authenticity, places of proofs and pedigrees" (2012, 171). Although these more formal forms of exclusion were the foundation of archives, archival gatekeeping has changed from overtly voiced authority to more subtle forms of exclusion, namely the privilege offered to scholars who can afford extended research trips and who have extensive credentials to get support from archival institutions. As a contingent scholar, I find myself somewhere in the in-between of this form of privilege. I have received support from my institutions, but also have had to privately fund at least half of the research for my book. I debated for a long time whether to mention just how much my contingent status for the past three years has shaped my approach to archival research. What is possible during my archival visits is directly tied to what I can accomplish within financial and temporal limitations over which I feel I have little control. While archives proclaim their commitment to diversity, they must also fund projects that interrogate the centuries of oppression interconnected with white supremacy, homophobia, and sexism that have shaped curation practices and archival scholarship.

Digital Archives

Many scholars who focus on in-person archives, including the ones I mentioned in the previous section, create their historiographical arguments by interpreting archival materials as traces of embodiment. In the same vein, in-person archival research requires scholars to place their bodies into the archives. So what happens when the archive and the scholar are remote—when there is no body to encounter the archive in "real" space?

Before the pandemic, I knew that digital historiography was a thing, but that it was not my thing. As early as 2007, Sarah Bay-Cheng has argued for digital archives as a means of capturing embodiment in ways that written documents of performance texts cannot:

> Rather than resist or lament such a development [of the rise of mediated theatre], we need to expand the tools of theatre history to include the formal analysis of moving images of theatre performance as a critical part of the theatre archive of the future, and as pedagogical tools today
>
> (40)

In a 2010 essay on digital historiography Bay-Cheng questions Diana Taylor's repertoire:

> Rather than contest Taylor's statement, I would like to trouble it by suggesting that the digital neither eclipses nor negates embodiment, but changes our relationship to the archive and thus constitutes a kind of digital repertoire that is closer to Taylor's formulation (both formally and politically) than prior documents
>
> (2010, 125)

Rereading Bay-Cheng's arguments from a decade ago for this essay was an eerie experience, because Bay-Cheng predicts how much technology would impact theatre of the future and warns that accepting the digital as part of theatre scholarship is an inevitability.

Without the ability to conduct in-person research at Williams's archives I had to adjust my focus during the pandemic. The shift to thinking through and exploring digital archives happened for me on June 1, 2020, the application deadline for working groups for the 2020 American Society for Theatre Research (ASTR) conference, which ended up being a virtual meeting when they cancelled their in-person conference. When I found "Stonewall Forever," the online website that serves as a monument created through a partnership between NYC's LGBT Community Center, Google, and the National Park Service, I saw immediately the potential for reading its contents as a queer digital archive, rather than merely a website or an interactive experience. The memories contained in the monument serve a variety of functions, one of which is not to impose a singular experience for the viewer, who is able to navigate videos, photographs, and a variety of other ephemera alongside community posts that speak to how the monument influences LGBTQ+ identities then and now. The contradictions presented in this queer archive allow participants to reflect on and experience the contested history of the Stonewall riots in a variety of ways.

The Cuban Theater Digital Archive is another example of pre-pandemic desires to make theatrical ephemera easily available to communities that do not have access to institutional archives. Housed by the University of Miami; the archive contains 2,800 digital objects including 92 filmed theatrical productions:

> CTDA, as a community archive, complements and extends the role of traditional archives and special collections in virtual space. Thus, beyond a digital portal to access content, it works with a more inclusive paradigm for the curation, distribution and reproduction of Cuban performing arts materials
> (2013, 7)

What would it mean if the goal of all archives were to digitize entire sections, prioritizing access and eliminating travel expenses?

Another benefit of digital archives is that scholars can actively participate in the making of virtual repositories that require no physical space to house or protect materials. The 2021 special issue for *Contemporary Theatre Review* "Outing Archives, Archives Outing" contains two reflections on the creation of digital archives. Melissa Blanco Borelli and Olga Lucía Sorzano reflect on making a digital archive of Afro-Colombian and indigenous embodied practices:

> The analysis of body movements, corporeal interactions, and embodied practices can contribute to understanding and processing Colombia's long history of violence and conflict, and the possibilities offered by digital tools to document those processes, guided our debates on how to imagine the archive
> (Borelli, Lease, and Mitra, 2021, 174)

Bryce Lease documents his curation of a digital archive about drag and transqueer performance from South Africa's Western Cape: "My work on the production of a digital archive made me both optimistic and pessimistic about the potential for this online forum to set queer collective memory in motion, both as a trigger and as a locale" (154). The practice of making a digital archive actively decenters the authority of institutional archives.

The contrast between my experiences with pre-pandemic and post-pandemic digitization processes affirms the challenges and possibilities of shifting towards a more accessible model. When I requested letters from an Edwin Forrest archive for a term paper in 2014 from a library in Philadelphia, I think they charged me less than $10 to scan 20 pages. I limit these requests, not just because of expense, but also because I view it as an imposition on the resources of archival staff. Contrarily, when I contacted Sarah Owen, the Director of Library Services for Independence Community College, which houses the William Inge Collection in Kansas, during the summer of 2020, she sent me every piece of correspondence between Margo Jones and William Inge for nothing. It took an afternoon of her time and saved me the flight and hotel for a task that would have taken me an hour or two to document. How much access would be possible if every library had proxies who could digitize—trained institutionally-funded employees willing to video chat with researchers about what they needed from the archive, and who digitize portions of the archive at the request of researchers, creating materials that would remain available to future scholars?

The Harry Ransom Center has a proxy list that Colleary has sent me multiple times, but I have yet to use one. The document says that rates are a matter of discussion between the scholar and the proxy. I would have used a proxy in September 2021 but was able to arrange with Cristina Meisner in Reference Services to get 100 free scans, a service that the HRC was offering to help patrons who were not able to visit during the pandemic. I had to wait two weeks, but I was so grateful to receive scans of the box of letters Tennessee Williams sent to his lover Robert Carroll (a significant find that was missing from my fourth chapter). My scans are usually blurry, and I must squint or pass over pages if I can't read them; theirs were not.

Although I am still learning how to dance with digital archives, the challenges presented by digital archives is no longer new. For example, Rudy Laermans and Pascal Gielen argue that the idea of a digital archive is an oxymoron: "'The digital' and 'the archive' are clashing notions because they refer to the basic, and opposite, characteristics of new and old media" (2007). If the future of archives is digital, what will be lost is physical access to the object, but there is also much to be gained. Although I have felt the magic of touching archival materials, I take away from the pandemic-imposed closures a strong appreciation of the efficiency and access offered by digital archives.

Towards a Hybrid Model of Archival Methodology

My separation of in-person and digital archives in the previous two sections only encourages me to argue that archival research could benefit from hybrid explorations to capture both the value of in-person experiences and the ongoing potential for digital archives. This is especially so in undergraduate classrooms, where asking students to conduct archival research might not be feasible, while asking them to play around with digital archives related to course material is easily accomplishable. Similarly, institutional archives need to allocate resources toward digitization to be more hybrid and provide more access. There need to be more projects like the exemplary work of Amy Hughes and Naomi Stubbs in their digitization of the Harry Watkins Diary, which included undergraduate students as part of the transcription process, making the archives easily accessible through a search engine on *The University of Michigan* website. Even though I cannot touch the dust on these 13 volumes, I can interact with Watkins's impressive documentation of 19th-century US performance because Hughes and Stubbs digitized their archival find.

When I try to separate in-person and digital archives, many questions emerge. Just because something is digitized does it lose its authenticity? Is the New York Public Library's Theatre on Film and Tape Archive (TOFT) still an archive even though the researcher accesses the performances through video screens? If TOFT were to make some performances available through the internet, would that fundamentally change how the researcher experiences the already mediatized performances? What difference does trekking into Manhattan to sit at a screen on the third floor of the Carnegie Hall branch of the NYPL make, versus viewing the same thing in my PJs from my living room?

In thinking through the potentials for both the in-person archive's materiality and endlessness and the digital archive's virtuality and comparative finitude, I will voice a few concluding points that offer an initial model for teaching of hybrid archival methods:

- *No archive speaks for itself.* Not only is there no one way to approach an archive, but the archive requires scholars to be transparent about how their subjectivities influence what stories they tell and how they tell them.
- *All archives are messy.* If an archive appears clean and ordered in a narrative, it is no longer an archive. Part of the excitement of archival research is sifting through a bunch of junk to find something miraculous. Ordering archives creates a glossy history that does a disservice to both academic readers and other audiences.
- *No archive can thoroughly reconstruct the past.* The archive is always mediated. Although in-person archival research may offer a more personal connection to the archive, digitization does not change that the objects in the archive remain traces—traces that the historian must contextualize.
- *There are no official histories.* Any scholar who offers their readers an official history via a claim that in-person archives are more authentic because you can touch the materials is lying to them.

Archival research would benefit from the exploration of hybrid teaching because this forces teachers and students alike to think about how they access and explicate evidence. Each piece of archival evidence requires an exploration of the limitations and possibilities of knowledge suggested by the trace of the individual embodied memory it represents.

For teachers and students of the archive, it is important to consider how a blend of in-person and digital methodologies has the potential to address centuries of elitism that granted the archive an authority that must be questioned. In her exploration of dance practice, Carol Bernstein describes how "The archive's existence is predicated upon the unsaid or the unwritten as well as upon what is explicitly given in language" (2007, 7). Similarly, Cook and Schwartz ask for accountability regarding systems of power that lurk within and dictate archival practice:

> by performing openly and accountably, we will begin to internalize accountability until it becomes the script by which we act. And so, as well, for performances respecting diversity, telling stories, broadening perspectives, refocusing on the research substance of our work. This does not mean that archives are no longer about power. Rather, power is shared, power is refocused, power is held accountable (2002, 185).

As Joseph Roach warns: "There is no reason to assume the innocence of the archive: to select is to tamper" (Reinelt and Roach 2007, 198). The path forward is to shift from teaching the singular, mythic Archive, to an exploration of the plurality of archives—both in-person and digital. I proposed this essay not fully appreciating just how many scholars questioned archival practices long before I visited my first archive. Why wouldn't I take my experiences with digital archives back into my in-person archival practices? And, just as importantly, why wouldn't in-person archives change their policies based on how closures highlighted the issues of access existent long before the pandemic?

Notes

1 Dimitrios Pavlounis reads the video game *Gone Home* as a queer archive: "Through this analysis, I also suggest ways in which digital games can help us think through the politics of archives and of queerness as a historiographical method" (2016, 579). Stephanie Springgay and Sarah E. Truman read a series of rocks as a queer archive:

> As queer archives of feeling, Stone Walks demand that we not think about what we can take from or collect of stones, or how we feel about stones, but rather to think in relation to their affective force, their quivering vitality.
>
> (2017, 861)

2 "The body is archive and archive a body" (Lepecki 2010, 31).
3 "Interview as an archive-producing process may embody various degrees of performativity for future researchers: archive-producing interviews may find ways to transcribe ephemeral oral statement into a semi-permanent recorded text, while the act of conducting interviews also alerts us to see interviewees as 'living' agents of archival potentiality, namely people who provide testimony to the production of archival knowledge" (Kim 2010, 200).

4 "The album assembled here is an archive of the exorbitant, a dream book for existing otherwise. By attending to these lives, a very unexpected story of the 20th century emerges, one that offers an intimate chronicle of black radicalism, an aesthetical and riotous history of colored girls and their experiments with freedom" (Hartman 2019, xv).
5 Carolyn Steedman concurs:

> Although 'Archive Fever' may have nothing at all to do with archives and the attendant practices of history, Derrida showed us a *place* in *Mal d'archive*, a building with an inside and outside, which is often a house (occasionally a home). He suggested that in an archive we are under some kind of house arrest.
>
> (2001, 11)

6 Halberstam calls the various cultural renditions of Brandon Teena's story an archive: "The Brandon archive is exactly that: a transgender archive of 'emotion and trauma' that allows a narrative of a queerly gendered life to emerge from the fragments of memory and evidence that remain" (2005, 24).
7 "It is organized as 'an archive of feelings,' an exploration of cultural texts as repositories of feelings and emotions, which are encoded not only in the content of the texts themselves but in the practices that surround their production and reception. Its focus on trauma serves as a point of entry into a vast archive of feelings, the many forms of love, rage, intimacy, grief, shame, and more that are part of the vibrancy of queer cultures." (Cvetkovich 2003, 7).
8 I highly recommend Steedman's exploration of the rag rug, as a particularly inventive way to think about archival research as weaving rather than synthesizing: "But what went into the rag that makes the rag rug, its own history of production, ownership and consumption, of wearing and tearing, deflects the use of this aesthetic" (2001, 116).

References

Bay-Cheng, Sarah. 2007. "Theatre Squared: Theatre History in the Age of Media." *Theatre Topics* 17, no. 1: 33–50.

Bay-Cheng, Sarah. 2010. "Digital Historiography." In *Theater Historiography: Critical Interventions*, edited by Henry Bial and Scott Magelssen. 125–136. Ann Arbor: University of Michigan Press.

Bernstein, Carol L. 2007. "Beyond the Archive: Culture Memory in Dance and Theater." *Journal of Research Practice* 3, no. 2. http://jrp.icaap.org/index.php/jrp/article/view/110/98.

Bernstein, Robin. 2009. "Dances with Things: Material Culture and the Performance of Race." *Social Text 101* 27, no. 4 (Winter): 67–94. DOI:10.1215/01642472-2009-055.

Borelli, Melissa Blanco, Bryce Lease, and Royona Mitra. 2021. "Outing Archives, Archives Outing". *Contemporary Theatre Review* 31, no. 1–2.

Colleary, Eric. Twitter Post. May 26, 2021. 6:13 PM. https://twitter.com/ecolleary/status/1397677387937157126.

Cook, Terry and Joan M. Schwartz. 2002. "Archives, Records, and Power: From (Postmodern) Theory to (Archival) Performance." *Archival Science* 2: 171–185. https://DOI.org/10.1007/BF02435620.

Cvetkovich, Ann. 2003. *An Archive of Feelings: Trauma, Sexuality and Lesbian Public Cultures*. Durham: Duke University Press.

Daston, Lorraine. 2012. "The Sciences of the Archive." *Osiris* 27: 157–187.

Derrida, Jacques, and Eric Prenowitz. 1996. *Archive Fever: A Freudian Impression*. Chicago: University of Chicago Press.

Echevarria, Roberto González. 1990. *Myth and Archive: A Theory of Latin American Narrative*. Cambridge: Cambridge University Press.
Halberstam, Jack. 2005. *In a Queer Time and Place: Transgender Bodies, Subcultural Lives*. New York: New York University Press.
Hartman, Saidiya V. 2019. *Wayward Lives, Beautiful Experiments: Intimate Histories of Social Upheaval*. New York: W.W. Norton & Company.
Hughes, Amy E. and Naomi J. Stubbs. 2018. *The Harry Watkins Diary: Digital Edition*. Ann Arbor: University of Michigan Press. https://quod.lib.umich.edu/h/hwatkins/.
Jimerson, Randall C. 2016. "Embracing the Power of Archives." *The American Archivist* 69, no. 1: 29–32. https://www.jstor.org/stable/40294309.
Kim, Suk-Young. 2010. "Finding History from the Living Archives." In *Theater Historiography: Critical Interventions*, edited by Henry Bial and Scott Magelssen. 197–207. Ann Arbor: University of Michigan Press.
Laermans, Rudy and Pascal Gielen. 2007. "The Archive of the digital an-archive" *The Digital Archive* 17. http://www.imageandnarrative.be/inarchive/digital_archive/laermans_gielen.htm.
Lepecki, Andre. 2010. "The Body as Archive: Will to Re-Enact and the Afterlives of Dances." *Dance Research Journal* 42, no. 2 (Winter): 28–48. https://www.jstor.org/stable/23266897.
Manalansan, Martin F., IV. "The 'Stuff' of Archives: Mess, Migration, and Queer Lives." *Radical History Review* 120 (Fall 2014). DOI:10.1215/01636545.2703742.
Manzor, Lillian, Kyle Rimkus, and Mitsunori Ogihara. 2013 "Cuban Theatre Digital Archive: A Multimodal Platform for Theatre Documentation and Research." *Information Technologies for Performing Arts, Media Access, and Entertainment*, Second International Conference, ECLAP 2013, Portugal (April 8–19): 138–150. https://DOI.org/10.1007/978-3-642-40050-6_13.
Muñoz, José Esteban. 1996. "Ephemera as Evidence: Introductory Notes to Queer Acts." *Women & Performance* 8, no. 2: 5–16. https://DOI.org/10.1080/07407709608571228.
Pavlounis, Dimitrios. 2016. "Straightening Up the Archive; Queer Historiography, Queer Play, and the Archival Politics of *Gone Home*." *Television and New Media* 17, no. 8: 579–594.
Postlewait, Thomas. 2009. *The Cambridge Introduction to Theatre Historiography*. Cambridge. Cambridge University Press.
Reinelt, Janelle G. and Joseph Roach. 2007. *Critical Theory and Performance*. Ann Arbor: University of Michigan Press.
Richards, Thomas. 1993. *The Imperial Archive: Knowledge and the Fantasy of Empire*. London: Verso.
Schneider, Rebecca. 2001. "Performance Remains." *Performance Research* 6, no. 2: 100–108. https://DOI:.org/10.1080/13528165.2001.10871792.
Springgay, Stephanie and Sarah E. Truman. 2017. "Stone Walks: Inhuman Animacies and Queer Archives of Feeling." *Discourse: Studies in the Cultural Politics of Education* 38, no. 6: 851–863. http://dx.DOI.org/10.1080/01596306.2016.1226777.
Steedman, Carolyn. 2001. *Dust: The Archive and Cultural History*. Manchester: Manchester University Press.
Taylor, Diana. 2003. *The Archive and the Repertoire: Performing Cultural Memory in the Americas*. Durham: Duke University Press.
The Center. "Stonewall Forever." Accessed June 26, 2021. https://stonewallforever.org.

Chapter 11

Building Trust Across Miles

New Play Dramaturgy in Virtual Rehearsal Rooms

Kristin Leahey and Shelley Orr

Theatre artists rely on strong collaboration for success, but teaching students how to collaborate presents challenges. Additionally, how does one foster robust collaborations on Zoom, let alone teach it remotely? Students can read about collaborative skills through case studies, and instructors can lead in-class discussions on the topic, but we contend students learn collaboration best through practice. In this chapter, we explore two case studies: MOXIE Theatre and San Diego State University's *BIG Night of Little Plays*, an annual event for which Associate Professor Shelley Orr facilitates and serves as a mentor, and the Fall 2020 season at Boston University's School of Theatre in the College of Fine Arts, which Assistant Professor Kristin Leahey collaborated on devising and producing. Each of us share our processes of mentoring emerging new play artists in remote festival and workshop settings, and reflect on the importance of cultivating dramaturgical relationships and responding to the ever changing needs of theatre students during this critical time.

Shelley Orr, San Diego State University: 36-hour New Play Festival

In our first case study, San Diego's MOXIE Theatre and San Diego State University collaborated on the *BIG Night of Little Plays*, an annual ten-minute new play festival, which started in 2015. In April 2020, it pivoted to all virtual. Together with my colleagues Prof. Stuart Voytilla (who teaches playwriting) and MOXIE Theatre's Casting Director Jen Berry, we matched eight groups of SDSU student playwrights and dramaturgs with professional directors and actors from the San Diego theatre community. Reflecting on my work with the 2020 festival, I share approaches born of the necessity to advise and mentor emerging dramaturgs in online collaborations.

In the theatre, instructors tend to feel that while we can teach the basic principles and techniques of theatre arts in the classroom, students learn best through first-hand practice. Practical experience serves as an essential tool for student dramaturgs, especially those new to the field. A challenge for those who teach dramaturgy is that often their undergraduate (and even graduate) students lack

DOI: 10.4324/9781003229056-15

any prior experience in dramaturgy. Acting, musical theatre, aspects of design, stage management, dance, and stage makeup are routinely part of the theatrical experience for students in primary and secondary education. But dramaturgy is typically introduced in college. My dramaturgy course sits at an interesting juncture; the course number indicates that the class is appropriate for advanced undergraduates and graduate students; however, I am aware that for many who take the course, this is their first direct, focused experience with dramaturgy. It is at once an introductory *and* advanced course.

SDSU offers a BA degree in Theatre. As a designated Hispanic-Serving Institution, one third of full-time students enrolled identify as Latinx/Hispanic. Another third identifies as white, and 57% identify as women. These demographics reflect the population enrolled in theatre classes. I have taught the dramaturgy course at San Diego State University every spring since I arrived in 2007. In teaching the course 14 times, I have made numerous changes to better serve my students' needs. One key change is that I have incorporated assignments that allow students to practice dramaturgical skills in real-world, collaborative opportunities as I found that my students need practical experiences to make their classroom learning meaningful.

In my course, we have always read essays on the role and the purpose of the dramaturg and discussed case studies by professional dramaturgs. But starting in 2015, in collaboration with SDSU playwriting professor Aurorae Khoo, I incorporated a weekend-long rehearsal process on a new play into my course. The playwriting and dramaturgy students produce a 36-hour, new play festival during which the plays are cast, written, rehearsed, and performed for the public (in that order). Working in teams, each dramaturgy and playwriting student pair is matched with two professional actors and a director engaged by the nearby professional MOXIE Theatre.

The advantage of this compact process is that students are able to experience a rehearsal room and collaborate with an artistic team without needing to commit to a months-long process. They each work on their own play, and I am able to stop by the rehearsals as they are all happening simultaneously on campus. In course evaluations, students often reflect on this experience as one of the most memorable and transformative of the class. Students regularly comment that they feel as though they are an essential part of the collaborative team. They share that their contributions and suggestions are valued by their collaborators. Often the dramaturgs are pressed into service to help pull off the performance, reading stage directions, finding props, or contributing in other practical ways. In the feedback on the *BIG Night,* I see students who now view themselves as full artistic collaborators, often for the first time. When classes at SDSU shifted to all virtual in mid-March 2020, the planning for the *BIG Night of Little Plays* was already well underway. Fortunately, this event does not usually happen until April to allow the students to absorb the techniques and approaches they study, so this provided us a few crucial weeks to adapt it to the new circumstances.

I gave my dramaturgs two assignments associated with the *BIG Night of Little Plays*. First, a low-stakes assignment to simply meet with their playwright and get acquainted. In class, we discuss for a few weeks how to build a relationship with a playwright and how to give feedback. How to best phrase and time the giving of feedback are topics that we discuss, but it is hard to absorb these skills without an opportunity to put them into practice. That is where this brief, intense new play process becomes extremely valuable. The second assignment is their participation in the festival. The participation itself is the work, so the written assignment that students submit is kept simple: students are asked to write a brief reflection on the process, their role in it, and any takeaways they gleaned during the weekend.

In most years of the festival, the plays are not written until the festival weekend has begun, "bake-off" style, where the playwrights are given a short, fixed period of time to write from a prompt, a common set of "ingredients" to incorporate into their script (such as a particular sound effect, line of dialogue, or bit of blocking). The schedule typically is as follows: on Saturday morning at 9 AM, everyone meets at MOXIE Theatre, the teams meet, and the actors perform two-minute monologues for everyone. During the modified auditions, the playwrights already know their cast but because the plays have not yet been written, part of the challenge is to write a script tailored to their actors. Because of the abrupt shift to distance learning and a state-wide lockdown, we were forced to cancel the in-person plans that we had to hold the festival. We moved the event date back by a couple of weeks to allow more time to plan. Diverging from typical practice, the playwrights wrote their plays before knowing their cast.

The consequence of this shift in schedule and the playwrights writing without knowing their cast was that we ran into challenges appropriately casting the plays. The playwrights, understandably, wrote plays that reflected their own visions, but as we had a very limited, volunteer casting pool with which to work, it was a challenge to provide each team with the actors that they needed to fit their scripts. We tried to cast appropriately, but we did not have actors to fit every play. In some cases, the playwrights adjusted their characters to better fit their actors (changing gender and/or age), and in other cases, when the actors were not able to match the character's ethnic identity, the process became more focused on developing the script. If we do this process remotely again, I would advocate for keeping the casting-before-writing step so particular actors become part of the "givens" for the playwright.

One of the most helpful tools that our student playwrights and dramaturgs had during the 2020 festival was an enhanced Zoom account that allowed them to host meetings of any length and size. While this expansion of the number of "rooms" available freed us from our typical challenge of securing spaces, the use of Zoom to rehearse had downsides. It was difficult to "drop in" and quietly observe the process without disrupting it. It was also difficult to have a "side conversation" with the dramaturg. The online rehearsal hall flattens the hierarchy in some helpful ways, as all contributions and contributors are given equal focus, but this format makes brief check-ins "in the hallway" difficult. While one can use the chat function to discreetly message one other person on Zoom, it can be difficult to have a free-flowing exchange with them via that channel.

When we meet in person, I can walk around the theatre building and drop in on the rehearsals happening to check on everyone's progress. When we gather over lunch, the barrier is very low to connect with everyone working on the project. In this new way of working, I had to make an effort to reach out to each dramaturg to check on their progress. The groups organized their own rehearsals and didn't routinely share that information with those not on the team. The autonomy was useful but also reduced the communal feeling of the festival. Uncharacteristically, I had relatively little knowledge of what was happening with each play until our abbreviated tech rehearsal. I reached out directly to each dramaturg at the end of every rehearsal day to keep lines of communication open, see how things were going, and ask what their team needed.

In performance, the collaborators made ambitious choices to stage the ten-minute plays as fully as possible with the actors on Zoom, each in their own homes, to an audience watching remotely. This involved a fair amount of experimenting with actors turning their Zoom videos on and off, trying out different lighting and different locations in the actors' homes, and finding props and costumes around the house. A play that was written for two actors in a car was cleverly staged with the actors sitting in their actual cars while performing the show.

Directors experimented with actors speaking to one another by directing their gaze toward one side of the screen in an attempt to make it look as though they were speaking to one another. Others worked with direct address into the Zoom camera as a way to have the actors speak to each other but also to the audience. In one play, the playwright set the scene on either side of a closed door; the premise was a romantic couple having a fight as one of them locked herself in the bathroom. This separation was effective on Zoom, as we saw one actor in her bathroom speaking to a closed door and her fellow actor pleading with a closed door in his hallway. The innovative approaches taken by the teams were inspiring, even when they were not entirely successful; it was useful to see how we could push the boundaries of the new tools at our disposal.

What did the dramaturgs take away from this process? They developed three main skill sets: networking in virtual spaces, creative collaboration with technology, and providing constructive feedback to their team. Some reported that they had challenges connecting with their team. It is difficult to have the more informal gabbing that happens before rehearsals, during breaks, and as one walks to the parking lot with collaborators. The teams are nearly all strangers to one another, and establishing a rapport can be difficult, but this process is also a skill that can be developed through relatively low-stakes experiences like this one. The students built up their repertoire of ways to connect with collaborators as well as their skills connecting through virtual platforms.

Dramaturgs were involved in brainstorming ideas to stage these plays in the most effective ways possible. They tried out different Zoom features, virtual backgrounds, and settings to help their teams create an engaging event that came as close as possible to staging the playwright's work. Dramaturgs were part of the process of discovering the strengths and weaknesses of the new platform and how to connect to virtual audiences. Giving playwrights feedback is always a delicate process. Especially when the playwrights are new, the relationship between the dramaturg and playwright is only a few weeks old, and the process has been shifted to a new modality. The dramaturgs navigated all these variables quite effectively to help their team reach their potential. I also learned a number of lessons about reaching out to students regularly, proactively asking them what they need, and supporting them as they become full-fledged creative collaborators.

Kristin Leahey, Boston University School of Theatre: Fall 2020 Virtual New Play Workshops

In our second case study, Boston University workshopped new plays by School of Theatre MFA playwriting candidates and BFA conservatory students. With the shift from full productions to workshops, peer collaboration and pedagogical mentorship became central. As a professor in Spring 2020, I quickly realized that time operates differently online. For students to process and retain material, engage with teachers and fellow classmates, and complete assignments, these activities became even more laborious. Simultaneously, students across the United States and the world encountered, digested, and responded to the racial justice movement not only personally but through their work as artists and learners.

I reflected on my pedagogy and deeply considered our students' passionate reactions to the racial justice movement in my work in our classrooms and in the new play workshops that I help curate. To better understand the unique culture of teaching and learning in the environment of a theatre conservatory within a Research 1 university, I offer the scope and some of the demographics of the School of Theatre. Annually, the School of Theatre receives between 1,100 and 1,500 applications for our highly competitive BFA programs in performance, and design and production. We welcome between 60 and 70 newly matriculated undergraduate students each year. In total, we enroll 275 undergraduate and graduate students. Initially, a majority of the undergraduate students have a goal to become professional actors but often discover they possess other passions in solo performance, playwriting, adaptation, theatre history, and dramaturgy through classes with playwright Kirsten Greenidge and myself, as well as other faculty, and seeing work of the upperclassmen. For instance, with the new play workshops all of the undergraduates who developed plays now identify as playwrights, who also act, or playwrights/actors/dramaturgs. Prior to these experiences, they exclusively identified as actors.

Because we are a conservatory with a strong belief in the liberal arts within a dynamic university, we offer a variety of classes and a multitude of performance opportunities for students, thus allowing for them to explore expansively. Many of our students are in the Kilachand Honors College or minor or double major in subjects such as film, international relations, or a language. Additionally, students are interested in social justice work, protest movements, and racial reckoning on our predominantly liberal campus through being exposed to many different styles of thought, including our new Center for Antiracist Research founded by Ibram X. Kendi. As BU strives to offer an elite education and experience, simultaneously it is an expensive, private, urban institution with many of the undergraduates and/or their families spending over $75,000 annually on their BU education. In the College of Fine Arts, the School of Theatre has limited scholarships per year. Also, some School of Theatre students attain merit scholarships through the university (outside the College of Fine Arts) and/or financial aid (Donovan).

Considering this diverse body of students, they pursue the disciplines of acting, design, technical theatre, directing, and writing, among others and/or multiple disciplines. Along with the staff and members of the faculty, the conservatory of students traditionally produces 30–40 shows a season. As the pandemic began during my second year at BU, I was just beginning to establish a dramaturgy program for productions. The dramaturgs receive extensive mentorship from me throughout the pre-production and production process. First, they create a dramaturgical protocol or extensive research packet, as pre-production work. At the same time, they collaborate closely with the rest of the artistic and design team on the concept of the production. They also perform a text analysis of the work and provide support, questions, and notes for playwrights on new plays. Subsequently, they attend first rehearsals and prepare and deliver dramaturgical presentations for the company. And they then attend rehearsal and designer runs and previews for the shows to provide more support and notes and, in many cases, create lobby displays or online resources to share their research with audiences. And, finally, they facilitate post-show discussions. Dramaturgs have become a vibrant part of the season, as they were in the fall of 2020. All of these steps transferred to the remote modality relatively seamlessly, as they didn't require a physical space.

Unlike the consistency of the evolving dramaturgy program in the season, much of the rest of the Fall 2020 School of Theatre season needed to be reimagined. Primarily, this adaptation was necessary because of the effects of the pandemic. And, similar to the rest of the university and the world of theatre, we needed to pivot to remote productions and readings/workshops or forgo the season entirely. Additionally, there was a call to action and for change from students responding to the racial justice movement and their own experiences in the School of Theatre. The production calendar for the School of Theatre is arduous, and students find it relentless in addition to classes, work commitments, and maintaining life necessities. From the students there was a desire to slow down and produce less. Additionally, they were concerned about the work the School of Theatre produces, which was predominantly by white, male artists and dominated by the MFA graduate directors choosing shows that fit their needs for their course of study. In the sophomore, junior, and senior classes in the School of Theatre, 40% of the students in each class identify as BIPOC and about 55% or more in each class are women and/or of expansive gender identities (Donovan). The students want to do more work that they identify with and have greater agency in bringing to fruition, hence the new play workshops were ideal. Typically, a season planning committee composed of faculty, students, and staff propose the season at BU, but the Director of the School of Theatre primarily decides the season. The originally selected season for 2020–2021 included many newer works; the writers possessed close connections to the School of Theatre. The Director also programmed Michel Marc Bouchard's *Christina, The Girl King*—an ambitious project for our student designers. Twenty-five more shows for the conservatory still needed to be selected for the 2020–2021 season when we moved to remote learning in the spring of 2020.

Rehearsals and productions already in process in the spring of 2020 attempted to adapt to Zoom. As with many other theatre education programs, directors assumed rehearsals could continue within the same traditional timeframes, assumptions which ultimately failed in practice. For instance, a very skilled director tried to transfer and maintain a production of *Anyone Can Whistle* on Zoom. It proved nearly impossible for students to sustain on Zoom for the same number of rehearsal hours, let alone simultaneously sing on the platform. Prior to remote learning, few of our faculty employed online learning tools such as Blackboard, and most lacked previous experience with Zoom. Considering the lack of prep time for the transition, faculty and staff did their best to adapt to the given circumstances and additional stressors created by the pandemic. Rehearsals sometimes ran for five hours on Zoom; directors attempted to sing-through musicals when only one voice could be heard at a time; and advisors tried to envision what pivots they could provide for MFA lighting design candidates, who needed bodies in spaces to do their work. Simultaneously, the global theatre landscape immediately halted. Productions initially were all delayed and then eventually canceled; offices shut down; employees furloughed and then laid off; questions began to be realistically raised if theatre would ever return, particularly if no vaccine became available.

As a pivot in the fall of 2020, the Director and faculty decided to pursue nine new play development workshops online rather than the traditional 15 or more fully produced productions. Workshops of the pieces by graduates and undergraduates, culminating in Zoom readings for virtual audiences, offered the students more agency, provided experiences conducive to the time constraints, and showcased more nontraditional, in-process work. The conservatory students acted, directed, "dream" designed, produced, and dramaturged these new plays performed on Zoom. This was the first time that students were granted so much agency, and so many women of color, queer women, and female playwrights became central to the season and were the creators of the bulk of the work. Workshops received only 29 hours of rehearsal, to decelerate the School of Theatre's frenetic production pace and combat Zoom fatigue. For many dramaturgs, this was their first experience working on a new play. For many of the playwrights, this was their first experience workshopping a play, and, in many cases, the first or second play they had written. For all of us, this was our first pandemic and this was our first experience working with students on Zoom to develop new work. One playwright stated in an interview:

> I think that Zoom theatre has opened up a new genre of playwriting. Specifically a moment that stuck out during the process was when we needed to add someone to read the stage directions. With Zoom theatre being primarily virtual reads, as a playwright, I realized the importance of stage directions. Since *Welcome Home*, I have been told that I am a playwright whose stage directions are almost their own character. I think that this was heavily influenced by the fact that my first playwriting experience was in the pandemic. I learned how important they are and therefore they have become one of the most important elements in my writing. (Playwright)

As an instructor, I trained as one of BU's Learn from Anywhere facilitators during the summer of 2020. Sponsored by the Center for Teaching and Learning and the Provost's Office, the Learn from Anywhere program provided us additional support in online learning, access to research, and to serve as contacts for our colleagues to transition to the online modality. "Trauma-Informed Teaching and Learning Online: Principles & Practices During a Global Health Crisis" (Baez), an infographic that was developed by social workers to assist pedagogues, became an indispensable resource (Figure 11.1). I used this document to inform both my classroom pedagogy and the way I contributed to the curation of the online workshop season. For instance, it recommends instructors to "create class routines or rituals." More or less, I shared a class agenda at every meeting, and I also built in recurring breaks. I used these practices to create consistencies within a world of inconsistency and emergency. Applying these principles to rehearsals and production, students met within a limited rehearsal timeframe. Creating these structures prevented exhaustion. They also aligned with antiracist practices, such as decelerating the rehearsal process, implementing individual check-ins and check-outs, establishing collective agreements and terms of communication, and encouraging and taking multiple breaks. Additionally, students self-selected to enter the casting process for the new play workshops and a majority of them were BIPOC, women, and LGBTQIA.

The rituals the artistic teams developed in their rehearsal rooms introduced a sense of calm and consistency, and also fostered a feeling of family. One playwright reflected on her collaboration with her director:

> I was really thankful to have had a process that was not as fast as what it would have been in person, because it gave me time to really sit with the material other than what I had written. One of the first discussions I had with

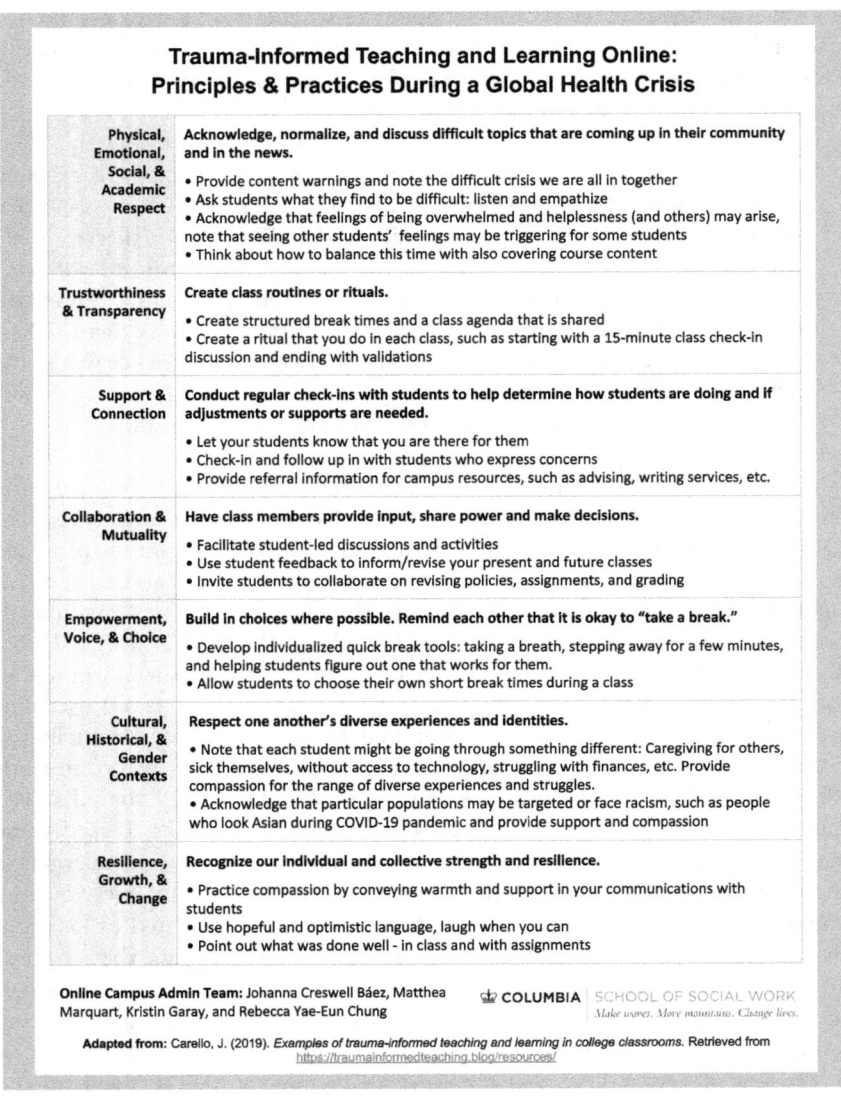

Figure 11.1 Trauma informed teaching and learning during a global health crisis.

my director was about materials that had inspired my work other than my personal experiences after she had prompted me with what made me write my play. I sat down with her on Zoom and went through movies, books, essays, YouTube clips, photos, and musical selections that I felt best embodied my work and how it came to be. (Playwright)

In addition to the collaborative nature of the forum of developing work via Zoom, students reported that the virtual rehearsal space provided some respite to the myriad obstacles they encountered in their work, school, and private lives because of the aberrant reality generated by the pandemic, confronting racial injustice, reexamining systems, and navigating the pandemic's economic fallout. The infographic also advocates recognizing "our individual and collective strength and resilience" (Baez). In general, our students practice this with each other and with me at BU, but I think there existed a hyperawareness, particularly being on Zoom, of the actions and words used in the remote space. Another recommendation raised by the infographic included: "Practice compassion by conveying warmth and support in your communications with students." We wanted to afford our students the agency to manage their own processes while supporting their needs. Additionally, we wanted to be sure that the designers could "dream" a palette that they could share and collaborate on with the entire artistic team and then share with the wider audience if the plays were eventually staged. As a mentor, I oversaw one of the projects from start to finish, meeting with the team during some of their pre-production meetings, advocating for them during the casting process, and attending runs and their final presentation. As an advisor for the dramaturgs, we met multiple times throughout the process and discussed how the dramaturgical work included but also went beyond the research, the creation of protocols, and immediate, in-the-room Google search findings. Even more than I traditionally do in my mentorship, I relayed to them how the art of new play development dramaturgy depends on building relationships; offering questions of the play, the process, and the trajectory of the work; and serving as another interlocutor in the rehearsal room and in meetings with the artistic team. I encouraged them to build strong relationships, even remotely or safely in-person, practicing social distancing with their playwrights and directors, so they were unified during this unprecedented time. Dramaturgs attended more rehearsals than they traditionally do, participated in casting, helped plan rehearsals and alternative activities for the teams, met with their cohorts over meals, and also met with me. They helped translate these new works for audiences online by designing PowerPoint Zoom displays, multimedia videos, and other forms of digital presentations. They curated music for pre- and post-shows and created websites for artists and productions. Throughout the process, the dramaturgs played integral roles in an attempt to adapt and also help translate the enthusiasm of their fellow artists during this time of change.

In response to these immersions, I surveyed the students about their engagement in their new play workshops and then, secondly, how they conducted themselves online.[1] In regard to challenges that students felt working online, they commented on the feelings of "isolation" and "remoteness" and the hardship of creating an "inviting environment." Also, they acknowledged technical difficulties. But they felt that working on Zoom also offered great benefits, allowing them to focus on the play development. One director described working remotely as "a choice" and not "all-consuming"; it created boundaries between rehearsal and life. In many cases they attempted to overcome the obstacles of Zoom, through the work itself. For instance, a playwright reported:

> The play was meant to emulate the feeling of shutting off the computer and going outside or taking deep breaths. Working remotely allowed us to further explore this concept, and the creative team made deliberate choices in the rehearsal room in order to nurture this sensation, such as prompting actors to bring in short videos featuring the outdoors. Prompts like these lent to a sense of community and solidarity. (Playwright, August)

Teams shared more dramaturgical material remotely than they customarily would, and they did so vis-à-vis PowerPoint, Google Drives, and Pinterest. In general, the playwrights commented on the workshop structure of creating "a relaxed atmosphere lacking the pressure of a finished product" and a desirable "flexible" process. They felt they could easily adapt the schedule to fit their writing needs. Also, many of the groups reported developing a deep camaraderie with their artistic team. A playwright said,

> The lack of physical resources available to us and the lack of a formal end result provided the most important resource of all: time. Time to focus solely on the strength of the text and discussions with actors that weren't tied up in their motivations for their blocking." (Playwright, August)

I asked them what each of them learned about their individual artistic roles. A director said, "I truly learned how to focus on the play, to generate conversation, refine my 'people skills.'" A playwright responded, "I feel more comfortable having a more hands-on approach to developing a script and speaking in a creative space." Another playwright said that by collaborating she realized they can be involved as much as she liked in the process—sometimes present and very active and other times observant and absorbing. A director said that they "creat[ed] a nurturing but also critical space." In general, the students articulated that the genre of new play making became one of their favorite forms of theatre, as well as an avenue of expression for them as directors, writers, actors, designers, and dramaturgs working collaboratively.

Looking to the Future with New Play Dramaturgy in Virtual Rehearsal Rooms

Despite seemingly insurmountable hurdles, both case studies demonstrate models that embody the effectiveness of the dramaturgical sensibility in teaching both collaboration and how to develop new work. Aspects of both processes will be preserved from this significant period of connecting remotely. The new play festival at SDSU will continue to be offered annually but will reconvene in-person. Proactively checking in with student dramaturgs will remain part of the protocol as will making use of remote rehearsal rooms when needed. The new play work at Boston University remains robust, but the conservatory program will return to the production of more pre-existing work, producing at least 20 shows during the 2021–2022 season. Important aspects that we will preserve from the virtual new play development model include: a focus on student-centered learning, applying a process-over-product lens, and implementing a cadre of antiracist rehearsal practices (practices this essay just begins to address). As demonstrated by both of these case studies—from opposite sides of the country—dramaturgy prevailed in inherently centering the creation process. Additionally, despite members of artistic teams working thousands of miles away from each other, virtual collaborations helped make visible the areas where both students and teachers need to continue to learn, reflect, and progress.

Note

1 I would like to thank the following students for contributing interview responses for the chapter and their incredible work on these new plays during the excruciating Fall of 2020: Henry Braff, Emma Foley, Rebecca Freeman, Samuel Theobald, Emily Trantanella, and McKayla Witt. To protect their identities, I have intentionally not attributed their quotations from the interviews. I would also like to thank my Boston University colleagues; fellow advisor and informal producer for this project; and additional interview contributor Associate Professor Kirsten Greenidge, as well as our Associate Director of the School of Theatre and Recruiter McCaela Donovon.

References

Baez, Johanna C., et al. "Trauma-Informed Teaching and Learning Online: Principles & Practices During a Global Health Crisis." March 2020. Columbia University's School of Social Work. Retrieved from https://academiccommons.columbia.edu/doi/10.7916/d8-gc9d-na95

Donovon, McCaela. Interview by Kristin Leahey. Email, October 2021. Playwright. Interview by Kristin Leahey. Email, August 2021.

Playwright. Interview by Kristin Leahey. Email, November 2021.

Chapter 12

Re-Making Rehearsal and Performance

Intersections of Collaboration and Accessibility in a Hybrid *Romeo & Juliet*

Dennis Schebetta

Traditionally, theatre artists build ensemble collaboration through engaging with each other physically in a rehearsal studio. But our efforts in the past to create this idea of "ensemble" could conflict with our efforts to be inclusive and allow for diversity. During the 2020 global pandemic, health restrictions and lockdowns forced all of us to imagine rehearsal and performance anew. Theatre artists discovered new methods of creating ensemble and collaborating online, often changing the conversation around collaboration and accessibility. In developing adaptive methods and redefining our flexibility, we better served those students who didn't have the access or privilege of being physically available for rehearsal. Our task now as theatre artists will be to continue to use these remote tools in the future so that we may enhance collaboration and access, to use technology to re-make a more inclusive rehearsal and performance space.

In this chapter, I will summarize my rehearsal and filming process for a hybrid production of *Romeo & Juliet* at Siena College in upstate New York. We began in-person rehearsals in January 2020 with a scheduled opening of April. When the college went remote, we transformed our plans for an in-person production to a hybrid film/video performance using the same actors, set and design elements—rewriting the script, planning scenes with a limited number of cast and crew, conducting hybrid rehearsals, and organizing a three-week shooting schedule in the early fall semester. Health restrictions prevented us from even performing a full run with our large cast and crew, much less filming it for online viewing (such as *Hamilton* on Disney+). One couldn't label what we did as a film adaptation, because we were not employing cinematography techniques with interior and exterior scenes (we did not, for example, have the budget that the National Theatre did when they adapted their professional version of *Romeo & Juliet* in 2020, directed by Simon Godwin).

I argue that a hybrid model of theatre production unlocks exciting ideas about collaboration as it also creates greater access and availability for both performers and audience. Furthermore, hybrid theatre production develops techniques for acting on stage and for the camera (both online and film). Whereas most

DOI: 10.4324/9781003229056-16

university acting curricula separate stage and camera into two different techniques, highlighting the differences in the mediums, a hybrid model brings the tool sets together, allowing students to experience overlap in technique as it also teaches them to adapt their skills to fit the medium.

Most importantly, health, safety and consent-based practices were tied to the ideas of inclusion in all ways, including the scheduling and production timeline. As any student could be quarantined at any time, the schedule needed to be flexible enough to modify and continue onwards, without any sense of guilt or shame being thrown at the student. The production accepted that the health of the individual outweighed the needs of the production.

While the traditional mode of "live" in-person theatre-making will always have value, this re-making of rehearsal and performance through a hybrid process liberates us to adapt to the needs of the ensemble, instead of the other way around. As conversations in our rehearsal rooms focus more and more on safety and both physical and mental health, as well as consent-based practices, how far will we choose to go to adapt our practices, not for the sake of a production, but for the sake of our student actors?

Setting the Scene: "A Plague O' Both Your Houses"

For our production of *Romeo & Juliet*, there was an image posted on social media of the ghost light sitting on a wooden platform of the set in the theatre auditorium of Foy Hall at Siena College. The light created dramatic shadows on wooden walls, slats and beams, reminiscent of an old mine, meant to represent the western frontier of Verona City. Students left that ghost light sitting there as they departed for spring break, but never returned for technical rehearsals as the college, like others, shifted to remote learning. The ghost light: this evocative image became the theatre world's symbol of the pandemic.

Many other theatres and schools had opted for some virtual presentation or remote reading to showcase the work students had done before the shutdown, but our team agreed that a public virtual presentation online would not convey the elements of this production. Set in the 1860s of a booming Nevada town in the desert hills, the production included live music, singing, dancing, and stage combat with whips, guns, and bowie knives. It was part wild west show and part classical theatre. The ensemble had collaborated intensely in-person to bring all these elements together, and the desire to share the work was like a flame that wouldn't die out.

In April, unsure of the future of the production, we scheduled a final reading with the cast on Zoom and recorded it, hoping to bring some finality and closure to all the hard work the cast and production team had done so far. An unsatisfying feeling loomed over us all, like the virtual background of the online reading, the image of the ghost light sitting on the wooden platform of our set.

A Hybrid Process

As I had experience with film production and direction, I pitched adapting the production into a hybrid theatre/film/video. At the time, I wasn't exactly sure what that would entail. I knew all the design elements were ready to implement. It could be a matter of solving the logistics of scheduling time on the completed set in order to film actors in costume with lighting, and then edit it. As it would be unsafe due to COVID restrictions to have all 16 cast members and dozen crew members in the building at once, it would not be feasible to simply film a run-through of a performance, commonly done for archival purposes. We hadn't even completed the technical needs of the production, and the students had not even done a run-through with the entire cast (several had conflicts or were out with the flu before the break). But film, unlike theatre, is not reliant on all actors being in the room at the same time, even if they are in the same scene. Film schedules could be broken up into using only an actor's time for specific scenes. After several meetings in April and May, and as the college's guidelines for returning to campus became more clear, we formed a strategy that might anticipate safety protocols and a method of working in this new way.

As the students would not return to campus until the following fall semester, the plan was to adapt the script into a screenplay in the summer and begin hybrid rehearsals in August, which would shift to in-person filming over a three-week period in mid-September. Ideally, the final product would be edited and completed by the end of the academic semester.

The strategy had to accommodate many factors: changing health guidelines, COVID status of the college, different schedules of the students, use of equipment, as well as potential delays due to anyone needing to be quarantined. Of great concern was managing the mental health, anxiety, and stress of the students.

Rehearsal Process and Timeline

It's important to note that much of what we were able to accomplish was because of the initial in-person foundational work done in the rehearsal studio before this hybrid process. From day one, the priority was on the actor's safety as we reviewed guidance for physical acting and movement, whether that was stage combat or intimacy. Having been recently introduced to the practices of consent-based work and intimacy direction by Claire Warden of Intimacy Directors and Coordinators (IDC) as well as the work of Theatrical Intimacy Education, it was important to me that students felt empowered and aware of their own boundaries. From the beginning of rehearsal, safety and health were vital to the success of the production, and this foundation was also beneficial throughout.

The online reading in April made me aware of a few benefits and challenges to the pivot we were about to make. First, the students were able to connect and be present with each other online, but as most of the students were trained only in theatre, many did not know how to work with the camera. Furthermore, many students didn't have a neutral space they could use at home or in their dorm rooms as an online "acting studio" and so were sitting at their desks, roommates studying on a bed behind them. Other students had terrible Wi-Fi connections and their faces would freeze or the audio would go in and out. The benefit of that was that it did cause the actors to listen in a new way, as suddenly the performance was not what they were used to. Before bidding a fond farewell and sending them to their "shelter in place" summer, I let the actors know that shifting from theatre to film was going to require different skills and a modified process that they needed to be prepared for. First, their intentions needed to be crystal clear, as the camera is like a microscope picking up every untruthful action. Second, the intensity of the moment, particularly in the language, still needed to be high; what they needed to adjust to was the shift from playing to the back of the house to playing to an audience of one (the camera). Third, we would be shooting out of sequence and sometimes they would have to play a scene with actors not physically present in the room (so would need to engage with their imagination and be specific). I also informed that some blocking may change as we made changes to adjust for camera angles.

The script changed formats from a play with five acts and twenty-six scenes into a film with fifty-five scenes, some of them as short as only a few lines, while the longest (Romeo and Juliet's balcony scene) was eight minutes of running time. The necessity of breaking up the script was not merely for cinematic reasons, but for health and safety. Scenes were altered so that only a minimal number of actors would be needed at any time. Although the theatre at Siena seated about 300), the maximum COVID occupancy would put us at our maximum when we included the crew and production team. Also, everyone, actors included, would be masked. As one of *Romeo & Juliet*'s plot points actually revolves around the complexities of a pandemic (the message to Romeo from Father Lawrence is delayed due to a plague), we embraced the aesthetic of a world that was dealing with their own outbreak. A simple added design element of a bandanna or cloth mask was integrated into the costume design and the world of our play.

Rehearsals began in late August with an online reading of the revised screenplay. Almost all of the original cast were available. With the aid of online auditions, missing roles were quickly filled. The first rehearsal was a review of important information about this shift of mediums, including reviewing the script revision. Scenes had to be altered for clarity as well as for safety, but also to ensure a shorter running time (less footage means less time editing in post-production). For instance, as the actors would be wearing masks, we cut lines referring to kisses such as "Thus with a kiss I die." Scenes were shortened and broken down with specific shot headings so that we knew what the final edit would look like. For the actors it meant that they would know when we broke up the scene to include close-ups or other angles to make it feel more "filmic." One example is the opening fight scene, which had the look and feel of a classic western stand-off. The rehearsal schedule was built for safety as well as for review as actors read through scenes online through the week. Rehearsals began in late August in the outdoor tent (one of the designated classroom spaces at Siena), or on the set in the theatre space as needed. This was essentially prep for the shooting dates which would begin in the second week of September. Rehearsal and shooting days were only on Sunday through Mondays and were never longer than two or three hours. For some actors, it was considerably less. One of the first and most important in-person rehearsals was the review of the stage combat sequences. Test footage of this rehearsal was edited together to give us some visual "storyboards" that we would use for a later edit, but also built confidence in the actors and production team. Fight choreography on film looks even more authentic than on stage, even when actors are practicing social distancing!

The greatest challenge of this project was that the production team had to create several contingency plans. Our main focus shifted from "putting up a show" to ensuring every member of the team was safe and healthy. The additional challenge was that most of the students and faculty were experienced with theatre production timelines, but not as well-versed with workflow for a film. In essence, the stage manager became the 1st AD and learned the importance of the shot list and how to schedule each scene for the day, juggling what actors might need to for a costume change or who can be released.

For filming, we set up three cameras: a stationary GoPro for wide and establishing shots at center and two other mobile cameras with student operators on either side of the house. After a few days of filming, we were able to find some ideal marks and placement for general blocking, with additional shots set up for any special moments such as close ups or shots to make it seem like there were more people on stage than there actually were. The benefit of not filming a live theatrical performance was that the cameras could be placed anywhere on the stage, even on the balcony, creating a filmic aesthetic, even though it was still being performed like a stage play.

A challenge for many of the actors was adjusting to the medium. Part of my job as director and acting coach was to remind them that their audience was an audience of one: the camera. As I coached actors, I related how filming is similar to the way we might stop and start and work specific moments in earlier rehearsals. The fact that the students hadn't done a run-through of the whole show in months was actually an advantage, as students found diving in and out of scenes reminiscent of the work they had done earlier. As an acting coach and director, my emphasis was on the adaptations and coaching them to specifically look at key focus points or open themselves up for a more interesting camera angle. As they all had lavalier microphones, projecting to the back of the house wasn't necessary, but the actors still needed to be clear and specific in their choices. Although Shakespeare is poetic and grand, there needed to be a balance of truthfulness that could work with the camera techniques they were learning.

Pedagogical Benefits of the Hybrid Process

When the lockdown occurred, like many theatre instructors, I was focused on the challenges and disadvantages of trying to teach acting or directing remotely, not to mention how to make some form of "live" theatre using remote tools. From working on this production, though, I recognized that there were pedagogical benefits to both remote and in-person experiences, especially as this process was a unique opportunity to examine performing Shakespeare's text in different mediums.

Most acting classes in undergraduate training compartmentalize the mediums of performance, with introductory classes focused on the basics of acting and then intermediate and advanced acting classes building upon that, but primarily centered around the live in-person theatrical experience. After this foundational work, students then engage in acting for the camera, whether that be for film, TV or web-based programming. In this hybrid model, we were able to examine the adjustments that actors had to make from stage to film *at the same time*. This was peculiar and demanding for all. One reason why we might approach training this way is that we are product-based or product-oriented; actors work on a scene from a play as if it will be performed in a theatre space or actors work on a scene from a film to be shot with a camera. However, this process made me realize how important it is for teachers to differentiate to students the way actors can craft for different mediums and how necessary this will be as a skill.

In the first remote rehearsals, I gave special guidance on camera technique. The benefit (although it also can be a drawback) with students acting on a platform like Zoom or Skype is that there is a self-view feature that can be distracting. But when teaching camera acting, it's a great tool to help them understand how the effects of different types of shots, camera angles, lighting adjustments, and sound techniques can help tell the story. This early foundational work supplied a vocabulary and understanding that I could refer to later on when filming in-person.

Using Shakespearean text for this hybrid approach was also useful in that in order to fill up this poetic text, they needed to embody the power of their instrument (voice/body). When they achieve that kind of clarity in thought, action and voice, only then will that specificity translate for working on the camera. As I kept telling the actors, "It's not about being smaller" as some believe, but about being specific and going deeper. As Michael Caine noted, the scale may be smaller, "but the intensity is just as great" (9). As we worked in the physical theatre space, it was easy for us to discuss the differences in playing to different mediums by physicalizing the idea of an audience in the theatre space as opposed to the audience of one, the camera. With soliloquies delivered directly to the audience, such as Romeo's, this process became even more advantageous in heightening this principle. In the balcony scene, for example, there were several moments of instruction to the actor where we discussed how Romeo would deliver a line out to the whole audience and then how he might deliver that line if it was just one audience member (the camera). The actor was excited by the realization that saying the line, "But soft, what light through yonder window breaks!" has the same energy and dynamic when spoken to a crowded theatre as it does to an audience of one. Building these skills of adjustment—not just artistic adjustments to directing choices, but technical adjustments to simultaneous mediums—is a skill that will be essential for actors entering into an industry that is ever-evolving. As more and more theatres integrate film, AR and VR into performances, an actor who understands how to adjust technique for different mediums will be highly valued.

Another benefit of this hybrid model was that the lighting designer was based in the west coast and still able to be included in all aspects of the process. In the early weeks of production, before the pandemic sent everyone home, we were already asking him to videoconference into production meetings. He was planning to arrive at Siena for technical rehearsals in April, but of course, that never happened. As we went into our film shoot, a travel ban for New York state was still in place. So, he continued to use the web videoconferencing to be "in the room" for all lighting design changes. He watched a live feed from the GoPro so he would know exactly how the lighting looked on camera. He then relayed changes remotely to the lighting technician at the lighting board.

Integrating Accessibility with Collaboration

Almost a decade ago, director, author, and co-founder of DNAWORKS, Daniel Banks, challenged the language used in theatrical practices when he wrote "The Welcome Table: Casting for an Integrated Society." In his argument, he references John Berger's *Ways of Seeing* and that our relationship to the world is based on how we see it, or how we think we see it. This issue is larger than just a casting issue, of course, and extends into our culture and practice, into our very definition of theatre as well as definitions of words like "acting," "collaboration," and "presence." In the past year and a half, we have seen many versions of "live" theatre, where actors have been collaborating and been present through digital realms. I have been resistant myself and in conversation with others who deny this idea that any type of hybridization of theatre with the use of film or video is no longer theatre. There is an emphasis on the actor-audience relationship dynamic inherent in the "live-ness" of theatre that the physical presence of both actors and audience in the same physical space creates something unique that cannot be replicated any other way. What we have discovered, though, is that suddenly theatre is able to connect and reach out to more than just a small audience. Audiences can interact not just with the digital actor, but with chats and messaging and the digital tools that the medium like a video conference platform might give us. With a hybrid performance, audiences in the physical space can have a completely different experience than audiences who may be watching through a virtual platform, both watching the same show through a different perspective. A wider audience reach means more accessibility as audience members may not be limited by their own physical disabilities or financial barriers to seeing the production. For recorded performances, this means audiences who may have a job or family commitments can watch at a later time.

Conversations about consideration of our actors, crew, and audience have been ongoing in the world of disability and access. Although theatres and departments may consider access for theatre-goers, many don't consider access as a primary and necessary tool of collaboration. Here, a dramaturg could be a useful ally and advocate in the room, as Seattle-based dramaturg Andrea Kovich explains in her essay "Envisioning Change":

> I envision a future where there are accessible options for theatregoers to engage in both virtual and in-person events. A future where accessibility is so intrinsic to our work that theatremakers automatically think about who can access what we are creating and how they will be able to do so. A future where organizations recognize accessibility as a core value along with equity, diversity, and inclusion, and where the depths of their commitment to these core values is apparent in everything they do. A future where there are widespread productions with integrated accessibility to amplify inclusion. (Kovich)

The challenge and the large question for us as theatre-makers, a question that Kovich poses, is that we are in such a rush to go back to "normal" when we have the option of choosing new ways of working, a way of moving forward, not back. This hybrid model could be one way of creating this "integrated accessibility."

During the pandemic, we all banded together because everyone was experiencing the same global event. Everyone was experiencing trauma in various degrees, some worse than others. We all made sacrifices on many levels and in doing so, had empathy for our colleagues and our students. In my region, there were many signs on the doors of shops and businesses with a mask on it and the motto, "Stronger together."

But as we work in-person regularly again, embracing practices in a post-pandemic world, remember that even if we did eradicate this one virus, there are myriad other ways that people can struggle or need accommodations and access. There will be other disorders, diseases, or disabilities. There will still be immunocompromised people or others suffering from mental health, stress, and anxiety. As we rehearsed or taught theatre in a time when we all felt vulnerable and needed accommodations, we also extended a mutual understanding that if someone could not attend in-person, it was with good cause related to health and safety (their own or others). But is this feeling of solidarity only something we can sustain when all are experiencing trauma, or can we extend the same empathy and be inclusive even if it is only a small number of the team? Can we make accommodations part of our theatrical practice in the same way we are embracing consent-based practices?

Banks makes an argument that theatre practitioners and educators can make conscious choices about how they create a season, or a production based on the talents of the casting pool (as well as the gender, race, sexuality identity, or ability). He states:

> What curricular changes could happen so that the first priority in planning an academic season is for directors to choose plays to fit the talents of all the students and give them room for personal and professional growth?"
>
> (22)

If we rephrase this sentence to extend consideration and asked, "so that the first priority in planning an academic season is for directors to choose plays that fit the *mental and health needs* of the students?" we may then consider alternatives to how we schedule auditions, callbacks, rehearsals, and performances. Technology has shown us that access is available if we are willing to make it a priority and engage in the work as if our life depended on it, because at one point it actually did.

By example, the rehearsal and shooting schedule of *Romeo & Juliet* was driven by the main objective of health and safety. We ensured there was only a limited number of students in each scene for filming. We kept specific times for costume and wardrobe, staggering actor calls to limit traffic. The shooting days were always under three hours because we knew that, even with masks, it would be more advisable for air quality to keep contact in the space to a minimum. The rehearsal and shooting schedule also consisted of only four days a week, with an understanding that students may or may not be able to attend. We shifted scenes for shooting on a daily basis, which is actually not that uncommon with film, anyway. At one point, a few students were not able to attend for their scheduled scenes due to contract tracing and possible exposure. We had anticipated that and it wasn't viewed negatively or with any shaming. We simply modified the schedule. Many of the students wanted to attend rehearsals and shooting, even when they had conflicts, not just out of duty to the project, but accountability to each other. From the very beginning of the rehearsal process, we created a culture of student empowerment, putting focus on health, safety, as well as consent-based practices (mostly related to stage combat and intimacy). Consent-based practices must be tied to inclusion in all aspects of the production including the schedule.

By its very nature, live and in-person theatre is exclusive. Accessibility will always be a challenge that must be considered. Actors and spectators gather in-person in a physical space, and that physical space only holds so many people. Even the largest Broadway houses or stadiums can only hold so many people. Conversely, exclusivity goes down when you consider that all one needs to view a film, television or streaming show is a monitor, a DVD Player, or web connection. Imagine a theatre that could hold millions of people—that's the potential difference.

Moving Forward

It may be helpful to think of hybrid performance on a scale ranging from zero to ten, rather than a binary relationship of live/digital. A production that has no scheduled in-person performance for an audience but is a video/film version could be a way of re-imagining technical and dress rehearsals to accommodate all students who want to be included. As many professional theatre companies are currently transitioning out of long work hours such as the "10 out of 12" rehearsal, the academic world should replicate that same professional and inclusive practice; there is no need to keep students tied up in a theatre building for an entire weekend. Allowing for video/filming techniques to be included in the process means finding ways of breaking up the time so that each student can give time needed. Students with small roles can adapt and be flexible, rehearsing and filming as they are able to, while lead actors, usually more experienced students, can take the heavier load and time commitment of rehearsals and filming.

Of course, the film/video model for online distribution misses the in-person actor/audience connection that feels like the essence of live theatre. A hybrid approach that attempts both an in-person performance as well as a remote performance is a way to give students the "liveness" of performance as well as the challenge of camera technique. This could be achieved in different ways, depending on the needs of the students.

Of course, not every theatre department has the technical equipment or experience to create a live theatrical version of a production as well as a filmed version for streaming. Not every theatre practitioner is familiar or comfortable with different mediums such as video or streaming. A university or school has to consider the cost of resources. The cost is not only personnel and equipment, but also a longer amount of time in preparation, especially for the administration, directors, and production managers. There is a cost in payment for theatrical live performance rights as well as streaming or video rights. As we were producing a classical work in the public domain, however, this was not an issue. With new plays and playwrights, this could be a viable option as performance rights could encompass several types of audiences, physical and virtual (The Dramatists Guild of America has recently recommended certain digital and livestream rights to contracts, as well as a new Inclusion Rider).

Even though it is an added task to produce and create a hybrid experience as I've outlined here, it is hard to imagine theatre in the future that doesn't include some kind of hybrid technology, especially as it concerns accessibility. Creating accessibility is a cost that many institutions are willing to invest in over the long term. Even now on Broadway and in many professional regional theatres, there is technology to aid audience members with disabilities, such as those with a sight or hearing impairment, not to mention accessible entrances and exits. So why not create that same accessibility for actors, as well? Even in our post-pandemic world, there will still be immunosuppressed people wearing masks. There will still be those with physical disabilities as well as those with mental health issues, anxiety, depression, or other invisible disabilities. As Clay Martin, Artistic Director of Spectrum Ensemble states:

> Because of societal factors like the COVID pandemic, the wars we have been engaged in for the last 30 years, and the historic trauma brought on marginalized communities over centuries, it is predicted that in the future

over 50 percent of our society is going to have a disability of some kind. This is not a niche market. This is your audience.

(qtd. In Valdez, 2021)

How you adapt your productions to meet the needs of your students is how you will move forward in reaching your goals for inclusion and accessibility.

For my part, what I'm hoping to take from this model of hybrid rehearsal and performance is a multi-dimensional methodology of theatre-making that integrates accessibility with collaboration.

References

Banks, Daniel. 2013. "The Welcome Table: Casting for an Integrated Society". *Theatre Topics*, 23(1).

Caine, Michael. 2000. *Acting in Film: An Actor's Take on Movie Making*, New York: Applause.

Kovich, Andrea. 2021. "Envisioning Change: The Future is Inclusive", *HowlRound*, March 29. https://howlround.com/envisioning-change

Valdez, Samuel. 2021. "The How and the What: Access, Justice and Disability Aesthetic", *American Theatre*, Digital Issue, March 26. https://www.americantheatre.org/2021/03/26/the-how-and-the-what-access-justice-and-the-disability-aesthetic/

Chapter 13

Walking Backward on a Global Tightrope

Interview with Nassim Soleimanpour about the Virtual Performance of *White Rabbit, Red Rabbit*

Marjan Moosavi

The conception of this interview happened while we were all in an unchartered territory of a transitional period, coming out of or (in some places) going into lockdown. We were neither totally back to where we were or, neither arrived at a new normal. The perennial question for many of us became how we can play and connect in this transitional time and liminal space? On a broad level, digital tools and virtual spaces have certainly played powerfully; they extended, augmented, and connected our body, mind, and presence. Under COVID-19 pandemic conditions that theatres were closed, theatrical practices and practitioners have experienced a forced shift into the digital tools and virtual platforms which influence the performance's verve and space.

On March 13, 2021, to mark the anniversary of closing theatres due to the COVID pandemic, Nassim Soleimanpour Productions in association with Aurora Nova and one hundred other producers all around the globe invited one hundred performers globally to stage *WRRR* in various stages: theatrical venues, prison stages, and virtual platforms. This conversation with Nassim Soleimpanour focuses on the global, virtual performance of *White Rabbit, Red Rabbit* (*WRRR*) in which we talk about the shift to digital forms and how this shift has affected the way liveness becomes constituted, what happens to his playwriting "machine," his audience's experience, perception, and interaction, how we might conceive of life and performance in post-pandemic, and how he characterizes his cosmopolitan vision and practice. The conversation was conducted via email correspondence during May and June 2021. It is indeed in continuation with the conversation we have been having in recent years as friends. But first, let me introduce the play and the playwright.

WRRR is the first play written by the Iranian playwright Nassim Soleimanpour in 2011 (Moosavi, 2016). Nassim (literally meaning "breeze") was born in 1981 in Tehran and is a graduate of the University of Tehran. Before 2011, when he refused to do mandatory military service in Iran, he was denied a passport. Unable to travel, he decided to make his play travel around the world. The official website of the play says it needs no set, no rehearsal, not even a director

(Soleimanpour's Official Website). It was in the 29th Fadjr International Theatre in Tehran that Canadian theatre artist Ross Manson got familiar with Nassim and discovered his artistic talent. *WRRR* premiered in Toronto's SummerWorks 2011 as a result of a collaboration between Ross Manson (Volcano) and Daniel Brooks (Necessary Angel). Since then the play has been translated into "more than 25 different languages and has been performed over 2,000 times by some of the biggest names in theatre and film," making it "one of the most toured plays in the contemporary history of theatre!" (Soleimanpour's Official Website). Soleimanpour is known for deconstructing the binaries of director/actor or actor/spectator. His aesthetics in his later plays also revels in such binary deconstruction. His 2017 play *Nassim*, directed by Omar Elerian, is a compelling theatrical example of playful encounters that foster cultural mobility and creates de-territorialized spaces of reciprocal tolerance and cosmopolitan attitude.[1]

In online, digital performances, the multimedia platforms and digital tools extend the performer's body and theatrical temporality and liveness, and the connected participants interact across media. In the course of the live, in person, performance of *WRRR*, due to the absence of the playwright and director, the extension of the playwright's body and mind and playwright-audience connectivity are already at play. The performers of *WRRR* in live performances have been described as the "proxy" of the playwright (Barnett 2014). These proxies combine the playwright's voice to their own unique personality and embodied presence and share it with the audience who has a physical co-presence. In the virtual space, this co-presence and the interplay could oscillate between moving through and across, or experiencing a total stagnation. Speaking about the audience's experience, a variety of conditions influence the digital audience's experience and perception. *WRRR* keeps the audience members in constant doubt about what is real and fictive. While watching, they even see that the usual distinction between different theatre roles becomes less stable. They feel in a sense manipulated by the playwright and his labyrinthian narrative.

Moreover, both *WRRR* and *Nassim* are tricksy plays with the narrator as a trickster at the center and in control. In WRRR, in addition to this playful narrator, we have a rabbit that appears as a trickster when it decides to hide its ears by playing a trick to be able to enter the circus, it is caught by a bear, the gatekeeper, and is persecuted by a herd of ostrich stormtroopers. Circus and its power dynamics could be a metaphor of a country in which coercive measures cause absurd or surreal circumstances. To many, this metaphor resonates deeply. Such a playful fable carries excellent potentials for interrogating the status quo, just like what we see in Soleimanpour's playfulness with theatrical structure and aesthetics. In our conversation, he also confirmed that *"WRRR* is probably one of the most political plays of our time" but this aspect must not overshadow the worldly vision that the playwright infuses in his aesthetics. He indeed warns us against reducing it to a play merely about the political context of counties, namely Iran.

Soleimpanour's worldmindedness infuses into his life and practice. The stories in *WRRR* or *Nassim* might be about individual cases, "a generation born amidst the hardship of the Iran-Iraq war" (Soleimanpour's Official Website) or attachment to Persian, his mother tongue while living an immigrant life, but they are deftly retold from a global perspective that speaks to everyone regardless of temporal and geographical particularities. That explains why even during the pandemic his *WRRR* once again garners him global attention. Soleimanpour's cosmopolitan humanism is an invitation for us to pass the confines of our national or cultural boundaries and expand our intellectual horizons to contemplate on such universal themes as limits of obedience, collective complicity, injustice, and playful disobedience.

The virtual staging of *WRRR*, with the widest outreach of audience ever, is a remarkable example of how digital cosmopolitanism could be actualized within the very borders of the "home." Perhaps it is still too early to evaluate the success of such global Zoom stagings in empowering digital communities to practice cosmopolitan ease during a global pandemic crisis. It is one of the questions that this interview wrestles with but what we are sure about is that like deconstructing the aesthetics, this virtual staging does deconstruct the binary of the home and the world by connecting people from all over the world and presenting to its audience momentous encounters via their computer screens. On the occasion of the global staging of *WRRR*, Nassim Soleimanpour Productions issued a statement entitled "Let There Be Theatre" that clearly reveals their attentiveness to accessibility, openness, connectedness, and community enrichment:

> The Invitation: You are invited to produce White Rabbit Red Rabbit [sic] on the 13th of March, 2021 completely free of charge. The performance can happen in any kind of venue, large or small, indoors or outdoors, whatever you have access to and which is allowed under your local COVID restrictions. You may keep all income you receive for the performance but you are encouraged to donate a portion of the takings to a worthy cause, to aid someone in your community in need of help. (Although it also would be completely fine if that someone is yourself.) All you need to do is to find a suitable performer who can be of any gender or occupation (it doesn't have to be a trained actor). It is imperative however that they do not know the play or see the script before performing it in front of an audience. Think of the most famous person you call your friend!
>
> (Soleimpanour Official Website)

Digital cosmopolitanism and communal outreach are at the heart of the global, virtual performance of *WRRR*. Networked digital technologies generate collective digital imaginaries for *WRRR*'s team and audiences to manifest various cosmopolitan dispositions: experience of cosmopolitan empathy and awareness of interconnectedness. This interconnectedness, although virtual, when dovetailed with cosmopolitan dispositions, fosters an ironic distance to one's locality, nation, and culture which engages the connected people in self-reflexivity and reciprocal tolerance. The global reception of *WRRR* shows that communal self-reflexivity and evaluation of values are deservedly embraced in the course of the play's digital spectatorship. In a nutshell, the Zoom staging of *WRRR*, technological intervention and the playwright's playful manipulation are complicit; any interplay becomes more fluid, reality becomes rootless, absence thrusts forward, imagination overflows, borders fade, and connectivity grows.

Marjan Moosavi: Let's begin by talking about when and how you came to the point to adapt *White Rabbit Red Rabbit* (*WRRR*), which took you about seven years to write, for the virtual stage. What changes did you make to the narrative and structure of the play? Followed by that, I would like to know whether you consider your adaptation of *WRRR* for the virtual version a forced shift or another audacious experimentation with structure and form?

Nassim Soleimpanour- There was an immediate demand from producers around the globe. But the play needed to be revised and I was not ready. When I eventually found the time, the dynamic of change appeared to be quite organic. I tried to stay faithful to the original narrative by creating substructures that serve the new condition. A substructure is a mechanism inside the bigger machine. Think of a cog. It has a design but not a defined purpose, not on its own. You put a few cogs together and we have a substructure that has a more advanced design and a clear purpose. Such combinations create a mechanism which in turn makes the big machine. When you ask an audience member to give you a dollar, for instance, you get yourself a cog that has a design but not a clear purpose. You make the actor imitate an ostrich, there's another cog with a design and without a purpose. But when these two cogs are put together you have a substructure that has a clear purpose: personal demonstration of manipulation. But will it suffice? The audience will walk out and think they were manipulated for no reason. So you would need to create other substructures with other clear purposes like social responsibility or moral licensing. And if you manage to create a handful of high-functioning, masterly designed substructures which are perfectly put together to serve a highly valued purpose, you have created a masterpiece, an extra piece of life created by a master. Adaptation is the art of remounting a machine without losing the original design and purpose.

Think of all the changes we went through during the recent pandemic. We did our best to adapt but not lose our purpose and design. We came up with new substructures which serve the old purpose and are as much as possible faithful to the original design. I still tend to buy bio vegetables from our local store, but the procedure to go in, the experience of shopping, and consequently the tradition of cooking and dining with friends have all changed. We now try to bike to a park, bump our elbows to each other instead of a hug, and assure each other that we have followed the hygiene protocols. As much as all this was far futuristic to years ago, it is now part of our culture that will shape our future. So in a way, we are constantly doing things that are simultaneously traditional and futuristic.

We do this to have a better understanding of the presence or as much as anything to survive and enjoy survival.

MM. Right, virtual spaces and technologies turn out to be suitable tools for this correlation of traditional and futuristic living. Many consider them slow-moving and alienating. At the same time, they also present new possibilities for expressivity and prefigurative performances on a global scale. Technologies can extend the performer's body, theatrical temporality, and spatiality. How does technology affect these aspects in your virtual adaptation of *WRRR*?

NS- Technologies are not necessarily slow-moving. I am sometimes overwhelmed by the speed at which things change. This challenges the natural notion of time and space profoundly. Something I adore in theatre but hate in daily life.

What interests you have already been challenged in the original script. The show plays on the idea of the absent playwright who borrows the performer's body and twists the concepts of time and location in order to transfer us or himself into another world, a world which is free, a world which never exists. In the virtual set up these notions are challenged further, especially since the audience and the performer are as absent as the playwright. In a way, no one is there, in the empty theatre from which we are all deprived. We all join the protagonist in his deprivation which presumably adds a new layer to the experience of the show virtually.

MM. Absolutely, the virtual encounters with the performer of *WRRR* create the possibility of collective experience of physical absence. Let's look at this collective co-absence from another dimension, the performers of *WRRR* in live performances have been described as the "proxy" of you, the playwright. These proxies bring to the audience your voice and yet add their unique personality to it through their presence in a shared space with the audience. On a Zoom stage, audience members see virtual proxies of you that are presenting your voice through a *virtual* (not a real) presence. The performance, also, is live, but not live in a conventional way. I am curious about your insight into this experience of liveness and how the audience members can perceive it. I know that you were *virtually* present in Laura Linney's performance.

NS- That's not unique. I've been also present in the stage shows every now and then. To my way of thinking, what matters is not my presence. What matters is the absence of all of us. What matters is that we are all forced to refuge somewhere we do not systematically belong. Skyping with your family does not make them present. It seems to me that they often become more absent when you meet them from distance. The virtual platforms market themselves as reunion opportunities while at their core they are testaments to our isolation. Any unwanted mass immigration doesn't only affect the refugees but also exert influence on the environments in which the immigration has taken place. This naturally applies to both the origin and the destination, but above all the trajectory which connects them. To my mind, all these beautiful empty spaces, the heart-broken theatres which had to sit idly and watch us move on without them, have also gone through tragic changes in the course of the pandemic. Not only systematically or financially but more deeply philosophically or even deeper existentially.

What I'm trying to say is that we ALL find new objectives and physicalities as we watch Laura's memorizing performance from her home and not on a TV set or a stage. We are all really in it together.

MM. To further expand on these "new objectives and physicalities," during the performance, the audience is simultaneously manipulated and empowered to engage in a complex intellectual interaction with a performer who impersonates two persons at the same time: the playwright and their own self, the audience members become active and activated to take action. What are your observations about the virtual audiences of *WRRR*? Are they more empowered and engaged during the Zoom performance? Are their interactions with the Zoom performance of *WRRR* different from the reaction of those present in its live performance?

NS- Not necessarily. Again, to my way of thinking, technology is often not the best solution, but actually, it often causes more problems. If you ask me, the main excitement of being a writer is to be able to dig back, and not only forward, into the critical moments in the past and embrace the misunderstood paradoxes, or shift the paradigms towards the unexploited emotional and intellectual reserves. So no wonder while the theatre market was pushing for the online version of *WRRR*, I was busy mentoring a new project which was to be read by the audience around the fire. I might not be a traditional writer but I know the answer can lie somewhere in the deeper older layers of the tradition. Sometimes you have to go backward in order to be able to move forward again. One definitely has to dig deeper if one dreams to build a skyscraper.

MM. I absolutely love this idea of "going backwards." On a broader level, it reminds me of what Walter Benjamin writes about the movement of history in his writing "Angel of History." I interpret it as doing a U-Turn. I believe many of us during the pandemic had to turn our back toward the future and look back on our past and present. Moving on from the writer's experience to the audience's experience of interactivity and risk-taking, I think in the non-virtual performance of *WRRR*, the audience interaction is fluid and unpredictable, however, the virtual versions do not give a chance to audience members to act out in physical proximity of the performer or other audience members. Instead, a few of the audience members take part virtually in reading lines or act out (while sitting in front of their monitor or laptop), the rest can use the chat feature on Zoom space to type their answers, but at the beginning, they are asked to refrain from typing in the chatbox during the performance. Still, I found this Zoom performance far more exciting than the one I watched in September (run by Shedinburgh), in which we were just watching the televised version of the play. In that performance, we have a limited body of audience who were present in the performance venue. What are your thoughts about audience participation in the virtual performance, given that virtual audiences could appear as more impetuous and even with no inhibition?

NS- I understand. It is not too long since we have all been exposed to such experiments in theatre. Most of us didn't know anything about the many tools you may find in platforms like ZOOM at the beginning of the pandemic. So I consider that all theatre-makers, managers, and even the audience will need time to absorb and eventually master their parts in this new game. If I agreed to revise *White Rabbit Red Rabbit* once, I might agree to do it again. This is the big silver lining here: suddenly the riskier experimentations were not immediately pushed to the fringe but surprisingly shaped a new mainstream. This might have happened overnight and probably might not last forever. But the experience of a global paradigm shift will stay in the market since it tugged at everyone's heartstrings, just like a simple hug found another meaning after the pandemic.

MM. I agree. There is a lot to discuss about the durability and longevity of such virtual experimentations. Speaking of risky experimentations and new meanings of hug during the pandemic, the COVID-19 virus made us in our quotidian life more vulnerable and doubtful about many aspects of our living on a personal and global level. In *WRRR*, on the other hand, the blurred lines between different theatre roles and the unpredictability of the script make vulnerability the whole point of acting in *WRRR*. Even as an audience member, I felt vulnerable, too; what if I am not admitted to the Zoom meeting in time, what if my internet disconnects, etc. What do you have to say about this similar condition? To what extent did you, as a playwright with a global presence, feel yourself and your theatre in a vulnerable situation?

NS- A cold-read feeds from fear of vulnerability. It's not only the uninformed performer or the suspended audience, even the stage managers and technicians have to be on their toes to be able to react to the unknown. Walking on a tightrope above a still leafy mysterious valley, that is how I feel about my life, just like how I feel when I perform in *Nassim* (the play) or watch *White Rabbit Red Rabbit* off or online.

MM. In one of your previous interviews, you have noted that as a playwright, you try hard "to shift the paradigm of theatre" (Alia 2014). I read it as your passion for generating new ways of conceiving and perceiving theatre, and you name your way and process of playwriting as "theatre machine." Do you think online performance via Zoom aids or hinders this machine and the shift that it attempts to cause in the theatrical paradigm? You have another play called *Blank* that is based on intensive collaboration with the audience. You have also referred to it as a "mechanism" and have described it as "a very weird machine" (Sulaiman 2016). How likely is it that you adapt it for virtual performance?

NS- Not unlikely. But I don't have any specific plans.

MM. You offer workshops and masterclasses in which you teach your vision and process of playwriting as a "theatre machine." Could you elaborate on your idea behind such denomination and your teaching philosophy?

NS- I try to apply the theory of machines to my education curriculum where the courses themselves are "teaching machines." In a way, we try to create simple machines out of words that can process a certain type of inputs in order to produce collaborative outcomes. How can we write a story together for instance? Can we create some rules which develop into a game that results in creating a story in which we all partake more organically as opposed to what traditionally happens in the more hierarchical structure of theatrical organizations?

MM. On March 13, 2021, to mark the anniversary of closing theatres due to the COVID pandemic, one hundred performers staged *WRRR* in various venues ranging from Pakistan, Panama, and Guatemala to London and New York, even a prison in Mexico. What is your perspective on this global staging? Can it be considered as a global embracing of living in absence and isolation or a global celebration of reunion with "heartbroken theatres"?

NS- It is a poignant attempt to adapt and survive. I have a lot of respect for the organizers and every single performer and the audience members who watched it whether in a theatre with hygiene rules, or virtually from an empty theatre, or from the performer's home.

MM. Let's wrap up this conversation with a subject we both cherish. Coming from Iran, moving transnationally, both of us see the world as our common home. We value a sort of cosmopolitan ease and embrace connectedness. In recent years, with the aid of multimedia and digital technology, both of us have been practicing a sort of digital cosmopolitanism in our work. I'm keen on exploring the strength of the global Zoom staging of plays like *WRRR* in empowering digital communities to practice cosmopolitanism ease, especially during a global pandemic crisis. What are your thoughts on this cosmopolitan aspect of your works, both in *WRRR* and in *Nassim*?

NS- I find it inevitable. Danish pastry for breakfast, Japanese Sushi for lunch, Tacos and Hummus combined for dinner? Nah, one cannot ignore that. I'm still working hard to become fluent in English and German. While a three-year-old can easily switch between more languages in the playground across my office. Is she Turkish like her father, Syrian like her mother, German like her neighbor, or English speaker like Spongebob? If she is lucky she will become an adult in a world in which none of these topics matter anymore and if I'm lucky she would decide to take her head out of whatever-new-technology she would use just for one day and instead read one of my plays. How can I keep up with her? How can I keep her close to my heart? I know I love her. She's the kid from the playground, you know? She always comes talks to me and my dog when we go for a walk. How can I stay her cool uncle? The one who's not just smart but is also fun. The one who loves the past but is open to the future. How can this love feed her for the rest of her life? She will get older soon, you know. But my plays will stay the same. Words are trapped in time. Words need to know how to escape time. Can I create emotion capsules out of words? Can I use them to transfer my thoughts? Maybe to a black teenager in China 2030, or an old Mexican-Palestinian in 2040, or a third person, one without nationality, without borders, or without time. Nah, one cannot ignore all this when one writes.

MM. Nor can someone ignore all this when they go into conversation with Nassim Soleimanpour!

Note

1 *Nassim* has been performed in 20 languages worldwide. In 2018, it was "performed in twenty countries within a two hundred-day span" (Soleimanpour's Official Website). The same year, it won the Off-Broadway Alliance Award for Best Unique Theatrical Experience. Until the global COVID lockdown in 2020, *Nassim* had been performed over 340 times with the same number of different performers worldwide. Since 2017, Soleimanpour has created other plays: *Cook, Down the Creek, October 2020*. For details about his workshops, publications, other projects and their reception, refer to his website www.nassimsoleimanpour.com. To read my review on *WRRR* and brief introduction of his earlier plays *Blank* and *Blind Hamlet*, read "Nassim, A Breeze From Iran that Stirred Global Theatre Scene."

References

Alia, Syar S. "ISSUE interview with *White Rabbit, Red Rabbit* playwright Nassim Soleimanpour." Interview with Nassim Soleimanpour. *Issue Magazine*, April 13, 2014. Accessed May 12, 2021.

Barnett, Laura "Nassim Soleimanpour: 'Why Can't an Actor Just Get Up and Start?'" Interview with Nassim Soleimanpour. *The Guardian*, August 2, 2014. Accessed May 12, 2021.

Moosavi, Marjan. "Nassim, A Breeze From Iran that Stirred Global Theatre Scene." TheTheatreTimes.com, 27 September, 2016. Accessed March 17, 2021. https://thetheatretimes.com/nassim-a-breeze-from-iran-that-stirred-global-theatre-scene.

Soleimanpour, Nassim Official Website. N.d. "Home." Accessed March 17, 2021. https://www.nassimsoleimanpour.com.

Soleimanpour, Nassim Official Website. N.d. "White Rabbit Red Rabbit." Accessed March 17, 2021. https://www.nassimsoleimanpour.com/whiterabbitredrabbit.

Soleimanpour, Nassim Official Website. Official Website. N.d. "Let There Be Theatre." Accessed June 27, 2021. https://www.nassimsoleimanpour.com/copy-of-down-by-the-creek.

Sulaiman, Yasmin. "Interview: Nassim Soleimanpour –'I Receive Thousands of Personal Stories from People, So I Thought I Owed Them a Story Machine" Interview with Nassim Soleimanpour. *Edinburgh Festival: The List*. July 19, 2016. Accessed May 12, 2021.

Part IV

Materiality/Ephemerality

Teaching Design and Production Now

Chapter 14

Reclaiming Materiality in Remote Theatrical Design Instruction

Michael Schweikardt

Introduction

I am a scenic designer, researcher, and instructor of scenic design currently living and working in State College, Pennsylvania, whose interest is in material, handmade expressions of thoughts and ideas. As a scenic designer, I make things. Sometimes the things I make are big, like sets that fill stages, and sometimes they are small, like drawings or scenic models. No matter their size, these things have jobs to do: sets represent worlds in which performances unfold, and drawings and models represent the full-scale designs being made. Sadly, once these things fulfill their purpose—that is, once their jobs are complete—they often vanish; sets are rarely saved, and drawings and scenic models are usually lost or discarded. As a researcher I investigate ways in which the material things of scenic design can be made to endure once they outlive their original purpose. As an instructor of scenic design, it is incumbent upon me to teach students how to generate material ideas for the stage. Historically, my classroom has functioned as a creative space where students gather to co-create new things, but in the age of COVID-19 the gathering of bodies posed an existential threat, and as a result, digital spaces became the default sites for learning. The swift turn toward digital spaces meant a turning away from materiality that was at odds with my practice, my research, and my pedagogy. In the university, hybrid options—ostensibly a combination of remote and in-person teaching/learning—were widely offered to students and instructors in the 2020–2021 academic year. But, in my experience, hybrid teaching/learning situations tended entirely towards the digital. To keep hybrid teaching/learning in balance, I carved out space alongside the digital for tool-in-hand reflection—an analog space where materiality could persist.

Using my own experience as a framework, this chapter will explore the practical strengths and weaknesses of hybrid teaching/learning during COVID-19, and outline my attempt to balance the digital with the analog in my classroom by way of weekly sketchbook assignments whereby students made material drawings shared in digital space.

DOI: 10.4324/9781003229056-19

Dissolving into Digital Space

In Fall 2020—the year that digital performance scholar Sarah Bay-Cheng refers to as "the infamous pandemic academic year of *Annos Coronavirus* (ACV)"—I was asked by The Pennsylvania State University School of Theatre to teach *THEA150 Fundamentals of Design*, a course I taught previously in 2017, 2018, and 2019, to undergraduate students studying theatrical design, technology, and stage management (Bay-Cheng, 2020). The stated objective of this course is to introduce students to the fundamental elements of design, which are described as "a basic set of art and analytic skills that form the foundation for all areas of design in the theatre." Being a 100-level course, most students who enroll in *THEA150* are first-year students, and, generally speaking, they arrive at this course having been backstage theatre makers/craftspeople in their high school theatre programs. Rarely do they arrive considering themselves designers/artists. I use this course to build a healthy ego in students by treating them as young artists. Students also tend to arrive unaccustomed to active collaboration with their peers. I ask students to recognize their classmates as their collaborators and I help them to build relationships with one another. And finally, students tend to arrive with a cynical attitude toward storytelling. Most notably, students often reduce their first responses to class play reading assignments to negative statements like, "I didn't like it," or "I didn't like the characters." I help students release their cynicism by exploring how storytelling requires empathy, and empathy requires access to and expression of their inner emotions. Achieving all the above relies on hands-on art making and in-class, in-person collaboration.

For reasons of pandemic safety, I was now to deliver this course in what Penn State designated as "MIXED mode"—note the use of capitalization (not mine) for emphasis—implying students would receive a balanced combination of virtual teaching/learning and in-person teaching/learning. What follows is the syllabus language the university provided to describe "MIXED mode" to students:

> This class will be offered in a "MIXED mode". This means you will be instructed through a combination of in-person and remote learning at the instructor's discretion. The objective of this Mixed Mode format is to meet social distancing requirements in our classroom space, while also providing students with opportunities for face-to-face interaction and access to specialized on-campus spaces and equipment as appropriate.

Although the above language states that course delivery would be left to my discretion, the university also mandated that students be given the option to attend class remotely, either synchronously or asynchronously, at their discretion, and that all students, regardless of how they receive content, be given an equivalent class experience.

Twenty-six students enrolled in the course, but with new classroom capacities lowered to 25%, the largest available in-person teaching space accommodated only ten bodies. I was offered an additional classroom at the opposite end of the same building with a maximum room capacity of eight. With only 18 of 26 bodies (split between two locations) accounted for, the decision for how to proceed was left up to me. The class was scheduled to meet Tuesdays and Thursdays and I briefly considered splitting the students into a "Tuesday Group" and a "Thursday Group." When the "Tuesday Group" would meet in-person, the "Thursday Group" would be assigned curriculum to be completed asynchronously, and vice versa, but I quickly decided against this. Bifurcating the students in this way would mean the groups would never interact with one another. That was no way to begin building collaboration among students who were destined, at least in part, to spend the next four years working and learning together. Besides, this plan continued to yield groups larger than single room capacities could accommodate; students would still need to be split between two classrooms. That, and the fact that I could not be physically in two rooms at the same time made it clear that Zoom would be an unavoidable element of course delivery.

Ultimately, on any given day I had 12 students attend class in-person, split between two classrooms, while another 12 students attended class synchronously remote. The groups of 12 students attended every other class in-person. Two students chose to remain at home for the semester and they attended all classes synchronously remote. I changed classrooms every other class meeting, meaning I saw students face to face every fourth class. Whether students attended class in-person or remotely, all students, for every class, in every location, were required to log on to Zoom from their personal computers or cell phones. It became immediately clear that headsets and microphones were required to understand each other through our masks and to eliminate the awkward delays and feedback that Zoom audio generates when multiple devices are in close proximity. As a result, even when co-present in the same classroom, students and I communicated with each other exclusively through our devices. Our "MIXED mode" classroom was pulled irrevocably into the digital realm. Nonetheless, I embraced Zoom as the only space where students and I could all be together, in a sense, to build community and collaboration.

Working in digital space (Zoom) meant that the significant number of students who ended up in quarantine over the course of the semester were able to continue their classroom collaborations with relatively little interruption.[1] It also meant that students whose schedules made it impossible for them to get to their classrooms, dorms, or apartments in time for class could participate via Zoom from outdoor tents set up by the university, or building hallways, or their cars, or any number of other locations they improvised. While far from ideal, this, too, allowed a significant number of students uninterrupted classroom collaboration. Being on Zoom ensured that students who remained at home received a level of collaboration commensurate with their student colleagues on campus. While I have no doubt the digital classroom experience was lacking compared to an in-person experience—technical glitches were legion and Zoom fatigue was debilitating—it was equitable in the sense that students, whose situations were wildly varied and no fault of their own, had similar experiences with the course delivery. I don't believe achieving this equity required reducing the student experience to the lowest common denominator, something I had feared, but rather, it was achieved by averaging out possible student experiences to something in the middle, to ensure that no student was left out or left behind. However, the more the physical classroom dissolved into digital space, the more I felt a need to reclaim the material aspects of the curriculum that allowed students to understand themselves as artists.

To that end, I revised an old semester-long sketchbook assignment whereby students created five drawings per week based on open-ended prompts.[2] The sketchbooks served as an analog space where students could reconnect with their body, mind, and spirit. In this space I got to know my students, and they got to know themselves, as over time the sketchbooks transformed into intimate spaces of self-reflection where students exorcized their fears and anxieties.

Reclaiming Materiality, or Why Draw?

I acknowledge that of the twenty-six students enrolled in the class, only nine were interested in areas of theatrical design that make regular use of drawing (scenic and costume design). The rest were interested in areas in which drawing is rarely used (lighting design, sound design, technical direction, and stage management). Nonetheless, there are good reasons for all students to practice drawing.

One reason, as historian of architectural drawing and author Mark Alan Hewitt argues, is that drawing develops cognitive action-perception feedback loops in the artist. In his book *Draw in Order to See: A Cognitive History of Architectural Design*, Hewitt explains, "When artists or architects begin a design, they initiate a continuous feedback loop of actions (drawings, sculpting, painting) and perceptions (seeing and judging the artifacts in front of them)" (Hewitt 2020, 26). With each loop between hand, eye, and brain, the artist sees what they are drawing more clearly. I tell students I have them draw to take advantage of the clarity Hewitt says cognitive-action feedback loops provide to reinforce their comprehension of the fundamental elements of design. Composition, line, shape, mass and volume, value, texture, and color can all be explored in a drawing. As students' hands draw various elements of design (action), their eyes see the results (perception), and their brains understand the elements better (cognition). While drawing is an exercise in cognition that provides opportunity to reinforce student learning, it is also an embodied practice that provides opportunity for developing awareness, presence, balance, and connectivity.

As described by practitioner of mind-body communication Daniela Razocher, "embodied practices are about experiencing yourself in the moment, strengthening your felt sense of self and building awareness" (Razocher 2020). When students draw as an embodied practice, they keep themselves centered and present in their art making. Students come to realize two key things: (1) their art is uniquely theirs, and (2) their art has value because their lived experiences have value. Razocher goes on to argue that two key elements of an embodied practice are intention and attention (2020). When students sit down, pencil in hand, their intent is clear—they mean to draw—and as the loop between their hand, eye, and brain is established, students become more attentive to their minds and bodies. As drawing draws students' attention to themselves, it creates a space where they can connect their thoughts and feelings to their bodies.

And of course, drawing leaves behind marks—marks that are visible and measurable, have size and dimension, speed and direction, and catch light. A drawing is a *material* record of the artist's thoughts and imaginings that can be read by others. American painter and teacher Robert Henri captured this notion eloquently when he said:

> There are moments in our lives, there are moments in a day, when we seem to see beyond the usual. Such are the moments of our greatest happiness. Such are the moments of our greatest wisdom. If one could but recall his vision by some sort of sign. It was in this hope that the arts were invented. Sign-posts on the way to what may be. Sign-posts toward greater knowledge.
>
> (Henri 2007, 10)

I read the above for the first time in the weeks leading up to the Fall 2020 semester and it made me wonder: might these sketchbook drawings leave behind a record—a series of readable sign-posts—of how students were responding to the world around them during the time of COVID-19? This question breathed new life into the sketchbook assignment as I came to see it as an opportunity for students to record the story of what promised to be an extraordinary moment in their lives. I had some confidence that when the semester came to an end, the sketchbooks would serve as a kind of time-capsule-in-drawing, but I was unprepared for the deeply personal ways in which students would communicate with me through the pages of their sketchbooks. More than just a record, students' sketchbooks emerged more like journals in which students revealed themselves to me in real time.

The Sketchbook Assignment

In order to inspire students to reconnect with their body, mind, and spirit through analog drawing, I rewrote many of my weekly prompts to promote self-reflection and self-expression in the students' drawings. My new prompts aimed to center the student artist in the process more than they had in previous years.[3] The revised sketchbook assignment I ultimately gave students looked like this:

Sketchbook

Artists use visual elements to give meaning to their thoughts and feelings, and to respond to words and music. Your theatre life will be filled with drawing, scribbling and doodling. The sketchbook is meant to establish the healthy habit of drawing daily and to help you begin to see the world as an artist. Each week you will make five drawings on the following assigned themes:

Week 1: Cats and dogs and other best friends
Week 2: The heart wants what the heart wants
Week 3: What I miss
Week 4: Sometimes at night
Week 5: I wish
Week 6: Beauty is in the eye of the beholder
Week 7: Where I come from
Week 8: My jam
Week 9: Yesterday
Week 10: Your choice
Week 11: Dance revolution
Week 12: Unbelievable architecture from your imagination
Week 13: When I grow up
Week 14: Clothes for gods and superheroes
Week 15: What I want you to know

You may choose the medium, but your drawings must be drawn by hand.

In past years it proved unmanageable to collect, comment on, and redistribute 20-plus physical sketchbooks on a weekly basis, so I had students submit their sketchbooks only once, at the end of the semester. This caused many students to wait until the last minute to make their drawings, resulting in work that was rushed and thoughtless, and, if students did draw daily, they received no feedback from me over the course of the semester. Now, even if I wanted to collect students' sketchbooks, COVID-19 protocols made it impossible. Taking advantage of available digital technology, I changed the way sketchbooks were submitted. Once a week I had students photograph five of their drawings with their mobile phones, compile them into a single PDF and upload it to Canvas. Although their work was being submitted as digital facsimiles in digital space, students were still making material drawings. Students made themselves visible when they made their thoughts and feelings legible in these drawings, while the measured flow of digital submissions encouraged daily drawing practice and made it possible for me to see students' work develop in real time. Moreover, it allowed for consistent instructor feedback on students' drawings.[4]

I cannot stress enough the importance of weekly written responses to students' work. The regular back and forth of drawing and response created a conversation between student and instructor. Often the conversation was literal.[5] One of the very first drawings I received was from a student studying technical direction and it included text that read "I've never drawn before, sorry!" This moment provided me an opportunity to begin to build a healthy artist's ego in this student. My perspective is that everyone can draw. Drawing is like handwriting; both are deeply personal and utterly unique to the person. In the comment section on Canvas I replied,

> No worries. And no apologies are needed. There is no expectation that you have drawn before. Frankly, this is exciting. Experiment and have fun. Interpret and make connections. Just do the work. And your drawings are excellent. You made art. Good job.

This student's drawing blossomed in the following weeks due, at least in part, to the encouragement he received, but I believe his growth was mostly a result of simply feeling seen. This was true for most students. They felt visible because they knew they had an audience and, being aware they had an audience, the students began to perform, both in the sense that they fulfilled their obligation to draw, and in the sense that they enacted themselves in the pages of their sketchbooks. Being enactments of self, every student drawing was unique. Nevertheless, trends did appear. I will focus on a few categories of performance that emerged in the students' drawings.

At some point during the semester, most students made a drawing of the exterior of their home, ostensibly representations of where they lived, or live, with their families. These drawings tended to be wonderfully naive and often colorful, not unlike the crayon drawings proud schoolchildren give to parents to hang on refrigerators. Many students made similarly naive drawings of their families. There were countless drawings of pets—cats, dogs, fish, birds, and reptiles of all types—and groups of friends gathered at concerts, hometown hangouts, or in basement rec rooms. At first, I read these drawings as nostalgia—as students describing a sentimental longing for the (recent) past—but I came to realize there were sharper edges. Most of the students were young—17, maybe 18 years old—which means, in many cases, they were away from home for the first time. I believe students were performing their yearning to return to the comfort and familiarity of their families and friends. This yearning was expressed in several drawings showing roads in forced perspective that lead the viewer away from their current place into the distance. As if to put a fine point on it, in one case, a student drew a sign above the road that read "Home: All Lanes." While it may not seem extraordinary for first-year college students to yearn for home, it is important to remember that due to COVID-19 these students had to forfeit their proms, graduations, and other rites of passage normally marked in the presence of family and friends. As someone who once participated in all of those rites of passage with my own family and friends, I can recognize the sense of closure they provided me as I ended one chapter of my life and prepared to embark on another. Students in my class lacked that closure and this was palpable to me in their drawings.

One student made an intimate drawing of two figures in an embrace. The drawing brings the spectator close to the figures, one of whom has their face turned away from the frame, while the other closes their eyes. Unconcerned with their audience, they shed tears of relief as they hug. For me, it is the longing for each other's touch that is the subject of this drawing (Figure 14.1).

Another student, while less practiced with the pencil, made a drawing that is no less exquisite in communicating their longing. Here again, two figures lose themselves in each other as they wrap arms in a tender embrace. But in this drawing the student confronts their audience directly, stating in the margin, "I miss hugs" (Figure 14.2).

Before they left home for Penn State, students were masked and isolated. They arrived here the same way: faces obscured, unable to gather, and not permitted to touch. This took a toll on students, not that you would know it by talking to them; in conversations they kept their feelings to themselves, but in drawings they performed their loss. Week after week, drawing after drawing, students expressed longing for physical touch. They missed kisses, cuddles, holding hands, and hugs—especially hugs.

In countless drawings students performed their excitement for experiencing new things, new people, and new ideas. And there were performances of bravery

Figure 14.1 A student drawing of two figures in an embrace.

Materiality in Remote Design Instruction 165

Figure 14.2 A student writes in the margin of their drawing, "I miss hugs."

as students expressed latent aspects of their gender identities, sexuality, and personal politics in their drawings. While the sketchbooks provided a place where students could freely try on new roles and experiment with different personae, I continued to sense the anxiety that permeated the drawings. For example, one student drew themselves sitting on a bed, their body rendered in a vibrating mass of chaotic black lines. Their face is hidden behind a curtain of long hair, and their hands are clasped over their ears. They seem to be trying to drown out voices of their own self-doubt by filling the air with the sounds of "shhh, shhh, shhh" (Figure 14.3).

But the drawing that haunts me most is a terrifying image of fear and worry. In it a restless figure floats on a bed, seemingly unaware of the crazed creature emerging from the inked-black darkness below them (Figure 14.4).

As students drew in order to make sense of themselves and their world, their sketchbooks emerged as places of performance where they could enact their feelings through the process of drawing. All told, more than 1,900 drawings were made by students over the course of the 2020 Fall semester. While it is true that embodied drawing practice served as ballast against students' ever-increasing digital experience, the drawings they made were submitted, and commented on, in digital space—and there they remain. In previous years, when I finished grading the sketchbooks, I would stack them in the corner of the classroom and inform students to come by and retrieve them. Few did. Most remained in

Figure 14.3 A student drawing of a figure trying to calm themself.

that pile, only to be thrown in the trash come May. This year, thanks to digital space, students' material drawings endure as a living archive of "the infamous pandemic year of *Annos Coronavirus*." What is left behind is a record of readable signs that recall embodied moments of students' lives. In the end, the sketchbook assignment achieved a balance between the digital and the material that earned it a "hybrid" status.

Conclusion

As I write this, in-person learning seems poised to make a comeback. For this I am glad. However, the painful pandemic pause has served a purpose. With the move toward digital spaces, instructors engaged in new modes of teaching and students made extraordinary things in spite, or because of extraordinary circumstances. After all, branching out into digital spaces in 2020 had enormous benefits for my class: it opened new spaces for collaboration; it made class delivery equitable for students with varied and ever-changing situations; it made the submission of material assignments more efficient and allowed for consistent instructor feedback; and it left behind an archive of embodied practice that captures the moment.

As we pivot back to more traditional, pre-pandemic modes of teaching/learning, what is to become of the work that's been done during the past year? What

Figure 14.4 A student expresses their anxiety and terror in a drawing.

from this time will we take into the future, and what will we discard? If the past year has taught me anything, it is that creativity, collaboration, and learning can flourish in any place, no matter the given circumstances. But maintaining balance is key. In Fall 2020 I learned that, when left unchecked, hybrid teaching/learning can slip entirely into the digital realm, but I also learned that, in the hybrid classroom, digital spaces create new opportunities for collaboration and equity, and emerge as sites where materiality can flourish. Now, as I look forward to returning to teaching post-*ACV*, I seek a balance of virtual teaching/learning and in-person teaching/learning. Just as I felt compelled in 2020 to carve out analog space for materiality to persist in digital space, today I am compelled to maintain digital spaces in the in-person classroom. Students and I will continue to meet and work in both places.

Notes

1 Penn State's quarantine policy in the Fall of 202 was as follows:

> If you have been in close contact with a confirmed case of COVID-19, you will be asked by a contact tracer to quarantine for a minimum of seven to ten days after your last contact with the individual. You will discuss quarantine living options

with the contract tracer. Students may quarantine by returning home, quarantining at their off-campus apartment, or by moving into a quarantine room on campus. You have the option to end quarantine after ten days without testing if no symptoms have been reported, or after seven days with a negative test on or after day five of quarantine and if you have no symptoms. You must continue to monitor yourself for virus symptoms for the full 14 days.

2 I originally inherited the sketchbook assignment from Professor Laura Robinson who taught the class before me. I immediately recognized its value and so I retained it as part of my syllabus.
3 In previous years my prompts were naive: logos, football, Halloween, etc.
4 Responding to 130 drawings a week required the assistance of Teaching Assistant Bea Chung.
5 There were dozens of drawings submitted over the course of the semester including text that communicated directly with the viewer.

References

Bay-Cheng, Sarah. 2020. "In Defense of 'Stuff': Teaching the Ephemeral Theatre of Things." *Prompt: A Journal of Theatre Theory, Practice, and Teaching*, Volume 1, Issue 2, August 2020. https://www.promptjournal.org.

Henri, Robert. 2007. *The Art Spirit*. 1923. Philadelphia: J.B. Lippincott Company.

Hewitt, Mark Alan. 2020. *Draw in Order to See: A Cognitive History of Architectural Design*. New York: ORO Editions.

Razocher, Daniela. "Exercise vs Embodied Practice." Bodies at Work (blog), 2020, https://bodies-at-work.com/en/exercise-vs-embodied-practice/#:~:text=Embodied%20Practices%20are%20about%20experiencing, at%20the%20most%20two%20options).

Chapter 15

Reframing Beauty and Gender in Stage Makeup

Charlene Gross

Theatrical stage makeup is traditionally taught in a sequence of live, in-class demonstrations, each lesson building on skills from prior lessons. While core skills in stage makeup may not be changing, how they are taught can evolve to be more effective. For example, the classical stage makeup education presumes students and characters identify as binary. Lessons often imply there is a more beautiful face to be achieved. Lastly, the class is taught through a series of live, in-person demonstrations. I propose there is a better course to be taught. One that teaches from a non-judgmental approach, where anatomical names of features are emphasized alongside how to contour them effectively, and that methods taught are decoupled from gender as often as possible. A makeup course, and the skills it teaches, can be improved and become more inclusive when evolving perceptions of gender and beauty are honored in the classroom. A classroom that provides lessons via video to bridge accessibility needs. One reframed for the needs of both remote-teaching and today's student perspectives, with particular attention to the shift from a face-to-face studio classroom to online learning approaches.

COVID-19 forced an immediate need to move classes remote for the majority of educators. For my stage makeup class, this meant figuring out how to teach a hands-on, heavily demonstration-based class remotely and, eventually, asynchronously. Prior to COVID-19, I had begun the move toward anatomical nomenclature over the traditional makeup terms, but the demand to move the entire class online laid bare an additional language gap some students had been encountering that I was unaware existed. It forced me to see all of these challenges and to wrestle them into opportunities to improve and how I present the material. As I developed projects and lessons for the online format, I made discoveries which we explore throughout this chapter. Many discoveries were rooted in concerns, questions, quandaries I had prior to Spring 2019. Classes had been disrupted. What better time to explore the guts of a class.

To explore these notions, I have divided this chapter into five tangibles that I am currently tackling and/or a quandary in my own teaching. For the purposes of this chapter, let's call them the conundrums:

DOI: 10.4324/9781003229056-20

[CONUNDRUM #1]: How Do I Define Makeup Terms Accurately in a Non-judgmental Way?

Reframing the Terminology to Guide the Conversation

The class is an introductory hands-on course of the basic techniques and tools used in stage makeup which explores the concepts of beauty, monstrosity, and gender. Each of these three sections has a series of projects. Each project begins with a lecture, followed by discussion, demonstration, and application. As I reimagined individual projects, the need to step back and reframe the language for the class became apparent. How can the course terminology, along with the project titles, be more inclusive to diverse student populations, and be as clear as possible to convey the meaning? How can I get away from traditional stage makeup terms that are less accurate and use terminology that is more direct and non-judgmental?

I started by covering the anatomy of the human skull. I discovered that providing a rudimentary understanding of the parts of the skull allows the student to better understand and, in turn, find the bony landmarks on the face. Bony landmarks are where the skull protrudes. These protrusions cause facial highlights to naturally occur. The areas under and to the sides of those landmarks are where lowlights, also known as shadows, occur. Understanding and seeing where highlights and lowlights naturally occur on the face, is key to makeup design. Features on the face can be manipulated with 2D makeup techniques through highlight and shadow. It is only the holes on the head that typically require 3D prosthetics.[1] If the student can understand the connections between the skull in tandem with the muscle, fat, & cartilage of the face they are more likely to succeed in stage makeup. What I have not historically looked at is any anatomy lessons that go beyond the skull. Knowledge of a detailed anatomy of the head positively impacts lesson outcomes. By reframing the language around the slim/stout project (see Conundrum #2), I hope my students find the additional connection between the details of skull features with the overall skeleton and the muscular system of the body. The skull and how it relates to the muscles, fat, and cartilage that lives on top of it suddenly become more relevant to how everything on the face, both on the surface and below, interact with one another.

Second, using the anatomical names of the face, it helps neutralize gendered stereotypes in the class around features. Referring to one's mandible or zygomatic arch is more exact than referring to these features as their jawline or cheek bone. It helps the student find the specific area I am referring to while also eliminating some of the slang often used.[2] If you eliminate the slang, it's two-fold. First you remove what that area for a female "should be." High cheekbones = glamorous woman; cut jawbone = masculine male. Second, it makes the language clearer for an ESL learner.

In the three universities I have taught this class, it has always been in a dressing room. A dressing room without a screen, white board, or way to present this information beyond a handout or using our own faces in the mirror. When forced online, I found a better way to demonstrate—videos. For explaining the skull, I now use medical videos showing the parts of the skull that rotate for 360 degrees, showing the inner connection points between the bones, and use color to light up the areas of the anatomy as the terms are used to illustrate the lesson more fully. Videos the students can pause and refer back to whenever they need throughout the semester.

Defining the Discipline-specific Terms vs Pop Culture (One Example)

Contours, when speaking from stage makeup and painting terminology, are an exploration of highlights and shadows. They are meant to define the facial anatomy already present. Manipulation, which I address more fully below, can change the appearance of the facial features. However, basic contours in theatrical makeup are only enhancing the natural highlights and shadows present on the face. When students hear the term "contours," they often think of contours in terms of Kim Kardashian's makeup. In 2012, Ms. Kardashian revealed how makeup artist, Scott Barnes, made her face appear so chiseled in a Glamour magazine article. She followed up the article with close up photos of the makeup in various steps on Twitter. Suddenly this makeup trick professional makeup artists used was revealed to the public. Street makeup rapidly adopted this look and extreme chiseled contours became the mainstream in fashion makeup. Students in 2021 often arrive in class using the term "contours" only to discuss highlights applied to the face in this fashion.

Contours, in classic theatrical makeup refer to both highlight and lowlight makeup. They emphasize all the features of the face. YouTube and TikTok are rife with makeup videos, but most of these celebrate "contour makeup" in a similar fashion to Ms. Kardashian. Let's call these "fashion contours." I accept that terminology shifts and evolves. As an educator and designer in this space, I follow fashion trends that will soon become fashion history. I need to know about the contours of the 2010–2020s in a similar way I know about the intense blue eyeshadow indicative of 1980s makeup. I also need to clarify vocabulary used in the class. Defining anatomical terminology, explaining areas of the face, and referring to all use of highlight and shadow to create the illusion of depth starts the process of successful students for the course.

Focusing on What Is Appropriate for the Character

Focusing on makeup that is appropriate for a character affirms the idea that makeup design is an integral part of character development. Theatrical makeup needs to stand apart from beauty and fashion makeup. Once students understand basic terminology, anatomy, and the fundamentals of highlight/lowlight application, I can move onto how a successful design begins with focus on the character. Some students have a difficult time distinguishing between applying makeup on their own face versus for a character. From the first lesson, I work to remove the individual—their particular likes, dislikes, and perceptions—and constantly reinforce that analyzing the character through the text will help define how to make a character look. This can help students lighten or even remove self-criticism of their own facial features and faces. I repeat over and over again throughout the early classes, for Stage Makeup, students are not putting makeup on for themselves, they are designing in service to a text and a character.

By defining terms as they relate to the course, you force yourself to accept the influence of the Karadashians... er, no... you realize the culture of today is the history of tomorrow and, it's important to be cognizant of both history and the present.

[Conundrum #2]: How Can I Convince Students, "There is Nothing Wrong with Their Face(s)?"

AKA... Ideas around Beauty

It is necessary for students to observe their faces in the mirror as part of the class. We look at how the light defines the anatomy. We move around the muscles and poke at the cartilage on our faces so we can explore how it moves and functions. If the student understands the way a face moves, the knowledge can be used to apply makeup to manipulate this appearance for the stage. I want my students to see the anatomy for what it truly is. I do not want them to see their anatomy as flaws. While I hope they are secure with their appearance when they first arrive in the classroom, they often look at their face and begin to recite a list of all the flaws with gusto: eyes too narrow or deep, lips too full or thin, jaws too weak or square.... The list grows and often students chime in with a list based more on insecurities than on actual anatomy.

During Spring of 2021, I found Tara Maginnis's video entitled, "There is Nothing Wrong with Your Face."[3] This is now an integral part of the class. Students may not realize it, but it is how I share what she long ago figured out. If they are told by me, the professor, "there is nothing wrong with your face" from the beginning and often, they are more likely to accept this. The professor is the authority and knows all, right? By acknowledging upfront and out loud there is truly nothing wrong with *anyone's* face, we can embrace, move forward, and use the face in the mirror as the canvas to create. I want them to see the opportunities each face provides to create different variations and looks... for a *character*.

Although slightly outside the scope of this chapter, I believe it is important to note my class, while situated in a BFA Theatre program, sits within a College of Arts and Architecture within a big ten university that has a heavy general education requirement. This stage makeup class is made up of performance, design, and technicians, but the majority of the students are fulfilling part of their general education requirement or taking this as their "fun" class. They come from Communication, Business, Liberal Arts, and Engineering Some love watching makeup videos online, some are part of thespian clubs, and some are Cosplayers. The mix of students shifts every semester Because of these factors, I am mindful of how my students perceive themself within what is often a very atypical class for them. I want to empower my students to be proud of who they are, and what they look like. I want them to feel confident if and when they are in a situation in a theatre, or anywhere, and someone says, "fix your face!" that they inwardly know that refers to their character's face. More specifically, the character's makeup because there is nothing wrong with *their* face. Here are a couple examples of how I do this.

The Corrective Face Project

One of the first full makeup application projects is the "corrective face." For a decade, I cringed inwardly every year when, "Project: Correct Makeup" came up in my syllabus. I started the section every time telling my students there is nothing wrong with their faces (even before the discovery of Maginnis's video). I would inform them that the term "corrective face" is referring to creating a basic makeup design for the stage.

> The term corrective can be deceptive. To say corrective implies that a feature or characteristic needs to be fixed. For stage, the term refers to making facial features more symmetrical and emphasizing those features… . [This is] considered the basic stage makeup of a performer. Its purpose goes beyond beauty makeup. Corrective techniques utilize highlight and shadow to shape the face once the stage lights wash out the features. Also, facial focal points must be emphasized so audience members can distinguish characters and expressions.
>
> (Townsend, 2019)

"Corrective face" is the term used in textbooks such as Laura Thadium (1999), Richard Corson (1990), and as quoted above, Daniel Townsend. The corrective face, while not meant to be derogatory, often is perceived that way by students. The "corrective face" typically addresses the so-called "problem areas" such as uneven skin color and textures, and asymmetrical features. Like most makeup techniques, it is simply about manipulating the appearance of facial features through use of highlight and shadow.

The phrase "corrective" long bothered me, but I didn't know what else to call it. The project's name change arrived when I started thinking of my course in a larger context of theatre design. I was working a large opera production professionally, and I told the chorus to apply "basic stage face, please!" The phrase was non-judgmental, straightforward, and precise. The basic stage face. That's all it is.

So why, if I am teaching in a pre-professional program and am a working professional designer, aren't I teaching the techniques and calling them by the names I use in the "real world"? I, the professor, should teach the makeup application that I, the professional costume designer, expect the performer to be able to do. How to contour their face so their features pop under the stage lights. How to scale this basic face appropriately whether the makeup is for an intimate black box or a large proscenium theatre. I maintain the same course objectives, and teach the same skills, regardless of the project name. The language is slightly altered and more direct to their contemporary sensibilities.

The "Slim/Stout" Project

The section that follows the troublesome "corrective" assignment was "Slim/Stout." This project shows students how to make facial features appear fuller or thinner by using highlights and lowlights to manipulate their appearance. While it seems direct, referring to facial features as "slim/stout" is not ideal. It (yet again) opens the door to students pointing out features they considered wrong and/or undesirable with their faces. Yet this was how I was taught these skills, how the book I started teaching the class was titled the chapter—so what else should I call these techniques to get the point across?

Sharon Sobel's book *Theatrical Makeup: Basic Application Techniques* shifted how I teach stage makeup. Sobel does a simple, yet complex thing: she calls the "slim/stout" exercise what it is. In Chapters 6 and 8, respectively, she calls it "manipulating the bone structure" and "manipulating cartilage, muscle, and fat." It's non-judgmental, anatomical, and accurate. In a similar fashion, Richard Corson et al. (2019) refer to this as "modeling with highlight & shadow," while the Kryolan Makeup Manual calls it, "alterations to the face" (Langer 2018, 34).

Focusing on anatomical language rather than the relative fullness or thinness makeup can produce was the key to connecting the lessons that hadn't consistently clicked. Previously I taught a basic facial anatomy, followed by a basic lesson on light and shadow early on in the class. What I never fully tackled was how the muscles, fat, and cartilage interacted with the skull to give us our particular, individual features. Teaching the ideas of "slim/stout" through this lens connects all the lessons in a more holistic manner. It fuses together the importance of understanding facial structure with how to create the illusion of three-dimensional features through the use of painting techniques. It's yet another way to increase students' awareness of how light affects a face. They are artists, and this is just one form of painting.

In addition, it has led me to teach in more concise steps: How to lay in the basic highlights and shadows on the face; How to use those highlights and shadows to manipulate the appearance of bone & cartilage[4]; *then* I teach the basic stage face. I define the objectives for each project. I drill down into the "hows" and "whys" more thoroughly, thus allowing myself and my students to understand the objectives better and in order to best teach them the skills they need.

While making another seemingly innocuous adjustment to my class, it went hand-in-hand with widening the variety of techniques under this project as well.

As I am examining the terminology, and how I teach these skills, I find a desire to provide more examples of what these skills are and how they are scaled for stage size appropriately. Teaching remotely allows for this through use of short, information packed videos. In-person class demonstrations do not have time to cover all of these techniques. As an instructor, I can be distracted, mistakes happen (that can't be edited out), etc. From here forward, regardless of mode of instruction, I am and will continue to adopt more video demonstrations. While I am creating video content, it does not all have to come from me. It is curated by me, for my specific class, but from across a wide variety of platforms. I will cover this more thoroughly in Conundrum #5.

In the future, I hope to provide more examples of how the Basic Stage Face should be modified to accommodate various size venues and vary the faces that are shown in the demonstrations. In-person classes are restricted to either my own face, or the face of a single volunteer. Video allows me to curate a diverse menu of examples. Thus, increasing the students' awareness of all the beautiful types of faces that are in our world- all the differences in features, skin tones, and facial shapes. Never would I have written that sentence pre-COVID-19. I assumed students knew this. It was not until the Fall 2020 semester when I had a student tell me in a breakout room that they, because they felt safe enough to confess this without other students around, had never been asked to stop and examine people's facial features, thus never cognizant of how incredibly diverse and beautiful the world can be.

There is nothing wrong with your face. Sometimes when you start out making students feel more secure in themselves, you end up showing them the beauty in everyone.

[Conundrum #3]: Is There a Commercially Available Equitable Stage Makeup Kit?

The Theatrical Makeup Kit

Theatrical makeup kits are great because as a required class supply, the instructor knows what the student arrives with and what basic set of tools they are using. There are fewer issues with requiring one specific kit. It saves the student from hunting and gathering multiple small, theatrical-specific tools and supplies. There is less concern about variation and allows the instructor to plan accordingly. Furthermore, the typical stage makeup kits have all the makeup and tools the instructors need to teach a basic makeup course. Once the student has a basic kit, they can add to their (literal) tool box as needed.

Ben Nye has been the gold standard for the stage makeup class—and for good reason. The quality of makeup and tools have remained consistent for decades. The kit does require matching the student's skin hue. You select the kit based on your base (foundation) color. Once the student's foundation color has been matched, the instructor places the order but it can take weeks for them to arrive.

Bookstores dislike ordering them because they are student specific and are hard to pre-order for the semester. Not to mention, if a skin hue was extremely dark or light, it wasn't always a great match. Regularly I found myself comparing other kits. I resisted the urge to switch because Ben Nye, regardless of the trouble it caused, was how I was taught and what I had grown accustomed to using in class. It was OK.

Enter COVID. In-person custom matching of skin hues was not an option. Classes went remote. I was not comfortable with matching the faces of students who were on campus; it was impossible to match students abroad in-person the variation in camera lenses, lighting systems and screens created a challenge to do it virtually. How, in a remote classroom, can I match skin accurately?

Makeup Is Painting

The key is to give students the tools. For me it was the Kryolan's 12-color foundation palette married with a deeper exploration of color theory and how that applies to matching and color correcting the skin. I leaned into my strong background in painting and applied it more deftly to this class than I had in the past. Using the foundation palette forced me to go more in-depth regarding color. It did not allow the students to simply use one of the three colors that arrived with the kit. Katie Middleton's book, *Color Theory for the Makeup Artist,* is a particularly good in-depth look at color theory applied to makeup design. I used some of Middleton's examples to teach more precise color matching and color correction. Her approach as a painter/makeup designer is a great fit for my own way of thinking, and I highly recommend the read for both the novice and more advanced designer for a fuller understanding on this topic.

Kryolan, doesn't let the student assume there's a perfect color because "it came in the box." It forces the student to look a little harder when they put on a foundation base. It also forced me to realize I wasn't fully drawing on my own knowledge to teach this class. I teach painting. Why am I not teaching makeup like I teach painting if they use the same techniques?

Kryolan does require a more attuned eye to match and mix accurately and can frustrate novice makeup designers because there is not an immediate "pot" of color to apply. Determining which of the 12 matches them best, just like Ben Nye's colors, is a bit of trial and error. Unlike Ben Nye, a palette allows for opportunities to adjust foundation colors, mix colors together to get a more accurate match. For example, if matching the makeup on the first day of class day wasn't correct or if a tan fades over the semester, there are 11 other options to choose. Using the Kryolan palette helps all my students achieve a more natural looking foundation color as well as gain a more holistic understanding of how color theory is used in makeup design.

I do not endorse, nor am I against any of these specific brands (nor am I compensated in any manner by any manufacturer). They all have their advantages and disadvantages. What I am promoting is being open to consistently trying new materials. These may lead to a better understanding of the hows and whys you teach something the way you do and, more importantly, to the development of any technique which minimizes subjective opinion of how something looks and maximizes repeatable and technically communicable skills.

Do not get stuck in the old way because it's comfortable. It may be holding both you and your students back. Be open to opportunities to challenge the students and yourself to learn additional skills and for them to learn the skills in a more comprehensive way.

[Conundrum #4]: How to Teach Gender Reversal Techniques in a Non-binary Way?

The Gender Reversal Project

Historically, the Stage Makeup Gender Reversal project is when female students make their face appear male and vice versa. It is often an exercise near the end of the semester as it incorporates a number of skills taught throughout the class, and demands students use skills specific to the opposite sex. The project reinforces lessons on bone and cartilage manipulation, this time emphasizing male or female characteristics. It is also a good way to incorporate a lesson on wigs, false lashes, and facial hair.

Many theatrical productions swap gender roles. It's a long held theatrical tradition. Yet in the classroom, I was increasingly concerned this project could, and eventually would, cause harm. The project begins with an assumption a student identifies as binary. It also assumes a binary student is comfortable enough with their sexuality to swap genders which may not be true.

My current stage make-up class combines lessons learned through textbooks, professional experience, and conversations with my peers. One particular breakout session, at one particular workshop, was incredibly formative in reimagining the class. It is where I discovered that I was not the only one challenging how stage makeup has been traditionally taught. Karen Kangas-Preston from Michigan State University offered that she had shed the gender reversal project years prior in favor of a Drag/Glamour project. Spencer Potter from Westminster College had done a similar transition, but gone a step further. His stage makeup class is structured, according to his syllabus, to "explore, develop, and challenge their (the student's) understanding of beauty, gender and monstrosity." This was the missing link.

By breaking the components of the class into the specific groupings of beauty, gender, and monstrosity, I could begin each of these sections with a discussion that questions what beauty/gender/monstrosity means. The discussion can engage and challenge the student to think and explore what these terms mean before they begin to design or apply the makeup project. The student can research and develop designs that not only demonstrate they have digested the skill being taught, but are challenged to explore what typifies, contrasts, or defies their norms. To paraphrase Potter, it thus furthers the student's understanding of the topic and creates a fuller, more interesting discussion and design.

The Drag Transformation Project

Thus the Gender Reversal Project has grown to become the Drag Transformation Project. The Drag Transformation Project meets the same objectives as the Gender Reversal Project *plus* it expands the range of skills the student can incorporate into this project. It also opens the conversation about gender in a less confrontational way. It emboldens the student to express themselves through the creation of personae. By providing students a spectrum of videos to choose from, the student can determine how/ who they wish to present themselves for this project. Videos that including drag queen, bio queen,[5] and drag king options.[6] Last, but certainly not least, the drag transformation project broadens the opportunities for guests.

I would take this opportunity to acknowledge how wonderfully giving the drag community has been in this process. They have been incredibly willing to share both makeup techniques and about their own journey. They have been universally eager to participate and share their process of transformation with the students. By reaching out to this community, my archive grew richer. In a moment when the world was shut down to live performance, time and space opened for these artists to share their abilities. The energy and effort that comes through with this project has been astounding. The project itself has been a raging success all around. Students are creative, invested, and highly motivated to show not only what they have learned throughout the class in this project and also more willing to share who they are/ want to be.

We live in a moment where escaping the confines of binary concepts of gender is accepted, and thus opens up the ability to explore the same escape for stage characters. Each time we tackle character analysis we can explore the gender spectrum best for a character. We need not live in a Victor/ Victoria restriction, and can just do what's right for Vic.

[Conundrum #5]: How Can I Embrace the Technical Challenges Opportunities of Remote Learning?

COVID forced an immediate need to move classes remote. For me it meant solving how to teach a hands-on, heavily demonstration-based course remotely and, eventually, asynchronously. As this essay illustrates, it laid bare an unacknowledged challenges some students had been encountering. It forced me to see these challenges and to wrestle them into an opportunity to improve how to present the material. I hope this conversation spurs a broader discussion which may include but is not limited to thinking in terms of language, digital, and learning accessibility. It may also include the accuracy of digital translation tools on your classroom platform, voice to text, and commonly used sites such as YouTube.

How to deliver the class was the first challenge. Many educators are overly familiar with what was asked of us: turning our in-person lessons into recordings of ourselves quickly and with little to no prep time. One untapped resource readily available for this particular class was the endless supply of online makeup videos. Three factors were evident when delving into these videos: (1) there is a need to curate; (2) there is a lack of good videos that teach the basic skills of theatrical makeup; (3) videos can help with unseen barriers to learning.

Need to Curate

My first step to online teaching was to comb through endless YouTube videos already available. Some were great, some awful, some were not how I wanted the skills taught. Remember Kim Kardashian's contours and how it has impacted makeup design in this millennium? It especially is rampant on YouTube makeup tutorials. Curious enough, the more specific the topic (animal transformations, facial hair application, applying false eyelashes, etc.), the easier it was to find the right video. What I did not find were the basic theatrical makeup skills: highlight/ shadow, basic stage face, and manipulating features. This led me reaching out to my network of costume colleagues and endless filming/ editing of lessons.

Your Living Archive

There are not enough words to express my gratitude for the generosity that occurred among educators. We found ourselves in the same boat, at the same time, and sharing resources was abundant. Anne Medlock in Texas needs a special effects video? Beatrice Gray in Washington needs some tips on contours? No problem. My network of professionals turned into a living archive from which I could draw and offer up to others in the same situation. We all shared our videos, the links discovered in the depths of the internet, and stayed in constant conversation when new resources were discovered or became available. When lessons didn't exist, I recorded, edited, and posted my own and shared them widely. The network of self-recorded and sourced theatrical makeup videos had begun.

Lessons Learned

Since incorporating videos I have learned breaking lessons into bite-sized videos yielded more consistent and complete viewing (easily tracked through analytics). Students can revisit, pause, and/or slow down to examine a particular moment in videos. Shorter videos are also easier to stream for those with internet accessibility concerns. The smaller the video, the more modular it becomes as a building block. If you wish to rearrange how you teach a skill, those smaller blocks are easier to arrange in different ways than one long video lesson. Bonus: Videos are reusable from semester to semester.

These lessons learned from using video forced me to reckon how and why stage makeup class leans so heavily on live demonstrations. Demos in class were often done either on myself (a middle age white woman) or on a student. Videos, on the other hand, can provide a more diverse set of examples for everyone. If I varied the faces in the videos, the variety of skin hues, facial features, and genders were more diverse. Having examples for themself (regardless of their age, ethnicity, skin hue), also informed how the techniques did (or did not) work on another face. Offering the class as remote asynchronous also meant my students in various time zones were able to watch and learn when it was convenient for them. It meant that students sharing their resources at home (computer, internet speed, quiet focus time) or who learned better in particular ways could choose when it was best for them to complete the work.

Lastly, the videos revealed how much slang I used. How often my sentences trailed off into nothing. How many individual questions were answered in the classroom. All of which was evident through the seemingly endless emails, direct messages, and discussion board inquiries especially in those first three semesters as I refined information on videos and class modules. It also pointed out a language barrier was more present than I realized- both in terms of theatre-specific language, learning disabilities, and with ESL students.

Be Aware How You Communicate

This newfound awareness opened the opportunity to explore how to better communicate. It forced me to prepare the lessons in a more concise way. It challenged me to be more precise with my language and experiment with how to present the information. Different lessons, not surprisingly, are more successful using different approaches. I found subtitles emphasized the major skill covered in that section of the video, provided the written name of a specific product, list resources, and/or reinforced a definition of discipline-specific terms. The written class outline I used to bring to my in-person class suddenly became subtitles to the video or a short video section unto itself. I found technical skills had more success with verbal narration over the demonstration. I used subtitles with the camera lens focused on the activity, not me, with limited verbal narration. This allows the students to see the action up close instead of trying to see around the other 20 people gathered at a table. They can pause the video and see the exact angle I hold my brush when I apply the contours. All of these approaches help with making a more equitable class regarding learning disabilities.

Moving Forward

By updating terms and reassessing my approach to teaching stage makeup, I am improving the accessibility of the class to all of my students. As I move forward, I intend to present my course both online and hybrid format, to address the widest student needs.

Incorporating a larger variety of examples of faces is my short term goal. I am working to find examples of many faces with a wide range of ethnicities, skin hues, and variations of the techniques for the lessons. My objective is not to necessarily provide every student a model who looks exactly like them. Rather, my hope is that by providing examples of people who represent a wide variety of skin hues, facial shapes, and gender identities, students will see how the techniques are universal while being exposed to the wide range of beautiful faces found in the world. I hope my students gain core skills and an understanding of how to incorporate them into a successful makeup design. I hope they keep asking themselves what makeup choices will define the character and emboldens their self-expression and ideas.

As the language of beauty and gender evolve, so should our classrooms. I challenge myself to continue to learn to continually evolve and improve upon my classroom experience. I will continue to look for ways to encourage open conversations about gender and beauty, and connect them to the class. I hope you found this brief look at how I approached this class, and these five conundrums useful. I have enjoyed that recent circumstances gave me the opportunity to accelerate a reconceiving of my class and expand into online teaching. I plan to continue evolving on the methods long used and hopefully make them meaningful entry points for my students—as they develop foundational skills which align with our current students and their needs.

Notes

1 Two eyes, two ears, one mouth & nasal=six holes. But you have two nostrils you say? The nasal bone is one opening and the cartilage that divides it into two nostrils is easy enough to make disappear with shadow.
2 For example, the "apple of the cheek" is typically a phrase used to indicate a positive female characteristic
3 Tara Maginnis is a costume designer and educator. Best known to me for the "Costumer's Manifesto," which was the largest costume related site from 1996 to 2008. Unbeknownst to me until early 2020, was she was a pioneer in class videos and online learning in the world of costumes starting in 2002.
4 How to make your nose look wider, thinner, shorter, longer; how to make your lips look thinner, fuller, and so on
5 Bio queen is a self-identifying female who is in female drag, or a woman pretending to be a man who is impersonating a woman.
6 Special thanks to the Center for Pedagogy in Art and Design through Penn State's College of Arts and Architecture. Their generous funding supported a series of drag transformation videos for this class.

References

Corson, Richard. 1990. *Stage Makeup*, 8th edition. Englewood Cliffs, NJ: Prentice-Hall, Inc.
Corson, Richard, Glavan, James, and Gore Norcross, Beverly. 2019. *Stage Makeup*, 11th edition. New York: Routledge.

Langer, Arnold. 2018. *Make-Up Manual*, 8th edition. Berlin, Germany: Kryolan GMBH.
Middleton, Katie. 2018. *Color Theory for the Makeup Artist: Understanding Color and Light for Beauty and Special Effects*. New York: Routledge.
Sobel, Sharon. 2016. *Theatrical Makeup: Basic Application Techniques*. New York: Focal Press.
Thadium, Laura. 1999. *Stage Makeup: The Actor's Complete Step-By-Step Guide to Today's Techniques and Materials*. New York: Watson-Guptill Publications.
Townsend, Daniel C. 2019. *Foundations of Stage Makeup*. New York: Routledge.
https://www.glamour.com/story/kim-kardashian-tweeted-out-pic
https://taramaginnis.com/manifesto/

Chapter 16

Lighting Design Dramaturgy and Practice in the Post Pandemic World of Online Streaming

The *Juditha Triumphans* Case Study

Christina Thanasoula

As a key contributor to stage dramaturgy, lighting design plays a pivotal role in theatre semiotics. Often described as the "glue" that puts together the three-dimensional theatre space (Pilbrow, 1997), lighting serves as a "magnifying lens" that draws the viewer's focus to particular areas or actions on stage. "Lighting design can do a great deal to ensure that things are seen by the audience in an order and with a priority that helps them to understand the story in a particular way" (Moran, 2017). But what happens when you add a second magnifying lens—the camera—that breaks the "well-glued" stage picture into fragmented shots? A forced sequence of camera shots changes the initial intended message; it distorts the performance's timeline, "creating a predetermined path or journey into the image" (Aitken, 2006). As lighting designer Robert Koenig (2020) notices, "we shouldn't have two different narratives running at the same time," but when designing for an online performance, this proves to be almost inevitable. Lighting design theatre practitioners are challenged to acknowledge the major differences in the processes and tools used in both theatre and film, in order to keep on achieving "best practice" in stage lighting design.

In this chapter, I will examine the differences between designing lighting for the human and the digital eyes and their impact on the dramaturgy of light. I will then argue how the roles of the lighting designer and the director of photography are being reinvented, to suggest that there is an obvious need for cross training in both practices. Then, I will walk the reader through the artistic and technical "maze" of designing lighting for my most recent online project, the opera *Juditha Triumphans*, staged at the Greek National Opera and recorded by Mezzo Opera Channel, to prove that lighting design training needs to build an interdisciplinary, cross medium identity, addressing both the traditional three-dimensional theatre space and the two-dimensional screen. What we are looking at is a new approach to lighting design, a cross pollination between the two genres that will create pleasing and meaningful images for both perceivers: the sophisticated-subjective eye and the less-sophisticated-objective camera lens. Hybrid theatre is in need of hybrid theatre practitioners who will "embrace digital transformation and build a workforce with the necessary skills" (Arts and Humanities Research Council).

DOI: 10.4324/9781003229056-21

#1 The Eye and the Camera

Seeing is a psychological process. "We only see what we look at. To look is an act of choice" (Berger, 1972). Live audiences choose where to look on stage, making hundreds of choices every minute of the show. The human eye responds to light in the exact same way it has responded for centuries, it is still attracted to it. What has been added is the medium of the camera, which interprets the visual stimulus differently. As Mike Baldassari (2020) observes: "theatre lighting is organic, since it addresses a real human organ. But the camera is an electronic device." Because of its technical limitations regarding brightness levels, contrast, and color, the camera offers a confined version of reality.

> There are major differences between the way your eyes see the world around you, and the version interpreted by your camera. You can look around freely, and quickly build up an accurate impression of your surroundings. A camera on the other hand, shows only a very limited segment of the scene. The flat image on the screen provides far fewer visual clues to enable you to interpret the scene. If those clues are not clear enough, you may misjudge what you are seeing.
>
> (Millerson, 1991)

Millerson suggests that it's better to keep the design simple in order for the cameras to be able to follow. Designers find themselves struggling with this superimposed simplicity: achieving balance between what the eyes see and what the camera can capture—and the digital content platforms can later on reproduce accurately—is like walking a fine line.

#2 Lighting Design Dramaturgy and Practice

"Rene Descartes used everyday metaphors to describe light, such as the use of sticks by the blind to replace their lost vision: like the stick, light touches the object under consideration directly" (Mirzoeff, 1999) making it visible to the spectator. According to lighting designer Ben Ormerod, the "stage is a kind of receptacle of meaningful objects" (Moran, 2017); lighting functions like Descartes' stick revealing them to the spectator. No matter who the viewer is—digital or human—and despite the technological breakthroughs concerning the lighting designer's toolkit, the main functions of lighting design remain the same: Visibility, Revelation of Form, Composition, and Mood.

Is the standard method of achieving these objectives still valid, though?

Three-point Lighting

Stanley McCandless' three-point lighting method of lighting the stage, developed in 1932, still guides the training and processes by which lighting designers learn their craft. Three-point lighting is probably one of the few parameters we share with camera lighting approaches and set-ups: for both stage and camera, the three needed directions are Key, fill, and back lighting. McCandless three-point lighting is in direct relation to the audience's point of view (POV), while camera three-point lighting refers to the camera's POV: the challenge is that these two POVs don't always coincide.

Properties of Light

The primal matter of lighting design is light with three main properties to be mastered: intensity, direction, and color. When it comes to stage lighting, these properties provide different information for the dramaturgy of the play. For camera use, though, apart from the dramaturgical impact, these properties have determinant technical impact on the image making, "as they directly affect what the subject looks like on screen" (Millerson, 1991).

The **direction** of light is relative to the camera's POV. There is a major difference in preferred directions as Baldassari notices: "45 [degrees] is the ideal angle for theatre, but once in film that has to come lower, those two worlds need to collide." Repositioning the camera changes the effectiveness of the lighting direction. So, what comes first? The chicken or the egg? To spice this up, lighting quality differences affect the contrast ratio and the lighting balance of the recorded image. For example, the technical impact of the directional hard-edge light of ellipsoidal spotlights is totally different from the shadowless soft light of a general wash.

When it comes to **color**, stage lighting designers looking to heighten contrast often use different color temperatures or very saturated colors, while "video systems are color-balanced to produce optimum color accuracy when used with white light of a particular chromatic quality" (Millerson, 1991). What this means is that when designing for theatre, you may wish to emphasize a shift in the mood by changing the color palette from blue to red-based hues. When it comes to film, though, you will need to pick your preferred wavelength right from the beginning and stay consistent with it, since any extra hue will look distorted on camera. Most of us have experienced a red looking orange on camera or else a bleached-out red.

Regarding **intensity** levels, the human eye is highly sophisticated, able to make educated guesses and "fill in the gaps." Human vision is a very complex process, one that has not been yet fully understood by science, that's what makes lighting design so exciting! "Eye and brain continually make allowances and adapt to local conditions. So, you seem able to detect details in shadowy areas, adjust to varying light intensities, instantaneously refocus. The video camera can only handle a limited tonal range" (Millerson, 1991). Lighting designers need to be conscious of these *dynamic range differences* between the eye and the camera. "The eye can process varying brightness levels while the camera is set to look best for only one specific brightness" (Ravitz and Baldassari, 2020). To give an example, a highly contrasted emotion-evoking stage picture will not be equally effective for camera use: it will either look underlit or overexposed, making it hard for the online audience to even distinguish details, let alone feel the atmosphere. So how much light is needed?

Relative brightness is a pivotal parameter for camera lighting. In stage lighting we usually aim for more contrasted synthesis, but the camera is not a great fan of contrast. Not all cameras have the same contrast ratio, though, you need to know your cameras' specs; training on how to use cameras is an essential digital skill.

Streaming Light and Shadow Online

Live streaming is proving to be a very demanding theatre subgenre: alongside the live audience's static single point of view sitting in the auditorium, designers have to equally consider the visibility needs of the digital spectators, watching the show through the multiple cameras' POVs which add extra, non-theatrical sightlines. "Close-ups are like using binoculars at the Opera" (Ravitz, Baldassari, Scott, 2020) but can you watch the whole show through binoculars, won't you feel disconnected?

In theatre, there are quiet and dark moments, when you need to sit back and reflect, but is this something that can be achieved through the camera lens? When it comes to a broadcast, long pauses create uneasiness, viewers will assume that there are technical issues and will not be emotionally available to be carried away by onscreen **silence** or **darkness**. Appia would insist on "shade being as necessary as light" for the stage synthesis, but camera practice fails to agree: darkness is streaming's biggest fear, as cameras lose their focus in the dark and need time to adjust and regain their focus after the blackout. Designers can't really count on blackouts in their cue synopsis, so no more snap to black!

Whereas specific amounts and qualities of light are needed for camera lenses to operate, light is still expected to have emotional impact, engage the audience's focus and be a building block as much as a cogwheel of the dramaturgy of the play for both types of audiences. The lighting designer needs to acknowledge the two medium's interconnected languages in order to design lighting effectively and creatively. One example is the use of spotlights: tight "pools of light" seem to have a huge visual impact for the live audience, but would you really consider using a solo ellipsoidal spotlight on a dark streaming stage? It would, most certainly, look poor, lacking any spatial reference to other visual elements that give information about stage depth and dimensions.

#3 Case Study: *Juditha Triumphans*

Lighting designers around the world are gathering empirical data and evidence accumulated "on the go," in a learning-by-doing process, about tools and skills needed to serve hybrid theatre. *Juditha Triumphans*[1] was my third experience designing lighting for broadcast, giving me the chance to reflect upon its potential outcomes and challenges. I had to consciously redirect my personal creative process, improvise with and re-master the different lighting disciplines, re-imagine the artistic goals, and experiment with priorities, in order to serve both audiences (even though a live audience was excluded after all). The lighting concept was tailored to a "less is more" approach, to help navigate both groups of spectators through the storytelling.

Juditha ended up being more evenly and brightly lit than it would have been if there were no cameras present technical limitations forced the lighting choices. I realized that lighting is the single stage element that is so deeply affected by cameras' presence, with side effects expanding to the collaboration between set and lighting. For example, some of the vertical surfaces of the white set had to be repainted by the scenic department, in order not to reflect too much light and "blind" the camera. In the camera rehearsal, we even had to cut the side lights that were sculpting the singers' bodies from hitting white vertical surfaces. Follow spot intensity levels were doomed to be very dimmed throughout the show, as their HMI super-bright lamp sources "cut through" the camera lens.

Streaming is, for sure, superimposing its technical needs to theatre and "we must harness the lessons we have learnt over the past year" (Arts and Humanities Research Council).

Lighting people for "Juditha": different POVs asked for different key lights. Live streaming is proving to be a maze of POVs! In a single run you need to get the best shots for every single POV, while in the tv studio you would be shooting for a week to prepare the different lighting setups needed for different camera positions. Meeting the cameras' needs is on top of your "To do list." The cameras' POVs vary. Close up shots that do not exist in live theatre are necessary when broadcasting. Having the camera zooming in and out results in seeing details that wouldn't need to be considered in a live show; for instance, the rig has to look good in close up, while also meeting the extended lighting needs of the show.

And then comes the **time** factor. *Juditha's* creative team had three weeks to prepare the show but only two days with the video crew. The lighting plot had to be super flexible, offering fast and versatile solutions. Moving lights played a pivotal role in designing both for the camera and the eye. We created a long list of palettes and presets that could be updated safely and fast. Most camera-oriented solutions had to be developed on the fly, in a blink of the eye, mixing hues and adjusting color temperatures up to the last minute, while staying faithful to the main lighting concept. Lighting creativity suddenly needs to be streamed down a very narrow and high-speed path with much more paperwork, *dos* and *don'ts* in hand.

#4 Lighting Budgets

Live streaming calls for technologically sophisticated, high budget lighting gear, making it very difficult for smaller theatres to fund it. To give some examples, lighting fixtures operating in silent mode are key, both to opera—no one wants to hear fan noise on top of the arias—and to camera. Rich color palettes, varying dimming curves and flicker free operation are all prerequisites. (Thankfully, manufacturers have come a long way in the past few years concerning refresh rates for LED sources.) Both wide zoom range specs, covering many lighting needs -from general wash palettes to tight spots for specials—and easily matching colors between tungsten, HMI and LED lighting sources are absolutely necessary when designing for camera. The human eye makes educated guesses about small differences in color and will read two similar tints as identical to quickly process the image, but this is not the case for the camera, which is much more sensitive to color variations, as already mentioned. Sadly, venues and companies operating on small, insecure budgets will be left out in the cold if they don't find the resources to upgrade their lighting gear.

#5 The Director of Photography and the Theatre Lighting Designer. One-person Army?

Twenty years ago we would never have been able to cover streaming lighting needs, as we didn't possess the technological resources to do so, that is why the stage lighting designer and the director of photography's paths have never been so similar. But reality has caught us by surprise: the post pandemic world has heralded the opening of remote online spaces and for the urgent need for an updated dramaturgy of light.

So, are these two roles merging into one? LDs need to become familiar with camera settings, color balance etc. and DPs need to understand the theatre-oriented emotion-evoking video output, in order to collaborate more effectively with each other. As the lighting designer's pitch-black stage canvas is expanding through the camera lens, we need to re-evaluate our long-trusted theatre tools and reinvent their use, while carefully reconsidering and chiseling the creative process almost from scratch. "We have entered an age where a presentation is preserved for some version of eternity, to be paused, replayed, and shared. This raises the stakes and makes an improved lighting approach more compelling than ever" (Ravitz, Baldassari, Scott, 2020). We most certainly need to re-imagine our craft and art, even though it may not be possible yet to apprehend what lighting design will look like in a decade's time. Live streaming is not something that is going to go away after the pandemic has ended: we need to recalibrate our mindset, redesign the system and reconfigure the rules. The streaming camera is a new stage element that has been violently added to the *mise-en-scène*, and lighting designers need to acknowledge its presence and actively contribute to its fine tuning, helping to incorporate it into the *"choréographie' of light and space,"* as this was originally envisioned by Adolph Appia (Palmer, 2015).

Note

1 The opera was composed by A.Vivaldi. It was produced by the Greek National Opera, directed by Thanos Papakonstantinou and conducted by Markellos Chryssicos. *Juditha* was recorded in April 2021 and was broadcasted by Mezzo Opera Channel in due time. More information about the lighting concept and design of it: https://www.livedesignonline.com/news/robe-triumphs-at-opera

References

Aitken, Doug. (2006). *Broken Screen*. New York: DAP.

Arts and Humanities Research Council, July 23, 2021. "Boundless Creativity Report." GOV.UK. https://www.gov.uk/government/publications/boundless-creativity-report/boundless-creativity-report.

Baldassari, Mike. *Designing for Theater, Television and Film with Mike Baldassari – Webinar*, Martin Professional, *YouTube*. May 21, 2020, Video. https://www.youtube.com/watch?v=ey54fwm0PoI&list=PLX8PNXe5hN6OGaUSGoRQHUUpS_j-5oHwV&index=59

Berger, John. 1972. *Ways of Seeing*. Oxford: Penguin Books.

Koenig, Robert. "Collaborations in Lighting—Directors, Programmers and Designers with Robert Koenig – Webinar." Martin Professional, *YouTube*, May 19, 2020, video, 1:38:28, https://www.youtube.com/watch?v=4cqV0cbMxJ0

Millerson, Gerald. 1991. *Lighting for Video*. Oxford: Focal Press.

Mirzoeff, Nicholas. 1999. *An Introduction to Visual Culture*. London: Routledge.

Moran, Nick. 2017. *The Right Light: Interviews with Contemporary Lighting Designers*. London: Palgrave.

Palmer, Scott. 2015. A 'Chorégraphie' of Light and Space: Adolphe Appia and the First Scenographic Turn, *Theatre & Performance Design*, 1:1–2, 31–47.

Pilbrow, Richard. 1997. *Stage Lighting Design: The Art, The Craft, The Life*. London: Nick Hern Books.

Ravitz, Jeff, Mike Baldassari and Greg Scott. 2020. "White Paper: Lighting for Live Streams." https://www.martin.com/resource/lighting-for-live-streams-white-paper.pdf

Chapter 17

Standby Life as We Know It... Life as We (Now) Know It, Go

A Case Study in the Hybrid Stage Management Classroom

Meg Hanna-Tominaga

"Following *this* schedule, we'll be able to accomplish *these* observable, assessable objectives." All course syllabi and lesson plans are theoretical frameworks within which we allow for upsets and pivots to best serve a class and its needs. Similarly, stage management is all about organization and preparedness, the facilitation and completion of observable objectives, and adapting to live challenges under pressure.

What a metatheatrical experience, then, Fall 2020 was for my stage management class. Much like running a show that must put in an understudy who knows none of her lines or blocking, teaching during the pre-vaccine pandemic pushed my preparedness and adaptability to extreme edges. I was certainly not alone. Every educator had to adopt "the show must go on" strategies for classes to survive, if not thrive, in Fall 2020. Pedagogically, I found the most profit in prioritizing key elements of stage management: emotional intelligence, the importance of flexibility, and clarity in communication. By modeling that these are transferable skills (to the classroom here, but to any discipline, really), I demonstrate that managing the protocols of a Covid era hybrid classroom was much like stage managing a show.

The main challenge I faced was in revamping this very hands-on course. Through what would normally be live, in-class activities, students needed to learn and apply the vocabulary, concepts, and skills needed to understand stage management and its vital role in theatre making. I would need to maintain these objectives and somehow provide experiential content within the confines of the newly imposed protocols and all the unknowns they were meant to address. Our college's pandemic response included an updated academic calendar: we would start a week earlier than originally planned, eliminate our fall break, and push the full 14-week semester straight through, ending the term at Thanksgiving. Ours was a "high flex" model; we had students who attended classes entirely online, joining the in-person students via Zoom. The "normal" in-person classroom, however, was also disrupted by strict new protocols and cleaning rituals that shaved minutes off both ends of class sessions. Furthermore, "high flex"

DOI: 10.4324/9781003229056-22

meant that students might suddenly go into quarantine for days or weeks at a time, perpetually shifting the online to in-person student ratio.

Incorporating and adapting to all these variables while studying theatre's constant and dependable division of duties and collaborative structure would highlight the critical role of the stage manager as the necessary stabilizing force within the creative chaos of a theatrical production. The question was: how would I do it?

Laurie Kincman's excellent *The Stage Manager's Toolkit* (Focal Press) had provided logical, linear structure for my past stage management classes. The text begins by discussing the various modes of communication, including a small section on Emotional Intelligence. As chapters progress, the steps of production are laid out neatly. Readers can learn all that pre-production entails, then the stage manager's role throughout the rehearsal process, and so on and so forth, culminating in the running of a show and ultimately, facilitating a post-mortem. My previous classes were all, of course, in-person; we went chapter by chapter in an era when nobody wiped down lightboard keys or feared sharing headsets. We'd pass out hardcopies of documents like candy. We could kneel shoulder to shoulder on stage, taping out sets for our actors to trample all over. Those days were behind us, it seemed, and the more I thought about how we stage manage, the more I thought about how I taught stage management, and how I needed, in this case, to perhaps manage more than teach. A flexible stage manager can navigate nearly any situation if they are able to identify and isolate the issue at hand. Here, I realized maintaining the course content was not an issue. Facilitating the students' experiential application of these objectives was the challenge.

Kincman's final chapter, "Teaching Stage Management," observes "(s)uccess as a theatre professional ... requires equal parts creativity and technique. To me this translates into time spent both on the foundations – the *craft*, and the advanced ideas and skills – the *art*" (245).

I did not abandon Kincman's text; each chapter still provided structural foundation and examples and anecdotes that helped illustrate the *craft*. However, with the ever-present fear of another lockdown, I wanted to frontload the experiential learning, or Kincman's *art*, and have the students calling shows sooner rather than later. I considered how we begin an individual production: almost invariably we start the rehearsal process with a table read. The cast sits together and "performs" the show from start to finish, relatively smoothly, and this is when the creative collaborators often connect for the first time. The table read is a preview and a promise of what a show will be. Should we be forced back into our homes for another round of lockdown, at the very least, akin to the table read, I wanted students to have the preview and promise of what their final *could* be.

I started the semester with just such a preview, focusing the first real lesson on emotional intelligence and the necessity for a stage manager to apply it at each step of their work. The emotional toll that the pandemic was taking on everyone meant that for the sake of sustainable mental health, students needed to be aware of how their emotions affect their work and that of others. Building these habits seemed critical. If the students were to successfully call a show at the end of the term and have a strong working rapport with their respective crews, then the promise of those connections needed to be made early on. If we were to go into lockdown and try to manage everything from isolation, this need was even greater.

As opposed to just studying the benefits of healthy social engagement, I tried to manufacture opportunities to experience them as well. When students were physically in the classroom, they were socially distanced, putting everyone just out of each other's peripheral view. A strange byproduct of the protocols was the eerie silence before every class; small talk all but disappeared, and I longed for the days when I had to implore students to pipe down. These moments are where a class's personality is formed; without them, it was very difficult to "read the room," not to mention the fact that the few folks Zooming in from home were unable to engage smoothly with their classmates. I soon realized pre-class chatter had to be intentionally devised. So, if we were going to be spending that day talking about costume plots, for example, the complicated organizational charts that show "who wears what when," I'd initiate a discussion *before* class about the students' own experiences with quick changes and elicit other costume-related anecdotes. Forced though they were, these informal chats were invaluable. They gave students the chance to build a little camaraderie and gave me the chance to manufacture student commentary that I could directly reference in the main topic of discussion once the actual class began; students' comprehension improved when they could connect their own experiences to the lesson.

In keeping with the idea of previewing the final, after impressing upon the students the need to be mindful of regulating their emotions, we then jumped right into the deep end of production. The students each created a bare bones prompt script: a shell with proper tabs for everything that would eventually be included. Initially, though, we would only create what the students needed for rehearsing and calling a show: a script with cue margins and backing pages, and their respective keys.

The script we used was short: just an excerpt from the show that our mainstage was producing. Students learned blocking notation in class; they attended (or Zoomed into) the rehearsal the night the scene was blocked, adding the notes to their backing pages. As you can well imagine, class lectures and textbooks are great for glimpses at the practice, but they are no substitute for actual production experience and its idiosyncrasies. Melding the creation of their first prompt script with a real production's rehearsal process both granted the students an opportunity for experiential learning and freed up class time to allow for assessment, discussion, and reflection.

Some students had to Zoom into those evening rehearsals. Since the camera was rolling anyway, I had the students mute themselves; I minimized their windows, then recorded the rehearsal. The recording was shared with all the students. They had their scripts along with the blocking notes they took during the rehearsals. After a "paper tech," where all the technical cues were added to the margins, the students could practice calling cues on their own time. For their midterm test, each student submitted their own video: they opened a solo Zoom room, shared their screen (showing the rehearsal video), and recorded themselves "calling the show" in the little window in the corner of the screen.

As much as I disliked the ever-shifting hybrid classroom, I freely admit that Zoom proved to be unexpectedly beneficial for practical pedagogy. Trying to maintain an educational equilibrium between virtual and in-person learners was dreadful. However, finding other ways to incorporate Zoom as a teaching tool rather than simply utilizing it as a communication medium was a profitable discovery only made through a willingness to be flexible in lesson planning and approach.

Typically, it would take two or three class periods to cycle through everyone's turns to call the show and the live aspect would sometimes inevitably give some students unfair advantages or disadvantages during testing. Now there was no need to have the students go one at a time; students could rerecord if they made a mistake (or be fine with their mistakes), and I could grade at my convenience. This proved to be a very low-pressure, low-stakes way for students to gain experience and confidence.

Additionally, with a few sessions now freed up, I could guide the class in addressing issues that arise when relying so heavily on templates, as we do in such a document-driven arena. Templates are all but indispensable for the organized stage manager, but without a solid understanding of document design, the "why" behind formatting decisions can be lost on beginners who assume that data entry is sufficient. In the theatre, where specifics are wildly different from show to show, understanding the template *and its elasticity* is vital, yet the time to explore these differences is not always available. Previously, if the content was correct and relatively legible, I would have to make do with general critiques and move on. I could offer "this is how it's done," but not always "this is *why* this is how it's done."

I used one of these "extra" classes to focus on an assignment that required students to take a Cast List template and reimagine it to fit the demands of a particular "show" to gain an understanding of how flexibility in documentation is key. Their homework was to create a document for this theoretical show that not only displayed what actor played what character, but also which prop belonged to each of those characters. I provided the information in the form of a logic puzzle, forcing the students to use their problem-solving skills to generate the content for the form. They then had to design this new document, clearly showing the information.

Each student's Cast & Prop List was as unique as the student who submitted it. I printed each submission and tacked them to the board so that everyone could see all the lists at once. What unfolded was a thoughtful and engaging critique session from which students could compare, contrast, and clearly understand why this font was preferable or that type of graph/grid made things difficult to find information quickly. Students were given the option to resubmit their work; nearly everyone did, and every new submission demonstrated a keener understanding of how the document's design can be as important a tool of communication as the document itself.

Streamlining my objectives also allowed me to better see the class's needs and adapt to address issues as they arose. As mentioned, our college opted to abbreviate the fall calendar by removing all our breaks. This made navigating the very stressful term incredibly difficult for the students, many of whom had additional burdens as frontline workers, caregivers to younger siblings who studied from home, and in more cases than usual, dealing with deaths in the family or reports of abuse. While it is sadly not uncommon to have students share personal trauma, the pandemic clearly exacerbated complex problems that our students were addressing beyond and in addition to class content. Having prioritized mental well-being from the start, and having allowed time for more practical assessment, I was better able to discern not just the students' stage management skills, but also whether a student might potentially require additional support from our academic or health counselors. I also recognized the need to lead the second half of the semester coupling intentional discourse regarding emotional intelligence with more typical assignments that focused heavily on improving their organizational and managerial skills.

In a class session I call "Sticky Situations," I posit "how would you handle this" from various happenings in my time working professionally. Students love the gossipy nature of some of the anecdotes, but the sessions are focused on how to decompress if emotions run hot or how to reframe a nerve-wracking situation with a fresh perspective.

The hybrid classroom is a terrible space for these kinds of sensitive conversations. Thus, for this exercise, I again used Zoom as a teaching tool. This time, I had *every* student Zoom in, and I was able to utilize the breakout room feature of the platform, where the whole class can be put into smaller groups for more intimate discussions. Groups of three or four were given separate "what ifs" to discuss and navigate, being mindful of the habits of healthy interpersonal engagement. We commingled again at the end, each group sharing their responses to the hypothetical problematic scenarios. The smaller group sizes created more opportunities for each student to engage in the conversations and get more out of the activity.

Another exercise that was bolstered by having everyone Zoom in was that of production meeting roleplay. Real production meetings are as fun as they sound: the artistic staff, primarily directors and designers, meet to discuss the page-to-stage process of their production. In theory, this is a practical and efficient way for artistic collaborators to ensure that the show and all its elements are cohesive, and with any luck, successful. In actuality, it is a room full of artists who may or may not be respectful collaborators, and who almost certainly have and want to share their opinion on everything. It is the stage manager's job to facilitate, mediate, and record the meeting in a written report. At worst, it is a nightmare, at best, a circus. Again, in the past, I would assign each student a position (i.e., scenic designer) and a monkey wrench (i.e., introduce scheduling conflicts). Students have always seemed to really enjoy this exercise, but the downside was that only one student got to play the role of stage manager. At the end of the "production meeting," we would discuss what was done or could have been done to keep the meeting on track and we'd have just the one student's production meeting notes for reference. It's great training for one stage management student; the rest of the class benefits, but only indirectly.

By moving to a Zoom format and recording the meeting, though only one student lead the meeting as stage manager in real time, now the other students could watch the recording and write up their own meeting report. It wasn't a perfect fix, I admit. However, in addition to everyone getting the practice of writing a meeting report, the feedback session, which was held after all the reports were turned in, was much more productive, as all the students were able to spy back from the stage manager's viewpoint. As an added benefit, while students were learning about the ins and outs of production meeting culture and etiquette, they were concurrently learning the emerging culture of Zoom etiquette, a necessity for future professionals. Over the course of the term, nearly every student had at some point needed to go into quarantine and attend class virtually; using Zoom was not new. However, these types of exercises were a chance for the students to be conscientious of their appearance and personal environment, intentional about the use of mute and chat logs, and well-versed in the smooth transfer of sharing screens.

As an instructor, always having a back-up plan for a lesson was tiring, but no different than a stage manager always needing to be prepared to pivot during a live performance. By prioritizing healthy and clear communication along with flexibility in the training of duties, by the end of the semester, students were able to apply their critical thinking skills directly to building their prompt scripts; every tabbed and sub-tabbed section was complete, with sample documents for every section. By the time we got to the student's finals, everyone had done so many virtual simulations that their overall performance was well above average compared to previous classes that only began practicing calling a show near the end of the term; the overall stress levels and personal interactions were demonstrably better as well.

There were upsets and pivots, as were to be expected, but the course functioned well enough to produce a confident cadre of stage managers. These students all gained a uniform base of knowledge regarding specific tools and methods of the trade and, not despite but due to the hybrid classroom, they have all had experiences that most closely approximate the intangible elements of stage management as well.

Reference

Kincman, Laurie. 2013. *The Stage Manager's Toolkit*. New York: Focal Press.

Index

Note: *Italic* page numbers refer to figures and page numbers followed by "n" denote endnotes.

Abraham, Kyle 81
academic ableism 3, 33
academic grace 32; benchmark aspect of 36; institutional citations of 41; permission models of 33
academic violence 33
actors-in-training 61
adaptation 148
Alexander, Frederick Mathias 36, 95
Alexander Technique (AT) 85–86; downward pull 88–91, *89, 91, 93*; end-gaining *vs.* means-whereby, the orders, inhibition, new direction 91–94; interoception and exteroception 87–88; mind-body unity 86–87; semi-supine as means to primary control 94–97
American Psychological Association (APA) 26
American Society for Theatre Research (ASTR) conference 116
archival methodology, hybrid model of 117–119
archive 109–111; digital 115–117; in-person 109, 111–115
The Archive and the Repertoire (Taylor) 110
Archive Fever (Derrida) 110
An Archive of Feelings (Cvetkovich) 110–111
asynchronous learning platform 27
AT *see* Alexander Technique (AT)
Auslander, Philip: *Liveness: Performance in a Mediatized Culture* 69
Avalon, Robyn 96, 97n4

Baldassari, Mike 184, 185
Baldwin, Neil 83
Banks, Daniel 140, 141
Barbarin, Imani 50
Barnes, Monica Bill 70, 74
Barnes, Scott 171
Barnette, Jane 2
basic stage face 173–175
Bausch, Pina 80
Bay-Cheng, Sarah 36, 115, 158
Beckett, Samuel: Worstword Ho 58
Beginner, Intermediate, and Advanced Intensives 57
"Beginning Tap II" 99–100
Benjamin, Walter 150
Berger, John: *Ways of Seeing* 140
Bernstein, Carol 119
Bernstein, Robin: "Dances with Things" 113
Berry, Jen 122
BFA Theatre program 172
BIG Night of Little Plays 122–126
Black Lives Matter movement 105
Blum, Susan D. 34; *Ungrading: Teaching and Learning in Higher Education* 33
Bly, Mark 80
bodymind 48–49, 51, 52
Bogart, Anne 61, 66
Böhler, Michael J. 32
Borelli, Melissa Blanco 116
Boston University (BU): Fall 2020 virtual new play workshops 126–132, *130*
Bouchard, Michel Marc: *Christina, The Girl King* 128
"boundless specificity" 61, 65

breakout rooms 102–103
Brook, Peter 67n4; *The Empty Space* 59
Brown, Camille A. 81
Bühler, Karl 62, 67n8
Butler, Lisa D. 45, 46; "Potentially Perilous Pedagogies" 48

Caine, Michael 139
The Cambridge Introduction to Theatre Historiography (Postlewait) 112
Cape Fear 37
"Cape Feare" 37, 38
care: pedagogy of 44, 51, 52n1, 75; practices of 49
Carello, Janice 45, 46; "Potentially Perilous Pedagogies" 48
Care Work: Dreaming Disability Justice (Piepzna-Samarasinha) 35
Carroll, Robert 117
Caruth, Cathy 50
centering space 75
choice 131; practice of offering 28
choreography 79, 82
Christina, The Girl King (Bouchard) 128
classical stage makeup education 169
classic theatrical makeup 171
Collaborative for Academic, Social and Emotional Learning (CASEL) 23, 24
collaborative policymaking 28
color, of light 185
Color Theory for the Makeup Artist (Middleton) 176
community 101–102
Community (television show) 52n3
compassion 11, 12, 15, 99
Conable, Barbara: *How to Learn the Alexander Technique* 89
Conceptual Blending Theory 67n8
contour makeup 171
contract grading 33, 34
Cook, Amy 67n8
Cook, Terry 109, 119
corrective face project 173–174
Corson, Richard 173, 174
COVID-19 pandemic 12, 21, 26, 99, 145; hybrid teaching/learning during 157; protocols, sketchbook assignment 162
Creative Drama for Mental Wellness 24
crip time 49
critical thinking 11
Cuban Theater Digital Archive 116
Cueva, Bert María 33–34

curation, to strengthen and enliven choreographic voice 83–84
curiosity, as artistic rigor 81–82
Cvetkovich, Ann: *An Archive of Feelings* 110–111

danceaturgy 83
dance dramaturgy 79; history of 80–81
"Dances with Things" (Bernstein) 113
"Dancing in the Dark" (Springsteen) 69
The Darkest Timeline 45, 53n3
Daston, Lorraine 114
Days Go By 70
deictics 61
deixis 61–64, *63*; imaginary 64–65; in theatrical media 62
Denial, Catherine 12
Derrida, Jacques: *Archive Fever* 110
Descartes, Rene 184
digital archives 115–117
digital cosmopolitanism 147, 152
digital dance studio 99–100; facilitating access and engagement 102–104; maintaining community and stress reduction 101–102; unintended consequences/student reflections 104–105; Zoom, limitations of 100–101
digital performances 71, 74, 146
digital platforms 16; conversations and lectures on 42n1
digital space 157; dissolving into 158–160; working in 159
direction, of light 185
director of photography 188
disability-informed pedagogy practices 48–52
discipline-specific terms *vs.* pop culture 171
Dolmage, Jay T. 33, 34
drag transformation project 178
dramaturgical process 81, 82
dramaturgs 122–128, 131
dramaturgy 79, 123, 124
Dramaturgy in Motion (Profeta) 81
Draw in Order to See: A Cognitive History of Architectural Design (Hewitt) 160

Echevarria, Roberto González 114
Elerian, Omar 146
emotional intelligence 190, 191, 194
Emotional Intelligence (Goleman) 23

empathy 11, 21, 47, 66, 99, 105, 141, 147, 158
The Empty Space (Brook) 59
"Envisioning Change" (Kovich) 141
"Ephemera as Evidence" (Muñoz) 111
equity-focused curricula 22
Esther Merle Jackson collection 113, 114
Eugene O'Neill Theatre 40

Fall 2020 122, 126–132, 158, 161, 167, 175, 190
Fallot, Roger 46
Fauconnier, Gilles 67n8
feedback loops 66
feedback process 17, 90; triple tier of 16
Ferdman, Bertie 73
Ferguson, James 73
film/video model, for online distribution 143
Fischer-Lichte, Erika 72
flexibility 190, 193, 195
flexible pedagogy 12
Foli 103
Forrest, Edwin 117
Freire, Paolo 13
Fricke, Ellen 62, 63
Frodahl, Julia 15; "Training A Million Compassionate Americans" 18

gender reversal project 177–178
"'A Giant Trigger Warning:' Performances of Trauma and Terror" 44, 48
Gielen, Pascal 117
Gilbert and Sullivan: H.M.S. Pinafore 37
Goleman, Daniel: *Emotional Intelligence* 23
grace 32; academic 32 (*see also* academic grace)
grade-based system 34
Gray, Beatrice 179
Greek National Opera 183
Greenidge, Kirsten 126
Grotowski, Jerzy 67n4; *Towards a Poor Theatre* 59
Gupta, Akhil 73

Haggard, Merle: "Mama Tried" 73
Halberstam, Jack 111, 120n6; *In A Queer Time and Place* 110
Haley, Jennifer: *The Nether* 36
Halvorsen, Lauren 36
Hammond, Zaretta 25, 26

Hanna-Tominaga, Meg 7
Haraway, Donna 13
Harris, Aleshea: *What to Send Up When It Goes Down* 44–45
Harris, Maxine 46
Harry Ransom Center 109, 110, 112, 114, 117
Hartman, Saidiya: *Wayward Lives, Beautiful Experiments* 110
Heirich, Jane Ruby 96
Hewitt, Mark Alan: *Draw in Order to See: A Cognitive History of Architectural Design* 160
"high flex" model 190–191
H.M.S. Pinafore (Gilbert and Sullivan) 37
Hoghe, Raimund 80
Horst, Louis 79
How to Learn the Alexander Technique (Conable) 89
Hughes, Amy 118
human eye 134
Humphrey, Doris 79
hybrid archival methods 117–119
hybrid performance 140, 142
hybrid process 136; pedagogical benefits of 139–140
hybrid stage management classroom 190–195
hybrid teaching/learning 157

imaginary deixis 64–65
The Imperial Archive (Richards) 114
In A Queer Time and Place (Halberstam) 110
Inge, William 117
inhibition, Alexander Technique 91–94
Inoue, Asao B. 19n3
in-person archives 109, 111–115
integrated accessibility 140–142
intensity levels, of light 185–186
intermedial space 73
intimacy 18; personal 71, 72; physical 72

Jackson, Michael 95
Jagers, Robert 26
Jimerson, Randall C. 110
Johnson, Mark 67n8
Jones, Margo 117
Juditha Triumphans 183, 186–187

Kardashian, Kim 171, 179
K-12 education 26, 30

Keep Going: 10 Ways to Stay Creative in Good Times and Bad (Kleon) 79
Keep Moving 69–71, 73, 74, 76
Kelly, Gene 95
Kendi, Ibram X. 127
Kershaw, Baz 61
Khoo, Aurorae 123
Kincman, Laurie: *The Stage Manager's Toolkit* 191
kindness: labor of teaching with 11; pedagogy of 12, 15, 18; ungraded pedagogy of 14
Kleon, Austin: *Keep Going: 10 Ways to Stay Creative in Good Times and Bad* 79
Koenig, Robert 183
Kohn, Alfie 33
Kovich, Andrea: "Envisioning Change" 141
Kritik 16, 17, 19n5
Kryolan Makeup Manual 174

Laermans, Rudy 117
Lakoff, George 67n8
Lamott, Anne 83
Lauren, Ellen 63
learner-centered online course 26–30
learner-centered psychological principles. 23, 26
learning: asynchronous learning platform 27; hybrid teaching/learning during Covid-19 pandemic 157; in-person 166; remote learning 99, 101, 105, 105n1; trauma informed teaching and 129, *130*
learning management system (LMS) 50
Lease, Bryce 116
Lefebvre, Henri 72
Lemon, Ralph 80
lighting budgets 187–188
lighting design 183; budgets 187–188; dramaturgy and practice 184–186; *Juditha Triumphans* 186–187; streaming light and shadow online 186
lighting design training 183
light, properties of 185
Limon, Jerzy 62
Liveness: Performance in a Mediatized Culture (Auslander) 69
live streaming 186–188
living archive 179
LMS *see* learning management system (LMS)

Maginnis, Tara 172, 181n3
makeup: in non-judgmental way 170–172; painting 176–177
makeup course 169
"Mama Tried" (Haggard) 73
Manalansan, Martin F. 112
Mandel, Emily St. John 36
Manson, Ross 146
manual deictics 61, 64, 66
Martin, Clay 143
materiality, reclaiming 160–161
McCandless, Stanley 184–185
McCombs, Barbara 26, 28
meditation 16
meditation-based pauses 16
Meisner, Cristina 117
mental health: conversations about 29; crisis 21
metacognition 14
Mezzo Opera Channel 183
Middleton, Katie: *Color Theory for the Makeup Artist* 176
Miller, Bebe 81–83
Millerson, Gerald 184
mind-body communication 160–161
mind-body unity 86–87
mini-line dances 78
"MIXED mode" 158, 159
modern dance 78
Monica Bill Barnes & Company 69, 70
movement training 58, 63
MOXIE Theatre: *BIG Night of Little Plays* 122–126
Mr. Burns: A Post-Electric Play (Washburn) 35–37; storytelling 37–38; text analysis 38–40
Muñoz, José Esteban: "Ephemera as Evidence" 111

Nassim (Soleimanpour) 146, 151, 152, 153n1
Nassim Soleimanpour Productions 145, 147
Nathans, Heather S. 112
The Nether (Haley) 36
New York Public Library (NYPL) 118
non-volumetric performance 58, 67n2

O'Connor, Tere 81
online performance 78, 151, 183
online reading 136–137

Index   201

online teaching 3, 4, 34, 97, 179, 181;
  Alexander Technique 85
open-ended prompts 160
the orders, Alexander Technique 91–94
"origo-allocating acts" 63
origo-relative language 67n8
Ormerod, Ben 184

pandemic performance life 78
Pavis, Patrice 61
Pavlounis, Dimitrios 119n1
Pearson, Mike 71
pedagogy: of kindness 12, 15, 18; spatial dramaturgy as 74–76
pedagogy of care 44, 51, 52n1, 75
peer-based grading system 17
peer review opportunities 16
Penn State: "MIXED mode" 158; quarantine policy 167n1
performance: digital 71, 74, 146; hybrid 140, 142; live streaming 84; meaning-making in 71; site-specific 70, 71, 73, 76; virtual 69, 70, 72, 147, 150
performance curation 79
performance spaces 69–74
Performance Studies: An Introduction (Schechner) 33
performance theory 25
performative consciousness 61
physical intimacy 72
Piepzna-Samarasinha, Leah Lakshmi: *Care Work: Dreaming Disability Justice* 35
place: multiplicity of 72–74; specificity of 70–72
Plants, Jen 26
Play Analysis (PA) 34–36, 39–41, 42n4
playwriting 123, 124, 126, 129, 131–132
point of view (POV) 185, 187
"positions of mechanical advantage" 95
Postlewait, Thomas: *The Cambridge Introduction to Theatre Historiography* 112
post-pandemic performance life 78
"Potentially Perilous Pedagogies" (Carello and Butler) 48
Potter, Spencer 177, 178
Prendergast, Monica 26
pre-recorded videos 102, 105n1
Price, Margaret 48
production meetings 194–195

Profeta, Katherine 80, 81; *Dramaturgy in Motion* 81
proximity 59
psychophysical unity 86

Razocher, Daniela 160–161
rehearsal process, *Romeo & Juliet* hybrid production of 136–138
remote learning 99, 101, 105, 105n1; technical challenges opportunities of 178–180
Richards, Thomas: *The Imperial Archive* 114
ritual, parts of 14–18
Roach, Joseph 119
Robinson, Laura 168n2
Roebers, Thomas 103
Romeo & Juliet, hybrid production of 134, 142–144; integrating accessibility with collaboration 140–142; pedagogical benefits of 139–140; "A Plague O' Both Your Houses" 135–136; rehearsal process and timeline 136–138

Saenz De Viteri, Robbie 70, 71, 74
San Diego State University (SDSU): *BIG Night of Little Plays* 122–126
Saratoga International Theatre Institute (SITI) 57, 60, 67n1; Virtual Skidmore curriculum 66
Sartre, Jean-Paul and Merleau-Ponty, Maurice 59
Saxton, Juliana 26
Schalk, Sami 48
Schechner, Richard: *Performance Studies: An Introduction* 33
Schneider, Rebecca 111
Schwartz, Joan M. 109, 119
Seattle Children's Theatre 24
Sedgwick, Eve Kosofsky: *Touching Feeling: Affect, Pedagogy, Performativity* 67n3
SEL-centered course 28
self-dramaturgy 82–83
self-management skills 29
SEL-informed curriculum 25
semester-long sketchbook assignment 160
settled hierarchies 33
shadow 170, 186
Shanks, Michael 71
The Simpsons 35
site-specific performance 70, 71, 73, 76

SITI *see* Saratoga International Theatre Institute (SITI)
sketchbook assignment 161–166, *164–167*, 168n2
Skidmore Summer Intensive 57, 67n1; *see also* Saratoga International Theatre Institute (SITI)
"slim/stout" project 174–175
Sobel, Sharon: *Theatrical Makeup: Basic Application Techniques* 174
social and emotional learning (SEL) 21–26; integration of 29; within theatre and performance pedagogies 22–23
social justice education 25
social media: dance on 78; and live streaming performances 84; as stage and gallery 79–80
Sofer, Andrew 45
Soja, Edward 70
Soleimanpour, Nassim 6, 145, 146, 153n1
Sorzano, Olga Lucía 116
space: centering 75; intermedial 73; relationships between 70; virtual 4, 69, 101, 125, 145, 146, 149; working within limits of 70–72
Springsteen, Bruce: "Dancing in the Dark" 69
stage awareness 61
stage lighting designer 188
stage makeup 177
Stage Makeup Gender Reversal project 177
stage management 190
The Stage Manager's Toolkit (Kincman) 191
Stahl, Robert J. 53n7
Staley, Christopher 3, 4, 7
Standing Statues 65
Steedman, Carolyn 113, 120n5, 120n8
Stevens, Fraser 76n1
Stommel, Jesse 11, 14
"Stonewall Forever" 116
storytelling 34, 158, 187; *Mr. Burns: A Post-Electric Play* 37–38
stress reduction 101–102
Stubbs, Naomi 118
Suzuki Company of Toga (SCOT) 60
Suzuki Cultures 57, 59
Suzuki Method 57, 60–61; actor explores in 58; intensity of speed and directionality in 65
Suzuki, Tadashi 60, 65, 67n4, 67n5
Sweetser, Eve 61–62; *Viewpoint in Language: A Multimodal Perspective* 62

tactile body image 62, 67n8
tap dance 99, 101
Taylor, Diana 115; *The Archive and the Repertoire* 110
teaching: affective approach to 12; critical thinking 11; labor of 11
"teaching machines" 151
teaching online 2, 5, 29, 36
technologies 57, 72, 101, 142, 149; digital 35, 147, 162; intermedial 73
terminology, reframing of 170–171
text analysis, *Mr. Burns: A Post-Electric Play* 38–40
Thadium, Laura 173
Thanasoula, Christina 7
THEA150 Fundamentals of Design 158
theatre for young audiences (TYA) 22
"theatre machine" 151
Theatre 101N 1
Theatre on Film and Tape Archive (TOFT) 118
Theatrical Intimacy Education 136
theatrical makeup 171
Theatrical Makeup: Basic Application Techniques (Sobel) 174
theatrical makeup kit 175–176
theatrical space 71, 72, 74
theatrical stage makeup 169
Theory of Mind 62
think time 53n7
3D prosthetics 170
three-point lighting 184–185
"through put" 18, 19n10
time factor, of light 187
Touching Feeling: Affect, Pedagogy, Performativity (Sedgwick) 67n3
Towards a Poor Theatre (Grotowski) 59
Townsend, Daniel 173
"Training A Million Compassionate Americans" (Frodahl) 18
training, transindividualistic potential of 59
trauma: and debilitation 51; and disability 44, 45, 49; and terror 44, 45, 47, 52
trauma-informed practices 45–48
trauma-informed scholarship 48
trauma informed teaching and learning 129, *130*
Turner, Mark 67n8
2D makeup techniques 170

ungrading 3, 12, 18, 33, 34
Ungrading: Teaching and Learning in Higher Education (Blum) 33

University of Chicago Consortium on School Research 24
US educational systems, inequities of 21

Vezant, Iyanla 18
Viewpoint in Language: A Multimodal Perspective (Sweetser) 62
virtual performance 69, 70, 72, 150; of WRRR 147
virtual realism 36
virtual rehearsal rooms 132–133
Virtual Skidmore curriculum, SITI 66
virtual spaces 4, 69, 101, 125, 145, 146, 149
virtual staging, of WRRR 147
Vivaldi, A. 188n1
Voytilla, Stuart 122
wait time 53n7
Walzing/Rhythmic Gait Analysis 103–134
Warden, Claire 136
Washburn, Anne: *Mr. Burns: A Post-Electric Play* 35
Ways of Seeing (Berger) 140

Wayward Lives, Beautiful Experiments (Hartman) 110
Webber, Stephen 61
What to Send Up When It Goes Down (Harris) 44–45
White Rabbit, Red Rabbit (WRRR) 145, 146, 151, 152; virtual staging of 147; Zoom staging of 148, 152
Wiens, Birgit 72, 73
Wilkes, Talvin 82
Williams, Tennessee 112, 114, 115, 117
Wombach, Abby 95
Worstword Ho (Beckett) 58
Zoom: *BIG Night of Little Plays* 124–125; collaborations on 122; Fall 2020 virtual new play workshops 128–132; hybrid classroom 192–195; interconnected dancers on 73; limitations of 100–101, 105; staging of *White Rabbit Red Rabbit* 148; working in digital space 159
Zoom fatigue 100, 103, 104, 160
Zoom gallery 73, 74

Taylor & Francis eBooks

www.taylorfrancis.com

A single destination for eBooks from Taylor & Francis with increased functionality and an improved user experience to meet the needs of our customers.

90,000+ eBooks of award-winning academic content in Humanities, Social Science, Science, Technology, Engineering, and Medical written by a global network of editors and authors.

TAYLOR & FRANCIS EBOOKS OFFERS:

- A streamlined experience for our library customers
- A single point of discovery for all of our eBook content
- Improved search and discovery of content at both book and chapter level

REQUEST A FREE TRIAL
support@taylorfrancis.com